One Fell Off
the Merry-Go-Round

Surviving Alcoholism in a Dysfunctional Family

KATHI STEWART

BACK COVER ILLUSTRATED
BY VANCE NESBITT

Fulton Books, Inc.
Meadville, PA

Published by Fulton Books 2020

ISBN 978-1-64654-961-0 (paperback)
ISBN 978-1-64654-962-7 (digital)

Printed in the United States of America

I pray that I may be used to lighten many burdens. I pray that many souls may be helped through my efforts. You are not alone.

—Kathi Stewart

To My Mother, My Best Friend, My Rock, also to my family and those special friends who supported me on this journey

Introduction

When it comes to living and growing up with an alcoholic parent within a dysfunctional family, the only way one can learn to live around the chaos and insanity is you have to give yourself a push and not be afraid to fall off the merry-go-round. It is the only way you will be able to learn to live, love, and be healthy. I use the analogy of a merry-go-round because that was how I saw my life growing up. Once I figured out what a merry-go-round was and what it did, I realized that is what living in my family felt like. We were forever going in circles, repeating the same scenario over and over again. I never was sure which horse I would end up on. What I did know was that once I understood the analogy that the ride was never going to end, all I ever wanted to do was to fall off and escape or pull the plug. I would pray the ride would cease to exist because it was not fun and it was not a happy memory. I sometimes would close my eyes and envision the ride going in circles so fast until I was dizzy and flying off of it. I could see myself on this beautiful horse. It was a unicorn with a cracked horn. Sometimes I would imagine grabbing hold of the reins and riding off to some secret beautiful place where there was no scariness and no trauma. Instead, the fear of running away to the unknown would make me cling and hold on even tighter than before. I held on to the reins that held the secrets.

Repeating and reliving the same scenarios on a daily basis, I formed three vital coping mechanisms. Those three mechanisms were hope, courage, and a sense of humor. Without these three elements, I would not have survived. You had to have a sense of humor at the sheer insanity of the situations. Sounds a bit odd and possibly a bit morbidly sick to say laughter gets you through the most horrendous times, but believe me, it did with our family. That dark humor at times turned into hysteria. It was black comedy at its ultimate best. Laughing through the pain, sorrow, shame, horror, and embarrassment was the only way to put medicine on the scars. No coping mechanisms can lead to the crash and burn, the sinking deeper into the abyss of depression, the sinkhole that can swallow you up into the darkness. At the age of five years old, I had not yet figured those mechanisms out. Let alone did I know what a merry-go-round was, there was no humor or laughter in witnessing the horrendous scenarios, especially when you see your mommy being hurt. It was not until I was much older and had survived many of those repeated situations that I could bring dark comedy into the mix as one of my many survival techniques. I hope that by telling my story, it may help someone else fall off their own merry-go-round of dysfunctional hell. Just a forewarning: try not to get too dizzy on my ride because I know each one of us has our own horse and pony show.

The Beginning

Where to start? I guess I will start at my earliest childhood memory. Anything younger than five, I guess I most likely suppressed it or blocked it out. My first vivid memory when I was five years old was my first inclination that my family was anything but normal. That is when this first story played out. It was a Friday night, not too late because I remember my brother and I were still awake. It was possibly maybe nine or ten-ish. I remember looking at the clock. It was on the number 10. I was only in kindergarten; I didn't know yet how to tell time. I was just learning my numbers 1 through 10, so I saw the hand was on the 10.

Mom was pacing the house and extremely nervous. My brother and I had been sitting on the family room floor, looking at picture books and coloring. None of us heard the car pull up, but all of a sudden, we all heard the loud pounding on the front doors. We had double front doors with a peephole. One remained bolted shut, and only one side opened. They were a very bright orange color. That is my mom's favorite color. Then some fumbling with the door handle as if someone was trying to break into our house. My mom quickly grabbed my brother's arm and my arm and practically dragged us down the hallway to our bedrooms. She told us in a very harsh tone to stay there. I sensed something was very wrong by the grip my mom had on our arms and the way my mommy was acting. After Mommy told us to stay in our rooms, she ran down the hallway out to the family room. My brother and I, of course, did not listen. We were curious like all children. We both snuck out of our rooms and quietly crept down the hallway to peer out into the family room to see what was going on. There we sat huddled in the hallway. I was holding my little brother's hand as he kneeled behind me. I had to

7

be the big sister, to protect him, so I was the first one peering out. Our little bodies were tense with anticipation of what was coming through that front door. I was holding my breath. Our bodies both relaxed with relief when it opened. Oh, it's just Daddy. That relief was short-lived because when I took one look at my daddy's face, my back arched with fear and the hair on my neck was all tingly. The look on my daddy's face was scary. He looked like a monster. That did not look like my daddy. That person looked mean. I knew something bad was about to happen. I quickly pushed my brother behind me as if my little body could shield him. I watched my daddy stumble into the house.

He loudly began yelling for my mother, "Get your fucking ass out here, bitch."

My eyes got as large as saucers. I felt my brother start shaking. Oh my, why was Daddy saying naughty words? And why was Daddy so angry at Mommy? My mom took a leap from the family room and ran toward the kitchen. I am not sure why she did that, but I think she did it because I think she spotted us out of the corner of her eye and she saw us watching from the hallway. Maybe it was panic or fear I saw in her eyes when she saw us crouched there. I think to distract my daddy from seeing us, she ran away from the family room toward the kitchen. It was her motherly instinct to protect us. Once she was in the kitchen, I could not see her anymore, but I could hear her turn on the water and the cabinet open. I was watching the kitchen closely, then I saw her lean far over the countertop in the kitchen, then I could see her clearly because her body was almost on top of the counter, hanging over. My eyes locking with hers, she took her hand and put it to her mouth in the shhhh position. I was trembling at this point, my little heart racing. I could feel my brother's little body quaking next to mine. I saw my mom come quickly out of the kitchen with a glass of water. She began shuffling her feet quickly toward him while extending her hand. I could see it was trembling with her head lowered to avoid his wicked stare. She reached out her arm with the glass of water toward him, some of it sloshing over the edge.

He looked at her with that scary face and said in the meanest voice I ever heard, "Bitch. Why the fuck would I want water, you dumb ass bitch." And then to my horror, he lifted the back of his hand and swung it, knocking the glass right from her hand. I watched water flying all over the floor as the glass crashed to the ground. Surprisingly, with the force that he hit the glass and my mommy's arm, it was amazing it did not shatter and break—probably because we had a big striped, shag throw rug covering the white tile floor.

Mommy grabbed her wrist, wincing in pain. She looked like a scared bunny rabbit as she tried to straighten up. She reached out to the wall to try to steady herself. Then she started to talk in a soothing soft voice, trying to calm him down, "I'm sorry, Kevin. Come on, honey. Come inside and sit here and rest on the couch. You must be so tired from work." She was saying this in this cooing, fake, high-pitched, sweet, soft voice.

As I was listening, I remember thinking how odd that was. Here he did something naughty and not nice, and yet my mommy was being as sweet as pie to him. That didn't make any sense to me. Her words only made him angrier and made the situation worse. The more she tried talking nice, the more horrible he got with his bad, ugly, naughty words—ranting and screaming and stumbling toward her. But because of his clumsiness, she was able to jump back, so he kept missing her. About the third time he tried, he fell into the side of the wall by the kitchen.

"Bitch," he said, trying to stand up straight. "Get the fuck over here and shut your goddamn mouth." My mom had finally stopped talking and said nothing. It was like she was a robot. Why was she letting Daddy talk to her like that? Why was Daddy saying all those horrible, mean, naughty words to Mommy? He then said as he slobbered, "Get your sorry fat ass over here, bitch, and give me some now."

Huh? I thought, furrowing my brow. What does that mean? What does he want her to give him? I didn't understand, but I could tell my mommy knew because she turned white, then her face turned bright red. I saw beads of sweat break out all over her forehead. That something was not something good, I could tell. There was a look of pure panic on her face. I was trying so hard to figure out what it meant to give me something. Because whatever that *something* was, I could tell my mommy did not want to give it or go get it. I then saw Mommy trying to move forward, I think to try to get away from our view, but her slipper caught the edge of the throw rug and she tripped and fell on her knees in front of him.

I heard my daddy say, "Just where I want you, you goddamn clumsy fat ass bitch." Snickering a sick laugh, he was like "Yeah, baby, that's right where I want you, on your knees." He grabbed the back of her blond hair and yanked her forward, toward his pants. Why was he doing that? She wouldn't be able to breathe if he put her face there, and why was he sticking her face on his private parts?

She twisted and tried to turn her head. "Kevin," she yelled, "you are hurting me!" When she resisted him even more, he grabbed her hair tighter, making her cry out in more pain, and then he slammed her head into the side of the closet doors in the family room. Because she was resisting and crying, that made him even madder. He then stood over her, repeatedly hitting her and slapping her. She tried to put up her hands for protection, begging him to stop. "Please, Kevin. Please, please," she begged, crying. "I'll do whatever you want," she said in a shrill voice.

He wasn't listening. His eyes were glazed over, and he looked like an animal. I was shivering and shaking. I was so scared for my mommy. Why? Why was Daddy hurting Mommy? Tears were streaming down my face. Mommy didn't do anything wrong. What should I do? Should I go try and stop Daddy? I was only five years old, but even at five, I knew I had to do something to help my mommy. I told my brother to stay where he was, his brown eyes wide with fear. I hugged him and said, "It's going to be okay." I whispered, "I'm getting Mommy help." He nodded. His amber-brown eyes grew even larger, like a big pool of chocolate syrup. I squeezed his hand to reassure him. I crouched, then crawled, and shimmied quietly like a little worm on the floor to my momma's work office, which was around the corner of the hallway. She worked part-time out of the house as a bookkeeper. I knew she had a phone on her desk in her office. It was a black old-fashioned rotary phone. My heart raced. Would I be able to find it in the dark? I was only five, but I knew I had to try. My mommy needed me. I quickly stood up and felt with my little hand and found the phone. Excitedly, I carefully picked up the receiver and dialed zero for the operator. That was what we were learning in kindergarten, along with our addresses and phone numbers, except we had just started to memorize that information. I panicked because I did not know my whole address. Would the operator be able to help my mommy? It was 1966. There was no such thing as 911 and no cell phones—only *0* for the operator.

I turned the rotary wheel on the phone and heard it ring on the other end. A voice came on the line. "This is the operator. How can I help you?"

I was scared to death. I was so afraid my daddy would hear me. In the voice of a five-year-old whose voice was squeaky shaky, I said in the loudest whisper I could, "Help, help! My mommy. Please."

The operator said, "Honey, I can't hear you. Please speak a little louder."

In a tiny tearful voice, I said, "Please, my mommy needs help. Please send a policeman. Send help. Daddy is hurting Mommy."

The operator said in a calming voice, "Why does your mommy need help?"

"My daddy is hitting my mommy, and my mommy is hurt. And he keeps hitting her. Please help my mommy. Please." At this point, I started to cry.

The operator talked quietly in a soothing voice. It was comforting. She reassured me that she was going to help me. "Honey, how old are you?"

I said, "Five."

"Do you know your address?"

"Not all the way," I wailed in a panic. "210 Care something," I whimpered. I tried hard to remember what I had been practicing. My street name was Clarion. It was too long and too big for me to memorize or pronounce correctly.

The operator, sensing my panic, said, "Honey, you did good. What's your name, honey?" I said Katie in a tiny voice. "Katie, I will be able to find out by looking up the number you called on, and then I will be able to send help."

I heard a loud bang. "Please," I said tearfully, "hurry." I don't know how she did it, but she was able to have the call traced. She asked me if I was okay, if my daddy had hurt me. I said, "No, only my mommy."

"Okay. Honey, the police are on the way." She said, "Is there anyone else in the house besides you and your mommy?"

"Yes, my little brother."

She asked, "Is he okay?"

I said, "Yes, we are hiding in the hallway."

"Good," the operator said. "Stay in your hiding place."

I was nodding even though she couldn't see me. Between my salty tears that were streaming down my face, my thoughts were *Why did she say 'good'?* From a five-year-old's perspective, there was nothing good about your daddy hurting your mommy. "I am scared for my mommy," I said. "Are they coming fast?"

"Yes, Katie. They will be there right away." She then asked in a kind voice, "Do you want me to stay on the line till they get there?"

"Oh yes, please," I whispered.

I heard another big thud, and so did the operator. She said quickly, "Katie, are you okay? Is that anywhere where you are?"

"No," I said. It's the other side of the wall. I looked through the crack in the door frame. It was hard to see because I was in the dark with only shades of light coming through the crack in the door. My father must have thrown my mommy against the outer wall of the office, and it was so loud it could be heard through the phone line. I heard a picture fall and crash into pieces.

The operator said, "It's going to be okay. The officers are coming."

"I'm scared," I whimpered.

She said, "Stay right where you are until they get there."

I said okay in a small voice. I crouched in terror. My daddy was still yelling naughty words so loudly that he did not hear the sound of the doorbell ringing. Finally, he heard the pounding on the front door.

"Who the fuck is that?" he slurred.

The doorbell rang again and loud knocking and a loud voice said, "This is the Prospect Police Department. Open the door."

My dad, stumbling his way to the door, was slurring and spitting. "What the fuck are they doing here? Did you call them, bitch?" He looked at my mother. My mom's head shook back and forth. "They have no fucking right to be here." He flung the door open so hard it hit the doorstop.

The police stepped into the foyer. I crawled quickly from my spot in the office back to my brother. I forgot I left the receiver off the hook. The operator must have disconnected because a few minutes later, the loud beeping noise could be heard in the deafening silence. I was scared because then I knew my daddy would figure out it was me. I just wanted to get back to Kent. My mother, with her left eye starting to blacken and turn blue, was looking frightened, shocked, confused, and perplexed as she heard the shrill beeping from the phone being off the hook.

One of the policeman said, "We are responding to a call we received from this residence that help was needed."

My mom shook her head, looking very dazed and confused. "No," she said in a shaky voice. "No one called for help." Her brow was furrowed, and her cheek was already expanding with puffiness from the welts.

The officer on the right said, "Yes, ma'am. We did receive a call from this home stating there was a disturbance. The operator notified the police department to respond."

Then my mom, looking bewildered, turned quickly and glanced at my brother and me. I straightened proudly and was nodding, feeling so confident and proud of myself and thinking Mommy will be happy I called for help, but when she looked at us and then turned back to the officer, I had a funny feeling in my tummy. She didn't look very happy. I then heard her say in a shaky voice, "We were just having a silly disagreement, Officer. Nothing is wrong." The butterflies in my tummy increased, and my shoulders sagged. My big balloon of achievement popped and deflated when I heard my mom say that. "Officer, it must have been my daughter. She must have misunderstood and called you. You know how five-year-olds are. They have an active imagination. She probably thought our talking loudly was a bad fight. It was just a tiny argument."

I stared in disbelief. *What?* I thought as my eyes widened. Now I stood straight up. I no longer was crouching as I went to stand behind my mom, crinkling my brow, very confused, very hurt, and bewildered. I didn't understand why she was not telling them the truth. As I stood behind her, I started pulling on her nightgown to get her attention. I said, "But, Mommy, Daddy was hurting you."

My mom laughingly said, "No, baby. Daddy and I were just playing."

I said, "But, Mommy, you got boo boos."

She shook her head. "Silly girl. She has such an imagination," she said to the officers.

I still was grabbing her nightgown, but she was ignoring me, putting her hand behind and grabbing and squeezing my shoulder as she tried to compose herself. I winced as she tightened her grip to silence me, and I did become silent. In my five-year-old little brain, I was thinking this very thing: What was she talking about? Daddy hurt her. My mom finally glanced down at me, and the look in her eye stopped me cold as she eased up on my shoulder.

There was a sad look in the officer's eyes as he looked at my mother and back at me and my brother. "Ma'am, that doesn't look like playing. Ma'am, are you sure you're not hurt? Are the children okay? We did receive a call for help. Are you sure you don't want help? We can file a report."

I moved slightly forward and was about to say something. But my mom squeezed my shoulder again to silence me, and she shook her head. By now, her lip was already purple and swollen. Her cheeks were puffy from the blows to her face. My mom calmly said, "No, Officers, sirs, thank you."

My dad then stumbled forward for the first time, slurring, "There is nothing to file. We just disagreeeeeeing, Officer. My wife— she just fell into the wall." He sloppily put his arm around her shoulder and yanked her closer to his wobbly body. "She just fine. A little bruised from the wall, but I take care of her. Both you can leave now," he said boldly and defiantly as his disheveled body wobbled and he clung to my mom. My father then reached out his other hand to pull me forward into the mix. "See, Officers, we just one big happeee family. Just having a disagreeeeement," he spoke in broken slang.

The officers were looking at each other with an underlying understanding in their eyes and a look of disgust, as if they had some kind of recognition of this scene being played before. "Sir," the officer on the right addressed my father and said, "there is no need to be belligerent with us. We are just responding and doing our job, and we're here to help and serve the community. That's why we respond to all calls. Let us do our job as we sort this situation out."

Seeing my father's face turn a beet red, an angry red, I knew he was steaming mad. His face had a wicked expression, and then it suddenly changed as if he realized the situation. It changed from looking like a mad bear to a scared bunny rabbit. He was trying to straighten up, but he was very wobbly. I wanted to giggle because he looked like one of my Weeble Wobble toys. "What do ya mean?" he slurred. "I am calm. Weeee just fine." He grabbed my mom's shoulder harder, and I saw her wince in pain and held her tight to him. "Right, honey?" My mom nodded vigilantly like a puppy dog.

The officer looked at him with disdain and disgust and said, "Sir, I just want to say this." He said in deliberate and in a strong voice and very slowly so my dad could comprehend, "If we get another call for disturbing the peace, we will bring you in and charge you for battery and domestic abuse."

Battery. I thought, *Why would they need batteries?*

"What?" my drunk father slobbered. "That's ridddicuulousss," he said. He then responded in childlike, whiney voice, "Disturbing the peeeeace in my own home?" When my dad saw the officer grab at his belt and the officer's hand was close to his weapon and cuffs, he knew they meant business. I think the reality hit him, and his demeanor immediately changed. He became quiet, like a mouse, and you could see he kind of had that fearful look in his eyes, like a deer-in-headlights look. For a five-year-old, at first, all I was feeling was relief that the policemen were here to help my mommy, my mommy whose bruises were already swelling and turning an ugly purplish

15

blue. Then my mommy said she didn't need help. But clearly with all the big words, I was confused. Like why did they want batteries for my daddy? What the heck was going on? Why was my mommy not telling them she needed them? Clearly couldn't they see my mommy was hurt? Then I saw my daddy change from mean to sort of nice, then he slobbered, "I am sorrrrrry, Officers, that we bothered you," with spit splattering out of his mouth through his teeth. "Thank you for coming. See, we okay," he said as he was hanging on my mother to keep from falling over. My brother and I were now cowering behind her. Then he released his arm off my mom's shoulder and stumbled forward toward the couch and plopped down there, drool coming out of his mouth and stains all over his shirt. "Kidzzzz." He waved his arm. "Come sit by your daddy." My brother and I looked at each other, not sure what to do. My mom pushed us forward to the couch. I didn't want to go, but we did. And my father took his hands and pulled us both to the couch next to him on either side of him and gave a sloppy wave of his hand, dismissing the officers. "Seee," he said, "We good, Officers." He said one more time with a sloppy smile, "See, me and my kidzzz are going to watch me some TV now." We were smooshed next to him, and I remember he smelled yucky. He was talking in childlike slang.

The officers looked at each other. I was watching them closely. They were hesitant to leave. My mom said, "Yes, Officers. Thank you for coming, but we are all right now."

Both shook their heads, and then I saw them turning to leave. *Oh no*, I thought, *they can't be leaving*. Why aren't they helping us? Why aren't they helping my mommy? The officers did not acknowledge my father. They looked at my mother and said, "Okay, ma'am. If you sure all of you are okay, we will be on our way."

My mommy nodded. My five-year-old brain kept repeating, No, no, no. Don't leave me and my little brother and my mommy alone with my daddy. He is going to hurt us. How can they believe my daddy? I don't understand. Tears quietly streamed down my face. I wiped them quickly away with the back of my hand. I didn't want them to see me crying. I wanted to be brave for my brother and my momma. My mom must have realized once they left that me and my brother may get the wrath of my daddy. She said, "Just a minute, Officers." She said, "Kids, say thank you, and off to bed with you both. It's late. Kiss your daddy good night."

I think she wanted us out of daddy's arm hold. Both my brother and I wiggled off the couch. Ooooooh, yuck. Why did she say that? He slurred, "Yep, give your daddy some lovin'," his dirty fingers pointing to either side of his cheeks. I so didn't want to kiss his cheek.

We did what we were told, and I took my little brother's hand and pulled him toward the hallway where our bedrooms were, but before I left, I started tugging on my mommy's nightgown in a panic. She turned at me with her blue-and-purple eye, put her finger to her swollen lip, and muttered, "Shhhh, Katie. Do what I said. Take your brother and go to bed. I will be there to tuck you in shortly." I cowered down because this time, the look in her eyes was not fear but anger. Now I was really confused. Why was Mommy mad at me? I grabbed my brother and pulled him down the hallway to my bedroom, bewildered and confused.

I heard the officer speak to my mommy one more time. "Ma'am, call us if you need us," the officer on the left said. I turned one last time and looked at him, and he looked me straight in the eye. His eyes had what I would later know as pity in them along with sadness because they were helpless to help us. He then said to me, "You two stick together." We nodded as we left the room. My little mind still could not comprehend that they were just going to leave without doing anything. Why, oh, why were they leaving when my mommy was hurt? The officer on the left said one more time, "You are sure, ma'am, that you are okay?"

My mom tried to smile. But her lip was too swollen, and the smile ended up looking like an ugly Halloween mask. "Yes, sir."

Hesitating, the officer on the left said, "Okay, ma'am." And looking at my father, he sternly said, "Sir, I trust you will have some coffee and get some rest? And we won't get another call from here?" My father, with his face looking at the floor, would not meet his eyes as he grumbled yes.

The officers turned and started to leave, and as I was turning down the hallway, I saw my mom's shoulders slump as she walked behind them, her feet slowly shuffling to the door. She looked worn and defeated. My brother and I stood one more moment in the hallway, peering at my mom and holding each other's hands tightly. My eyes were racing to the couch where my daddy was already tipping over his head and falling on the couch pillows. I grabbed my brother's hand and pulled him down the hallway to my bedroom. I started to shiver mostly out of fear because I was so scared at what was going to happen after she shut the front door. I hope Daddy doesn't move off the couch. I didn't even realize I was holding my breath. I let out a sigh of relief. My brother and I had climbed into my double bed. I then heard the front door shut and the locks turned. Silence. More silence. Then I heard the rumbling noise, sounding like a snorting pig. Good. I think Daddy is sleeping. I felt my little body release the pent-up tension of being clenched in fear for so long. I could feel my brother's hand was trembling. I put my arm around him and hugged him. "It's going to be okay, Kent."

He looked up at me with those amber-brown eyes and said, "Are you sure, Heart?"

See, he called me Heart because my mommy called me Sweetheart and he couldn't say *Katie*, so he started calling me Heart. It was a cute nickname, so we didn't correct him. "Yes, it will be." I squeezed him tight. Even though Mommy had let the nice officers leave without their help, everything was going to be okay.

I heard a loud sigh. It was Mommy, then I heard muffled sobs. They lasted a couple of minutes then stopped. I had a tummy ache. I felt like I was going to throw up. I heard my Mommy shuffling down the hallway. She came into my room and walked to the bed. She knelt beside the bed next to me and whispered, "We are going to let your daddy sleep on the couch. Do not wake him up in the morning. Stay in your rooms and play when you wake up. Understand?" She looked at both of us, her face grotesquely purple and blue and her mascara smeared under her eyes, but what was that look in her eyes? Anger? Fear? Then she said in a harsh tone, "Which one of you called the police?"

My brother sunk deeper in the pillow. Without any hesitation, I proudly said, "Me, Momma."

I felt so grown up and proud of myself, but that left quickly when she said in a very hushed, harsh whisper, "Don't you ever do that again, Katie? Do you hear me?" She grabbed my shoulders and with a stern look, said, "You could have gotten your daddy in a lot of trouble, and that would have been way worse for us. And he would have hurt us more."

What? My great achievement was quickly taken away from me. My head was filled with confusion. I was hurt, my eyes filling with tears. "I don't understand, Momma. I was only trying to help." I whimpered, "Daddy was hurting you."

What she said then shocked me. "Sweetheart, he didn't know what he was doing."

What? I thought. My five-year-old brain could not comprehend that answer. How could he not know he was hurting Mommy? I said, "Mommy, how could he not know he was hurting you? He was hitting you, Mommy."

She said, "People do things they don't mean to do when they drink." Why was my momma sticking up for Daddy? I was so bewildered. Here I thought she was going to be so proud of me, so happy I called for help that I was a big girl and figured out what to do. She then said in a very stern voice, softening it as she saw my hurt and confusion, "Baby, I am not mad at you. It's just you should never have called the police. Alcohol makes you do crazy things. Your daddy—he didn't mean it. If he would have gotten arrested, then we would have had to get him out of jail and he would have been so mad at you. I would never want him hurting you or your brother."

"Mommy, are you are telling me that you don't call the police for help?"

She nodded. "Because, honey," as she tried to explain, "it makes things more complicated afterward." I still did not understand. So the message I received as a five-year-old is that you just take the abuse, take the punches, and never call for help. So there I lay in bed, hugging my four-year-old brother, trying to be his protector, and feeling bad because my momma was mad at me for calling for help. Instead of praising me, she said I was wrong for calling the police. As a five-year-old, it was so, so confusing, and I felt so hurt and sad.

Then what my mommy said next was even more upsetting to me. "It really is none of the police's business, what happens in our house. We don't want anyone to know what your daddy did."

What? *Hmm*, I thought, furrowing my brow. That means you don't tell anyone that you are getting hurt? And you should never call for help? I frowned again. Now it was now beginning to dawn on me. I understand now. So this is what all mommies and daddies do? Daddies drink and get crazy, and it's okay? They fight and do bad things to each other, and it is okay for that to happen and you should never talk about it or tell anyone?

My mom hugged me tight and patted my head, but all I felt was hurt, confusion, and bewilderment. Here I thought I was the big girl, the hero, that I was helping my mommy. I thought I was doing a good thing, but clearly I did the wrong thing. My mommy took my brother and put him in his own bed. After my mom tucked us both in our rooms and in our beds, a few minutes later—as he did almost every night after she tucked us in—my brother would sneak out of his room, or I would sneak into his room; and we would huddle together, hugging each other for comfort. This would be a ritual for many years when the drunken beatings continued to happen throughout our childhood and elementary school years. We would lie there in fear, holding our ears, not falling asleep—scared for Mommy—and fearing that our daddy would come down the hallway and hurt us. It is so ironic to me that I could remember those images so clearly as if they were yesterday, just like that wicked scene when I was five years old. That scenario at five years old would be the very catalyst of my education on what I assumed was a normal family. It would also be the way I viewed what mommies and daddies' relationships should be. Of course, now I know it was anything but normal, but how would I know? I would believe for many years that was a normal relationship. For years, I was to consider this to be acceptable behavior between a husband and wife, between a mommy and daddy. It's all I ever saw. It was all I was exposed to growing up. Isn't that what all mommies and daddies do? So how could I ever possibly know what a healthy relationship was when I grew up when that was the only thing I ever witnessed or was exposed to at such an early age? How would I ever be able to actually be in a healthy relationship or form a healthy, loving relationship? Obviously, that was a cycle that I would have a hard time breaking as I became an adult.

There are many different types of alcoholics and alcohol abuse. My dad was not the normal alcoholic, meaning he was not the "drink your brains out every day" kind or the "come home from work and drink a case of beer" or "a fifth of scotch and pass out" kind that you read about in books or see on TV. Nor did he drink every day. He was what you call a binge drinker. He could and would go for periods of dry spells where he would not touch the sauce, sometimes a few days, sometimes a week, sometimes even a month. Those were his dry spells, his dry drunk periods. During those times, it would take him at least several days to become human. He would be irritable and unapproachable. He would eat tons of sweets, down tons of coffee, and smoke tons of cigarettes to get him through those dry drunks and grouchy withdrawal periods. I do, however, remember a time, and I believe it was when I was about fourteen and my brother, thirteen, when he quit drinking for a whole year. That was the year we had a glimmer of hope. We felt peace, we felt safe, and we felt somewhat normal—whatever *normal* is in a dysfunctional, sick family. My dad actually changed that year. His personality was quite different. I cannot really describe it, except to say he actually developed a personality, and he became a decent human being. Again, there was that glimmer of hope of being a normal happy family.

That first vivid memory when I was five was only one of many that has haunted me for close to forty-nine years, and to this very day, those memories and scenes remain with me like a VHS tape or what we now call a DVD movie that can be started, stopped, rewound, and replayed in my mind over and over again. It is amazing to think how the brain and mind works and how events such as the one I just described to you can be remembered like it was yesterday or suppressed at will and be so vividly clear when it happened so long ago. I am falling off the merry-go-round by writing and purging these scars and memories. I am making peace with the pain. I want to change the course of the ride and stop the continuation of the rituals, the secrets and the repeating dysfunctional behaviors, relationships, and scenarios.

One long-time ritual that happened in our family occurred on every other Friday night. If the clock struck five p.m. and my dad was not home, we realized that it was going to be a bad night—a very bad, bad night. We never knew what to expect except that it was not going to be fun. It was going to be frightening and scary. Sometimes the early evening would begin with my mom calling her best friend down the street. She would round up her three kids and me and my brother; and we all get loaded up in the Ford station wagon, and we would go from bar to bar all around the Old Orchard area, looking for my dad's car in the bar parking lots. All the places where his drinking hang outs that he and his buddies from work would frequent. My mom was frantically trying to find him and get in there and salvage any amount of the paycheck that would not have been sloshed away on booze. Us kids, not knowing how serious and sick the situation, used to play a game trying to guess which place he would be at, and who guessed it first was, yep, the winner. Yes, we thought that was fun, but really, it was a pretty sick, sad game. Here is the ironic thing: we always managed to find him. Most of the time, finding him was useless because by the time we located him, the money, well, it was already gone, and he was mooching off his drinking buddies or one of the barfly women who was always hanging all over him, thinking she found a sugar daddy. See, I found out in later years that he would pretend he wasn't married and pretended he didn't have a family to swindle more drinks from them. Once we found my dad, my mom would go in, and we would wait in the Ford station wagon with bated breath to see if my mom was able to come out with some money. Even if it was hardly anything, my mom, being the upbeat and vibrant lady, would make a joke of what she would come out with and had accomplished, trying to make a sordid Friday-night fun. If she ended up with a lot more than she expected to salvage, then we would end up at our favorite family eatery, Lum's in Wheeling, Illinois, best place for fish-and-chips and fried clams. Us kids always prayed for finding more money because we loved Lum's!

One of the worst events that happened during all those years of endless drunken binges was the most frightening incidents that could have resulted in the worse tragedy ever for our family. It happened to me and my brother when we were teenagers. That was, I believe, my breaking point—when my feelings, if I had any other than fear for my father, ended. I began to have no emotional attachment anymore to my father. As a little girl, I adored Daddy when he was sober, but as a young teenager, I abhorred him. It was what he did to my brother and how he treated him, plus the fact that as I became older and developed physically, his direction of affection was somewhat lewd. It was that behavior and that awful night when my dad almost killed my brother in a drunken fit of rage; that was when my emotional connection ended. It was a night that I shudder when I think of what could have happened. See, all those years when my brother and I were growing up, my mom never really did anything for herself. She never went out or did anything for her own happiness. She was always too terrified to leave us kids alone even if we were old enough to stay by ourselves. Her life revolved around keeping up the facade of our perfect family and protecting me and my brother from the hands of my father. We had the picture of a perfect family to every soul in the neighborhood, to every immediate family member, cousins, aunts, and uncles. It was what my mom wanted everyone to believe, so my brother and I went along with the charade. Mom—well, she did not really have a good life. She was too afraid to ever leave us alone in the event my dad would show up drunk. As we got older in our teenage years, she felt a bit less fearful and a bit more confident that we could handle ourselves, so every once in a while, she would venture out to play some coed volleyball, her favorite sport. After all, we were young adults. We did not need a babysitter anymore.

My brother and I we were in our teens on this particular evening. My mom loved to play volleyball. My aunt, her sister, had asked her to be a substitute on a team. Mom had been very depressed and at a low during this period, so she needed to get out and do some physical activity that could get her out of the insanity even if it was only a brief interlude. My brother and I encouraged her to

23

go, assuring her that we would be okay. I do remember that before she left, she begged us to please just stay in our bedrooms. She was only going to be gone maybe for approximately an hour and a half to go play volleyball. It was already late afternoon, around four p.m. We were home from school, but we had no way of knowing if Dad was coming home or not. After all, it was a Friday night and a pay-day. I remember she was so hesitant, frowning as she said, "If your dad isn't home by supper, please promise me you both will just stay in your rooms, and don't come out. Let him just pass out on the couch." In any other house, that would be a ridiculous request. In our house, it was considered normal. I was seventeen, my brother six-teen. My brother and I agreed to do that. We promised her. During that hour—time frame around 5:30 p.m.—I remember that as the minutes ticked by and he still wasn't home, my anxiety increased a hundred fold, and I was getting angrier and angrier. It irked me so much that we had to be ruled by his drinking and his vile behavior. I remember thinking how ridiculous that we did nothing wrong but yet we were the prisoners. We were the ones quarantined to stay in our bedrooms and not venture out of them. I was like a pot simmer-ing to a boiling point. I was so mad that he was doing this to us. I was sick of having to walk on eggshells all the time. I was sick of being ashamed. I was sick of having to have secrets.

Everything was always revolving around if my father was going to come home sober or not. As I was boiling in anger, I remember finally hearing him stumble in and come in the house around six thirty-ish. I began hearing the pantry where the stash of sweets was stored in the kitchen being ripped opened, cabinet doors slamming shut, stumbling stomps on the floor, and then a loud crash as he flopped and collapsed on the couch. I had been in my room playing my 8-track tapes on my 8-track stereo, trying to keep my racing mind busy and my anxiety and anger in check, and then all of a sud-den, something snapped in me. All that pent-up rage and anger that was held in for all those seventeen years shot out of me like a bomb exploding. I totally lost it. Yes, me, sweet little Katie, the good, kind Catholic girl was a raving lunatic. I don't know who that girl was, but she definitely was full of rage, full of built-up emotion and full of hate. She was out of control and exploded like dynamite. Everything that I had been feeling all the years growing up came pouring out. I was so angry at my life, our family's life. I just didn't care what the consequences would be if I riled him up enough to get him up off the couch. I truly hated him. I hated what he was doing to our family. I hated what he looked like—sloppy, disheveled, sour-smelling, and reeking of cigarette smoke and stale coffee and body odor. He disgusted me.

Of course, I did not want to break the promise I made to my mom. So I followed my mom's request and did not leave my room. The only thing I did not follow was not using my voice. I started yelling from my bedroom door every foul-mouth obscenity that I knew. "You goddamn son of a bitch. You fucking alcoholic pig. I hate your fucking guts. You are nothing but a piece of shit. You are such a fucking asshole. I hate you, you motherfucking piece of shit. Get your smelly, filthy ass off that couch and come down here so I can say it to your face, you piece of shit." The "F" bomb had gone off in my brain, and it was unstoppable. Oh yes, the good little Catholic girl was on an obscenity rampage. The girl who was incredibly, painfully shy and quiet as a mouse, who had no self-esteem and was afraid of her own shadow, had grown into a tiger. I think I would have won an award for saying the word *fuck* over five hundred times within an hour. I would have to go confession and do penance every day for years if our parish priest had heard me.

Of course, my poor brother was freaking out. "Sis, come on, stop it. You are going to get him all worked up and riled up. He is going to come down the hall and beat the crap out of you, and I am going to have to make sure he doesn't kill you." My brother, a year younger than me, was now five feet, eight, and me a mere five feet.

I said to my brother, "I don't give a rat's ass. I hate him."

My brother put his hands on top of my shoulders. "Sis, please," he begged. "Katie, just calm down."

The more my brother tried to calm me down and shut my bedroom door to drown out my verbal screaming, the more crazy I got. I just didn't care anymore. It was as if a time bomb was set off in my brain, and it had exploded. The bad thing was that this explosion was going into a deadly war zone. Because of my unleashed fury and rampage, I was now entering into the minefields of hell, and I thought I was ready for combat, but the bad thing was, I was dragging my poor brother into combat with me. You know the story when you have this major adrenalin rush, you have the sense that you are absolutely invincible. I was not even thinking about the consequences of my foul, vile ranting rampage and what a horrific disaster it could lead to. I just kept going no matter how many times my sweet brother asked me to stop. My brother, who was always the calming presence in our lives, with his polite, courteous, calm demeanor. He was my hero, my protector.

I am sure you can guess what eventually happened. About forty five minutes of yelling down the hallway insanely, all hell broke loose. The foul, vile verbal rampage had finally done the job. My verbal obscenity or bashing had riled my father up enough for him to drunkenly slur and yell down the hall, "Shut the fuck up, you little cock-sucking bitch, or I am going to come down there and shut your mouth with my fist."

Hmmm. Can you wonder how I responded to that sweet fatherly response? That was all I needed to hear to start the whole vile F-bomb and more all over the place. I spouted loudly, "Go right ahead, you motherfucking piece of shit." Yep, my reaction and response was that of an insane person asking for the smoking gun. The next thing I knew, I had succeeded. My plan to stir his sorry ass off the couch worked. Then it was as if everything was in slow motion. All I heard was the thud off the couch and the pounding footsteps.

My brother's face was full of panic, frustration, and anger, but mostly fear. He looked at me and said, "Great job, sis. Now look what you did."

I was so out of control with rage and hate. My state of mind was total defiance. My body was full of adrenaline. My answer was "Well, I really don't care. Let him beat the shit out of me. He is a motherfucker, and I hate him." I pushed my brother out of the way, and I ran down the hallway to meet my dad halfway. I put my face right up to his sour, foul-smelling mouth. I could feel his vile, hot breath in my face. I wanted to puke, but I held my ground, lifting my chin defiantly and just waiting for him to smack me. Yes, that was how crazed I was at that moment. Then I said, "Go ahead, you lowlife, lousy piece of shit. Beat the shit out of me. You're nothing but a drunken motherfucking *asshole*."

Yep, that was all he needed. He slapped me hard. I barely felt the sting, but my neck reeled back with the blow, my head hitting the hallway wall. There was a ringing in my ears. That didn't stop me from going on and on, spewing out obscenity after obscenity like a record stuck on repeat. The blows started at my face and were continuous as I put up my hands for protection, trying to fight back at the same time with slaps and punches of my own. Because of my high adrenaline rush, I did not feel a thing. I was actually beyond feeling anything. That was how much the adrenaline and hatred took over. They say your mind has the power to numb the pain. That is the truth because I felt nothing.

After the third blow to my head, my brother, who had been trying to pull him off me to no avail, finally pushed him hard enough for him to stumble and lose his footing. My brother then pushed in between me and my dad. My brother, always my hero, shoved me aside. When he shoved me out of the way, I fell back onto my knees to the floor. I was to the left side of my brother. My brother, God love him, was always there for me, my hero, my protector. Here he was again, stepping in to stop my dad's brutal attack, because I provoked the craziness. Anyone who has seen someone on drugs or is drunk knows that although they are impaired, they have the strength of a bear. When my brother interrupted his attack on me, it only made matters worse, and it angered and enraged my drunken father even more. I looked up from my knees, trying to use the hallway wall for leverage. That's when I experienced true fear. To my horror, I saw my father grab my brother by the throat. The look in my father's eyes was not even human. It was like an animal attacking its prey for the kill as if he was going to eat him. His bloodshot eyes were glazed over and glassy and bulging out of his head. Saliva was running down his chin. The stubble of his growing beard, that appeared on his face made him look evil. As I scrambled to my feet, I looked down at the floor. To my horror, my brother's feet were not touching the floor. They were dangling a foot off the floor. My father had lifted my brother by his neck off the floor. My brother who was already five feet, eight inches tall was backed up against the hallway wall, and he was being strangled by my father. Oh my god, what have I done? My heart was racing in sheer terror. My eyes were like saucers filled with fear. All I kept thinking was that I didn't have time to call the police because my brother will be dead by the time I do.

Sheer panic gripped me. Sweat was dripping from my face. My heart was pounding out of my chest as I thought, *This is my fault. My brother is going to die, and it's going to be because of me and my stupid mouth.* I jumped up and started pounding on his arms to break his hold, but my mere five-feet body and a mere 110 pounds did nothing to break his hold. I was like a tiny bug he didn't even feel. He did not even bother to swat me away or move his grip. I felt so helpless. I was filled with fear, remorse, anxiety, guilt, and panic. This was all my fault. "You motherfucker!" I yelled. "Let him go!" I screamed in such a fierce high pitch it sounded like a siren. He never even winced. He did not hear a word I said. He had my brother up so tight against the wall he was knocking family photos to the ground. My brother's eyes were beginning to bulge, and I could see the light draining from them as he was turning a grayish blue. It was at that very moment Mamma bear came running in to that horrific scene. Because he was taken off guard as she barreled into my dad on his right side, it was hard enough that she was able to knock him off balance to where he had to release my brother in order not to topple over. He even fell into me; at which point, I shoved him hard enough for him to fall to the other side of the hall wall, knocking off more pictures and shattering glass over the floor. My brother crumpled to the ground, gasping and choking.

Now my father steadied himself, and his bulging bloodshot eyes and rage are now redirected toward my mother. As he transferred his anger to my mother, the fight moved out of the hall to the family room, along with the yelling and screaming continuing from room to room and ending in our royal-blue velvet living room, which we always referred to as the Blue Room. Before running to the Blue Room, I hugged my brother and told him I was so, so sorry. He was holding his neck, choking. He croaked, "Go help Mom." I ran from the hallway to the Blue Room. I could not tell who had the upper hand because things were happening so fast and quickly. That's when I saw my dad grab a handful of my mom's hair, and he was slapping her like she was some rag doll. As I watched that scene again, my five-feet size had a complete rush of adrenalin. Again, I snapped. That's it. I was going to take control, and I was not going to let that son of a bitch hurt anyone in my family again. I ran up and with the force and strength of a tiger and the strength of probably four men put together. Yes, me—110 pound, 5 feet-tall teenage girl pushed my mom away so she was able to break away. Then with all my might, I made a fist and pulled my fist back. I swung so hard like I was swinging a bat for a home run and took that fist, closed my eyes, punched him so hard in the eyeball, and took that bastard down. He fell to the floor writhing in pain as he was holding his eye.

I looked at my mom, who was kneeling on the floor and trying to stand up, her eyes wide and shocked. I bent to try and help her to her feet. As I was doing that, her very first words out of her mouth were, and I am quoting her, "Oh my god. I just hope you punched him in the bad eye, not the good eye."

Hahaha! Yes, here it was, the black comedy in the insanity. See, my dad had a glass eye from, believe it or not, a non-alcohol-related injury where he was nailing something into the wall at our house and not wearing safety glasses. The nail went into his eyeball, and he lost his left eye and had it replaced with a horrible glass eye that never looked right. And for twenty-five years, he had at least four to five surgeries on that eye to save parts of the nerve, but ultimately, it was horrible, with the draining and infections. It was the way the eyeball was damaged that the glass eye always was draining, and it had to or it would get infected. It was ghastly looking. That along with his dentures that he would take out, he looked like a first-rate homeless bum. The years of drinking had taken a toll on his once very handsome looks.

I looked over to my mom and said, "Mom, did you really just say that?" I kind of giggled.

She nervously laughed herself, and she said, "Well, I am not about to be stuck taking care of a blind drunk for the rest of my life. Don't you think it is bad enough I have to deal with this shit and worry myself sick that one of you kids will be hurt?" She stated it rather than questioned.

I nodded, and Mom and I ended up in a fit of nonstop giggles. After our hysteria subsided, I said, "Mom, I punched him in the bad eye, not the good eye."

Yes, I know what you all are thinking. That is not funny. In a horrific event that finally ended without death, some families cry. Not us—we began to laugh hysterically because we had been through so many of these terrible scenarios it was becoming comical. I think that is the comedown from the anxiety, the nerves, and the fear. After what seemed to be several minutes of giggling, we saw my brother slowly walking toward us. I ran to him to see how he was. Bruises, big black-and-blue marks, were already forming on his neck. I felt so awful and incredibly guilty. I also thought, *Thank god it is Friday and the weekend, so no one would see it at school and maybe they would heal by then.* But they didn't, and he would have to wear a turtleneck shirt for a week before they did.

I remember hugging him so tightly and crying. I sobbed. "I am so sorry I caused this to happen."

He squeezed me tight and said, "Sis, it's okay." He said, "Do me a favor and next time, don't yell so loud and keep your door shut." He chuckled even though he was serious.

My mom let my dad lay there in a stupor on the blue carpet floor, where he eventually passed out. He laid there, drool and vomit seeping out the side of his mouth. It was disgusting. Mom, my brother, and I—well, we just got up as usual and dusted ourselves off and ordered a pizza to be delivered and hugged one another tightly. The three musketeers. I remember feeling so guilty for so long after that night, for doing that to my brother and my mom. If I hadn't been so crazy-filled with anger, none of that would have happened. I shudder to think my brother could have been killed. Yes, that, by far, was one of the most frightening scenarios, along with that one I so vividly recalled at five. In actuality, there were so many traumatic events and scenarios. I am not even sure I can remember to list them all. Those two that I just told you about are the ones that haunt me the most.

I can't even count on how many altercations and accidents that were alcohol-related that my dad was involved in. I cannot even chronicle them all. In 1977, my dad was arrested in the neighboring town for a DUI and lost his license. He actually had his license suspended many times. Some of the legal documents to attest to that, I have, but not all of them. I even remember a time when my mom got a call from some nice officer who stopped at the site of an accident my dad had when he ran his car into a tree. When he drunkenly stumbled or rather fell out of the car, his glass eye popped out onto the asphalt. That's how the officer found him, kneeling and stumbling around and looking for his eyeball. He was lucky he didn't fall on it and crush it. The officer called to tell her that he was intoxicated and that he impounded the car and that he was not going to book him but she needed to come and pick him up. And that between my drunk father and him, they were able to retrieve the glass eyeball. What a fricking circus scene that must have looked like. I cannot believe we kept these situations secret from friends, family, and neighbors, but we did.

The arrest in the neighboring town—well, that was way too close to home. That was in the town where I knew most of the kids that went to my rival high school. That was such an embarrassment to me. I was sixteen, and I knew so many kids who attended that high school who belonged to my church parish. I was sick for weeks to my stomach, praying no one would find out. My mom left him in that local jail overnight that time. It was safer than springing him while he was drunk. He also was arrested and jailed in 1997 in McHenry County. Before the seriousness of DUIs and driving while under the influence of alcohol, my dad had managed to pay off, get lawyers, or get off many of those incidents when he was pulled over for drunk driving. Most of the time, he just received a ticket for crashing and destroying a vehicle from an accident. My mom later told me long after her divorce that all the counties did finally start getting smarter with technology and once computerized, began connecting the dots.

That's when the laws started toughening on drinking and driving or driving with a suspended or revoked license, and MADD came into existence. Once they connected the dots, that was when he spent time in a federal prison. For how long, I do not know. It was long after my parents were divorced, and I was estranged from him.

At around the time I was sixteen came the point that my mother's relationship with my father was just barely civil. They were not sleeping in the same bedroom. He was on the couch. There were no affectionate displays of love or touching that had long died out, and Mom no longer wanted to do the pretense of pretending life was perfect, at least on the inside of our house. On the outside, it was a different story. She still pretended at parties, on vacations, and at holiday gatherings that everything was just peachy and perfect. On the inside though, there was no physical touch happening anymore when he was sober, and when he was drunk, she would lock her door. He also had started staying out all night long, so he was getting his dick fulfilled in other ways—either with Rosy, his hand, or the slut bar floozies. My mom knew that to be true, and she didn't care anymore. I think she was actually relieved. Her relief at having his unwanted affections coming her way was brief because he then started making sexual innuendos and advances toward me. That freaked the living daylights out of my mom and, of course, scared the crap out of me. As a little girl, I had always adored my daddy. I after all, I was Daddy's little princess. I could wrap him around my finger and do absolutely no wrong in his eyes. I cannot say that was true of my brother. He was always the scapegoat. No matter how hard he tried to win my dad's approval, nothing worked. He could do nothing right. It was always me. I was the one he smiled at and who he would light up for when I was around, and I was the one who could do no wrong. Of course, I loved that kind of adoration as a little girl, but as I got older and saw how my dad treated my brother, my guilt would be huge. Mom saw it too, and she would really compensate for all the negativity my brother received at my father's hands. And she also used me to do the dirty work of getting my father to do things she couldn't get him to do. All those years growing up, I know my mom didn't mean to use me, but she did. She used that daddy's-little-girl syndrome to her advantage, and I don't blame her that she did.

As I got older, I hated it. I resented doing it as it became very clear to me that I was the only one who could get my father to do anything. Mom knew it and used that to her advantage to manipulate him into doing the family thing with us. I think she thought if we did things as a family, everything bad would be swept under the carpet and only the good times would be remembered. Not really the case, but it did keep up the perfect family image to the outsiders looking in. And of course, we always took pictures of these times so that we looked oh so happy. We, of course, got the great opportunity to experience beautiful places on vacations, fun excursions to brighten up the dark night before. This would happen every time after one of his beating drinking binges occurred. I began to loathe it. It would start with my mom asking me to talk to my dad, who was passed out on the couch, and start cajoling him and begging him to get up. It would start out like this: I would kneel down next to the couch. He always had his back facing the wall. I am sure because he did not want to see our faces. I am not even sure the man felt remorse or just pretended to be remorseful. Not even sure he remembered what he did the night before. I would start quietly with begging in the voice of a tiny young girl. "Daddy, it's okay. We know you didn't mean it." I would chant that about five to ten times, sometimes even thirty times and sometimes even fifty times or more. Then I would pat his back with my little hand and rub it to try and stir him to move, anything to get his attention, and then the chanting, begging, and cajoling him would be repeated. "Please, Daddy. Come on, get up. Let's do something as a family today. Mommy said she wants us to be a family. Let's do something together. Mommy isn't mad at you. Please, Daddy, do it for me. I love you, Daddy. It's okay that you came home late. We love you, Daddy. We won't say anything about last night, Daddy. Please, come on. It won't be any fun without you. Mommy has something fun planned, Daddy. Come on, Daddy. I'll make you some coffee. Give you some of your favorite donuts. I promise we aren't mad at you. Come on, Daddy. Pleeeeeeaaaaase." Yep, that's how the routine would go every time. On and on, the begging would go, and it would always last about twenty to thirty minutes, sometimes even an hour and sometimes several hours, and then finally it would work.

For a little girl between the ages of five years until her teenage years, you can imagine how demoralizing and how exhausting that task would become. Yet in the beginning, I was proud to do it. I felt like I was the chosen one, like I won an award. I felt empowered, proud that I was the only one that could get him to do something, to be able to get a positive response and action from him. But in the end, I was the loser because I began resenting it, dreading it, and hating it so much. It made me angry, and my anger rolled over toward my mom, who I adored. I resented her for asking me to do it each time. By the time I turned about the age of fourteen, I stubbornly would not comply, and then by the time I was sixteen, I absolutely refused. This was the end of my rope. I could not stand the dysfunction of it all. I absolutely resented Mom for asking me. I hated feeling like I was obligated to do it as the only thing that would make my mom happy to get him up off the couch. I had severe low self-esteem, depression, and anger. I was a teenager going through hormones. This whole scenario depressed me and made me somewhat suicidal, on the verge of a breakdown. My mind was mixed up and messed up, and my body was telling me something was very wrong. And I was scared. I was terrified of all those feelings. I hated my life. I was embarrassed by my father. I wanted no one to know or find out how we were living, how he was a drunk. This was a very dark time for me as a teenager.

When I finally turned eighteen, my mom finally got the courage to actually file for divorce. This would be the first attempt. The sad thing was, she did not get good advice. She hired a lawyer that was recommended by a friend, but the guy was a total pushover. My dad, on the other hand, had his drunken buddies that he worked with get him some high-ranking lawyer who was a crook and knew the system. See, all those drunks stuck together and had to make sure they took good care of one of their own because if he was protected, they, too, were protected. There was some kind of sneaky payoff going on because the judge, no matter what evidence of abuse that was factual, leaned in favor of my father. His lawyer made allegations that we made up the beatings, and the fear and the abuse was nothing more than a joke and something we all said to make him look bad. My poor mom saw everything she worked so hard for slipping away. What a sick bastard, and all of them should have been ashamed of themselves for doing that to her and to me and my brother. Needless to say, my mom dropped the proceedings because she would have lost everything. One of the reasons my mom finally filed that first time was because when I was eighteen years old, I became so depressed I almost attempted suicide. It was a lame attempt because I tried to cut my wrists with a Legg's Shaver. I was just trying to get my mom's attention. All I did was make a bunch of scratches. It was a scare tactic. I wanted to shock my mom into doing something. I did not have the courage enough to actually slice my wrist even though I felt like wanting to die. I was too chicken, but it was enough to scare my mom into getting me professional help. I went and saw this psychiatrist for six months, and about that time, my mom served my father the restraining order and divorce papers. This was close to my eighteenth birthday. My father was a loser. He had no empathy in his heart. He didn't care about anyone but himself. He was such an unethical human being. The court proceedings happened very close to when I was turning eighteen. My dad had the audacity to have the sleazy lawyer subpoena my psychiatrist. This was the ultimate humil-iation and such a betrayal to me. I remember my face was red, and I broke out in a sweat as I heard my life story and my feelings being picked apart in an open courtroom. I felt like everyone was staring at me. There were many people inside the courtroom. My psychiatrist had to go on the stand and be questioned all about me. Here I was sitting there like I didn't even exist, and they were airing my private thoughts and feelings in front of me and the entire filled courtroom. His lawyer tried to make me look awful, that I was this hormonal angry teenager making it all up. Then he made my mom look like she was some money-hungry liar putting me and my brother up to saying all these things to make my dad look bad. I felt like everyone in the whole room was staring at me. I never was so humiliated in my entire teenage life. How my dad could look himself in the mirror after doing that to me was beyond my comprehension. When my mom realized what was going down, that her lawyer was not fighting for her rights and our rights, she decided to drop the case and reconcile with him. That was right before I turned eighteen. I remember that I was so angry with her when she did. I did not understand the circumstances. I wasn't mature enough to understand what was happening. All I kept thinking was he was coming back into the house and we were going back to hell. That's when I told my mom I needed to get away for a month before starting cosmetology school. I graduated from high school in May. I turned eighteen in June.

I told my mom I was going to visit my best friend in California for a month before I started beauty school in August. She agreed. I think she was relieved that I was going so she would not have to worry about me at home if my dad was around. I was afraid to leave her, but I needed an escape. So I ran away for a month and left her to deal with the beast. The freedom from not having to live in fear was pure heaven. It was one of the best trips I ever did. I came back and started cosmetology school, and it was the same scary ritual over and over again. Although this time, I was a young adult exploring my own wings and sowing my own oats. When I started cosmetology school, there were students in my class of all ages, and I was probably the youngest of the lot. Everyone else in my class was in their twenties and thirties and of legal drinking age. Well, that did not stop me from blossoming out and opening those wings to fly. Those new friends were able to get me a fake ID. I started going out to happy hours and, of course, drinking, dancing, and bar hopping with them. A whole new world and lifestyle using my fake ID and experimenting with alcohol. It did not occur to me that I was playing with fire. I was curious and wanted to see why my dad liked it so much. I wanted answers, and I got them. It felt good when I was tipsy because I didn't have to feel anything. Period. I felt free and uninhibited. One great perk was that my friends in cosmetology school were super tall. When I say super tall, I mean super tall. One was five feet, eleven, her boyfriend six feet, three; another girl was six feet, two, her boyfriend six feet, eleven; and me a mere five feet, two inches. So I would sandwich myself in between them when we would go out and just walk right in. Everyone was so busy looking at this giant group of people they never even saw me. It worked. What can I say? This was the first time I started experimenting with social drinking. I liked this newfound freedom, and I also wanted to fit in and be part of the in-crowd of new friends I just met. I didn't want to be this outcast outsider who did not fit in or was a nerd, plus I was beginning to love the numbing of not feeling any emotional pain. After my first euphoric drink, I understood. I liked that feeling. The only exception was the massive hangover. I couldn't understand why he wanted to feel so awful especially when I was hugging the porcelain toilet, vomiting for overdoing it, and then waking up with a severe hangover and massive headache. That was awful. That felt awful. How could he do that every other week, weekly, or ever? It was disgusting to feel burning acid bile come up in your throat and have a headache the size of the Eiffel Tower. Is that how he felt after one of his binges? I refrained from doing that too often because I hated that feeling of waking up sick and hungover. The scary thing was, I still secretly loved the beginning feeling of being all tingly, the euphoria of escape, escaping feelings and emotions. I tried to suppress that I liked it.

Mom and I continued living the next six years in that house with my father. We were constantly pretending and walking on eggshells. It was scary because Dad was becoming more and more demonstrative and sexual toward me. My brother—well, he just could not take it anymore. He was eleven months younger than me, so he immersed himself in school and work. And he practically was living at his high school sweetheart's parent's house. He was never home. By the time he was twenty-two, he had saved so much money he was able to put a down payment on a three-bedroom ranch house in the neighboring town. Then he proposed to his high school sweetheart, who was nothing but a selfish, conniving bitch who was using him. My brother was such a sweetheart. Because of the way he was raised with me and my mom, he had such sensitivity toward females along with a very rare kindness and innate empathy. Unfortunately, like all of us, his self-esteem and self-worth are low. He never realized how handsome and how incredibly attractive those sensitive attributes were, and that was why girls in school flocked to him because they saw this gorgeous, tall, dark, handsome guy who was sensitive to a woman's feelings. All my friends would beg me to have him ask them out because they saw it too. He was so nice and never realized that he was so sought after, which made him even more attractive, but instead of choosing a giver and choosing wisely, he chose a taker. He was young and in love. He knew nothing about relationships and what a healthy one should look like. Like me, he was clueless. He was too young and trusting to know love. He just wanted an escape. When you are a giver, a people pleaser, a taker usually sees your light and finds you. Sadly, that was what happened. The person he chose was as nasty as you could get and evil. You couldn't warn him because he thought he was in love. Plus he wanted to escape out of the hell we were living. So he did at twenty-two, leaving me and my mother to deal with the animal. We were on our own and had to handle Dad's binges, abusiveness, accidents, arrests, and DUIs.

One day, I finally looked at my mom and asked her why the hell she took my father back when I was eighteen. She finally told me the truth. I empathized and understood, but I also felt incredibly sorry for my mom. She deserved to be happy. It was not until I was twenty-three that she finally was at a point where she had things in order and enough documentation on his infidelity and DUIs and arrests to refile for a restraining order and start the divorce proceedings. That was when I was twenty-three years old, and that was when she finally divorced him. By the time I turned twenty-four years old, we were free. The house was finally a safe haven. We could live in it without living in fear. It was like a big weight was lifted off our whole family. The funny and ironic thing is that no one believed us when we started speaking the truth about what really was going on behind closed doors. We had kept such a good front up and kept those secrets so well that they were all incredulous at the horror that went on behind the bright orange front doors. There was no point to try and convince them now. By this time, I was completely estranged from him as I could not stand the sight of this man who was my father. I said to my mom, "Maybe we should be having a divorce celebration party." She laughed. When my mom had finally kicked him out, he didn't try to battle or fight it anymore. I think he knew we were done. We were not going to take his bullshit anymore.

Now my mom was single again and is such an attractive lady. She started living her life, going out and making friends, and going on dates. It was fun to watch her blossom. But see, when you are codependent and not healthy, you're a target for the needy or a beacon to an abuser. The good guys that make you feel uncomfortable because it is healthy, well, you feel smothered and they turn you off, all because they're feelings that you have never experienced before. That's what happened to my mother and also to me. Mom and I were both on the dating circuit, and my experience with the dysfunction that I grew up with did not lead to very healthy choices in my relationships. Neither did my mom make good choices in that department. It seemed both of us were targets. We leaned toward the men who needed help and seemed weak, men who needed fixing, but really men who were control freaks and abusive. Men who put on a face of being kind and good-hearted but were hiding behind the facade and in the end were selfish, self-centered, negative, toxic, controlling, and abusive. Subtle at first, but full-blown when they had you in the palm of their hand. A taker, an abuser, is someone who wants to be in control, someone who is emotionally needy. Mom, my brother, and I didn't know what a healthy, loving relationship could be. We never saw it or ever experienced it. It was like we all felt that was what we deserved. All three of us were and are enablers and codependent people. It's our giving nature, our need to fix everything, the people-pleasing syndrome. My brother is not as bad as my mom and me. I did not know how to be any other way, but I am finally learning after many painful experiences. Through my high school years from the time I was fifteen, I dated many nice guys, but those nice guys who probably were the cream of the crop and would have been awesome partners were dumped like hot potatoes. Their genuine kindness and love for me made me uncomfortable. The minute they got close to me or wanted a more serious, intimate relationship, I took the high dive and ran. They were too nice to me, and I was not used to nice. If they did not have a problem that needed fixing, I felt helpless. It was like I was looking for the rotten apple, deep down wanting to be treated badly because that was what I was used to, the behavior that I knew so well. Yeah, I know, that's sick. Well, I was sick. I always managed to find someone that seemed nice on the surface, but the core character was not; and all of them had some flawed, sick personality trait that was not normal, and always they were needy souls. They were needy, but this was my illness, that innate feeling and need to fix, help, and enable. If I was not doing that, then I would get these crazy thoughts that if I acted like this and loved them like this or did what they wanted or liked, maybe they would love me more, thus losing my identity even more. Not thinking that by putting my feelings and emotions under the carpet and solely behaving the way I thought that other person wanted me to behave, I was feeding the unhealthy merry-go-round ride once again. I felt that I did not deserve anything better. I felt I was not worthy of being cared for and treated with respect. I accepted bad behavior more easily because it was the abusiveness I was totally used to getting back all my life.

The first time I fell in love, I was nineteen. And yes, my dad was still around, and it was awkward trying to cover up for him. The guy I was with at first seemed wonderful. They always do in the beginning, when it's that high infatuation love, or campaign mode, as I call it. Then after a period of time, the surface behavior whittles away to show the true colors coming out. The true character of my first love came out after a year of dating. He was very selfish, a taker, controlling, condescending, and a verbally abusive narcissist. Because of my low self-esteem and my fragile state of mind, I allowed him to treat me like a doormat and enabled him to talk down to me—all the time thinking there was something wrong with me and that I deserved it. I would think, *What am I doing wrong that he is being like this to me?* I dated that person for three years before finally, after falling into a deep depression, I came to the resolution that I had to end it. That was only because the dynamics of the relationship had changed so drastically and my friends kept pushing me to see the light.

Deep down, I knew he was emotionally abusing me. It was over after the first year, but I kept holding out and holding onto something that was never right to begin with. I finally had a wake-up call during our third year together. I still had not slept with him, although I kept him happy in so many other ways except for making love, and I am sure you can imagine what that means. In the beginning of our blossoming relationship, when after a month I refused to sleep with him at nineteen, I clearly remember him use that condescending, judgmental tone of voice telling me I was frigid, that I needed to loosen up. He said I needed to let go, let love happen, and make love to him. I was nineteen, almost twenty, and I knew absolutely nothing about making love or had any intimacy or sexual encounters except going to third base. I was born and raised as a good Catholic girl. Yes, I was a virgin and wanted to wait till I got married. That had been hard-core pressed upon me since Catholic grade school. I was head over heels for this guy. He made my heart race. We both seemed to fall hard and quick after a month. He talked about marriage. We began looking for houses together. I was smitten. It was a whirlwind. He saw me every night from the first night I met him at a local dance club. So when the pressure-cooker jerk came on strong after a month about making love, I froze. I let him intimidate me and make me feel bad for holding on to my values. On our fifth date after seeing each other nonstop every night, Sam had the nerve to give me a book on how to make love to a man and lecture me about the facts of life. I should have known then that he had little respect for me or for any woman, but I took the book like a good little robot and, of course, was hurt and humiliated and felt guilty about how I felt. I remember reading the book and feeling humiliated. Yet there was something inside of me that held my ground and I would not sleep with him. That was the only thing I still had control over, and I just felt like he did not love me enough, that if I did, that was all he was really after. Like I was a prized trophy, and he was trying to reach the finish line for the win. He was used to getting his way, and it irked him that he couldn't. I just felt if I gave in, he would dump me like a hot potato. I had such low self-worth.

One day, I remember in the last six months of our three-year relationship, he finally said to me, "Katie, I only want to see you on weekends, not during the week. That's because I work so late and it's hard to get together during the week."

So odd because we had seen each other every day either at my house or his apartment every day for two and a half years, and then all of a sudden, he was having this late-night work ethic? Wow. Hurt, sad, and confused, I agreed to his rules. "Okay," I said, not wanting to upset the boat.

I loved him, so I followed his wishes. That should have been one more major indicator that something was not right. Everyone knows that if someone is too busy for you and doesn't make time for you, they really don't care about you. Of course, when you love someone deeply, you become desperate to do anything to keep the relationship alive. You agree to stupid things. You act stupid. So I sat at home drowning my sorrows alone. I started feeling very sorry for myself, so I started picking up a bottle of wine on my way home from work a couple of nights during the week and having a few glasses to numb my loneliness. Most of my friends were married already by this time, so I had no one to really hang out with. I knew alcohol was a depressant, and I also knew it was the very thing I hated my dad for. But I still did it, and while I drank alone, I would worry that my dad would come home drunk. Then there were the times after a half bottle of wine, I would call my friends sobbing. My friends would all say, "Katie, we saw him out at a club, and he was with another girl. You are too good of a person to be with him." Then the ritual would happen the very next day. I would confront him. He would make up a story. I would accept it, even though deep down inside, I knew he was lying. See, I was always the good girl, the respectable girl to bring home on the weekends to Mom and Dad and the rest of the family. It seems this is a pattern I would repeat in other relationships throughout my life.

The relationship lasted like this for another six months until I finally had the courage two months before my brother's wedding, where he was asked to be a groomsman, to break it off. I remember I started out with hope in my heart that I was going to tell him I was going to start dating other people. I was hoping he would all of a sudden have an epiphany of how he was treating me and suddenly change. Haha! I was wrong. He said, "If that's what you want to do, Katie," patting me condescendingly on my back. I felt like a dog. Not the response I wanted to hear. I wanted the Prince Charming response. I wanted him to profess his undying love, for him to say, "I am so sorry for making you feel small"; for him to say, "I love you and would do anything to make you happy." No, he was telling me, "Yes, go out with other people." *No*, I thought. That is not what I want to do, but I did. I, however, forced myself to go out with other guys. It was awful because the guys I went out with were truly nice guys—good, kind, loving guys that I didn't give the time of day to, who really treated me well and really liked me. All I kept thinking about was Sam. I was miserable when I would go out with them. I only followed his rules and dated them during the week because I did not want to miss seeing Sam on the weekends. I was his puppet.

The sad thing is, those two guys I dated were total gentlemen and treated me way better than Sam, who I was in love with. I remember one of them saying to me, "I know what you are doing, Katie. You're only seeing me during the week so you can see Sam on the weekends. You have to make a decision. It's either him or me. I care a lot about you and want to be with you, but you have to make a decision." Ralph was a great guy—kind, fun, and respectful. "Let's start by going out Saturday night."

I cringed. Oh no, I was found out. It was so obvious what I was doing. Of course, what did I do? I said, "I am sorry, Ralph. I can't. I am going to have to choose Sam."

Ralph was crushed, and that was our last date. "I hope you know he treats you horribly."

I said, "I know," and walked away.

I was so dysfunctional. When I finally came to my senses—not because I wanted to but in my heart, I knew I had to end it—I got the courage to break it off from Sam six weeks before Kent's wedding. That was in April, when I finally had the nerve to break it off with Sam. I tried to hold off till after the wedding since he, after all, was in the wedding, but I couldn't wait. This was around the time I had met Jack on a blind date. I knew I was going to be so devastated breaking up with Sam that I started doing volunteer work at the local hospital gift shop to keep my mind occupied during the week nights. I did not want to come home alone, alone with a 1.5 liter bottle in my hand that was fast becoming my best friend and especially alone in the house with my father. I remember telling my brother I broke up with Sam. Kent was supportive, but not my former sister-in-law. She was so angry with me. All I asked her was "Please do not partner me with him in the wedding party." I was nervous enough for my brother because he had my dad involved in the wedding. I did not want any horrible situation erupting between me and Sam to add to the already tenacious evening. I kept asking Kent if he knew what he was doing by having Dad at the wedding, but my brother felt this need to follow protocol and family rituals and the need to win my father's love. Not me. I was so done there. I was terrified my dad would drink excessively and ruin it. I was totally stressed out, both my dad and my ex-boyfriend at my brother's wedding. My father did drink in excess, but thankfully the excessive part of it did not happen till toward the end of the reception where he sadly got hammered and started his belligerent behavior and most of the guests had already gone home. I did make it through the wedding despite having to deal with Sam and his arrogant, sarcastic, condescending behavior. I remember Sam's parents and his sister, who I had become so close to through those years, were at the wedding. They said to me, "We love you, Katie, and you deserve someone so much better, someone who treats you right." That made me feel good, but also sad. Oddly because I am me. I still keep in touch with Sam's family, and that's forty-nine years later. I even was a bridesmaid in his sister's wedding, he wasn't even asked to be part of her wedding or wedding party. That should tell you something right there. Many years later, I found out that he finally did marry in his forties and never had any children. It's funny, the paths we take in life.

I met Jack right before Kent's wedding as I said before, and even though it was four weeks before the wedding, I did not ask him to the wedding. I was under enough stress to worry about how my dad was going to behave and how Sam was going to act to have to deal with a potential new guy. How I met Jack is a story in itself. On the first night I volunteered at the hospital, I met Jack's mother, a lovely

ONE FELL OFF THE MERRY-GO-ROUND

woman whose name was Harriet and who had been volunteering in the hospital gift shop for years. She was training me on my first night in the gift shop. After several hours of talking and conversing, she began badgering me, asking me if I was single and if I was seeing anyone.

She said, "I think you are so sweet. I have two sons that I would love to give your number to."

I said, "Uh-oh. I just broke up with someone I had dated for three years, and I am taking a break from dating."

Lo and behold, she would not give up. She called me the next night and asked for my number again. Catching me off guard and because I simply wanted to get her off the phone, I rattled my number off to her, thinking there was no way one of her sons would call. From that first night meeting her at the hospital, apparently, she went home and told both her sons. The older one was not interested, but the younger one, Jack, who was seeing someone, was intrigued. So that is how I met Jack—on a blind date through his mother.

At my brother's wedding, I made a decision that if I were to get married, there is no way in hell I was having my father anywhere near my wedding. When I finally broke it off with Sam that month before, he was as condescending as ever and tried to make light of all he did. He had manipulated me for so long into thinking I was a nutjob. He had cheated on me with the bridesmaid at his best friend's wedding that was out of town in Michigan. He made up some story that he was the only one who could go since it was an out-of-town reception that he could not take me as a guest, that none of the attendants were bringing guests. A lie, which I believed. Yes, I was stupid. I wanted to believe him. Then I found out the truth that he was cheating. That was my last straw. So I told him it was over. I asked him back for all the things I had at his apartment, and I also asked him to reimburse me for the tires that I purchased. After all, here I was, making a third of what he took home as an analyst for a big corporate firm, yet I was paying for everything. Yes, I was dumb, and yes, I was the dysfunctional enabler and doormat. When he would not respond to my calls and emails for the payment back, I did become nutty. One night, I was so upset thinking about it I drove to his apartment complex and pounded on his patio window to open up. His apartment was on the first-floor level, and you guessed it, I was drunker than a skunk. He pretended not to be home. When he did not respond, I did the next best thing. I stole his golf clubs out of his car and his Weber grill top on his patio and held it hostage. LOL. Yes, that was pretty silly, nutty, and pretty funny, but you do *crazy* when fucked up and under the influence of alcohol.

I remember him calling the next day, and in his condescending way, he said, "Now, Katie, why would you take my Weber grill top and my clubs? Don't you think you are being a bit immature?"

I said defiantly, "No. I am not returning them till I get payment back for the tires." I held my ground. Payment for the tires arrived, and I dropped off my hostages the next day.

In the interim of all that happening, I continued to volunteer at the hospital, which ended up being a positive thing in my life. So when I met Harriet, Jack's mother, as I said earlier, I was adamant that I did not want to become involved with anyone for a long while. But she was very persistent. All I thought was *What crazy dude would call some girl that his mom got a number from?* Well, Jack did two weeks later, and we went out on a blind date. Four months later in August, we were engaged. How did that happen? Yes, it was crazy. I will explain that a bit later.

I remember Sam's best man and his wife felt bad about our breakup and asked me personally to come to the wedding and to bring a guest. I felt very uncomfortable, but my friend who was dating his friend and is also in the wedding party insisted I go to show Sam I was moving on. I asked Jack if he would be willing to go, somewhat explaining the dynamics. He said, "Sure." I was a nervous wreck, driving to the wedding ceremony that was in June. My stomach was in knots. This would be the first time since April I would come face to face with Sam. We also drove my girlfriend since her boyfriend was in the wedding party. This seemed to ease the tension I was feeling. Jack didn't seem fazed at all. He actually seemed to be enjoying himself. After the ceremony, we went in line to the receiving line.

Here it was coming, the first face to face with Sam. I went through the line, my hands clammy and sweaty. I got to Sam. He had that charming smile and said, "Hello, Katie. You look very lovely." Always the charmer. He took my hand and brought it up to his lips. My heart lurched.

I said, "Hello, Sam. The wedding was lovely." I then said, "Sam, this is Jack. Jack, this is Sam."

He looked at Jack and dismissed him with one look, but Jack had another agenda. He boldly held up his hand for Sam to kiss. My eyes widened in disbelief as Jack said, "You're not going to kiss my hand too?"

There was an awkward silence as Sam gave him a scowl. My friend who was behind Jack started giggling. I started giggling too, and then it was over. We were shuffled further down the receiving line. That was when I actually started looking differently at Jack, seeing him as someone different from Sam.

Things were starting to finally look good at our house and started becoming more peaceful. Mom was finally divorced from my dad. Their marriage ended shortly after my brother's wedding in the month of June. I was thankful that Jack only met my father once during that whole time. My brother's wedding was the last event my dad was at that we pretended to be a family. I was so relieved when it was finally over, and my mom had the locks changed on the house. I finally felt safe in my own home. I was not the least bit sad that he was gone. I was relieved. The relief I felt was like weights falling off a weight bench. I was on a brush off negative road and on a high when Jack called me that April. I remember I was home, getting ready for volleyball when the phone rang.

"Hi, is this Katie? This is Jack." I didn't answer as I furrowed my brow, trying to remember. Did I know a Jack? He said, "You met my mom at the hospital."

I was like *Really? This dude is calling me? The son of the mom I met at the hospital?* "Okay, which son?" I said. "Are you the younger son? Or the older son?"

He said, "The younger."

He was twenty-one, and I was just turning twenty-three in June. *Great,* I thought, *young and immature.* I was not sure if I should be flattered, but I was very flustered by the call. He started by saying his mom spoke so highly of me and that his brother Peter did not want my number, so he took it. He asked me out to go dancing. All I kept thinking was what weirdo would ask a girl he didn't know to go dancing, and who would get a date from his mom? And hell no, I am not going dancing with someone I never met. So I suggested we meet at a local pub and watch a hockey game. He was a sports fanatic, so that was right up his alley. He would not take me seriously when I kept saying that I would meet him there. He insisted that he come pick me up. I was not happy, but when he arrived at the door, I was pleasantly surprised by the piercing blue eyes and blonde hair and engaging smile. He was five feet, six to my five feet, two. We went out and had a great time, laughing, drinking, and drinking a lot. I remember that I never laughed so hard when the bartender engaged Jack in conversation and then challenged him to drink a shot with no hands in a rubber shark without spilling it. Jack took the challenge, and guess what? Yes, he was wearing the Land Shark shot all over his white shirt. During the date, I never spoke about my father. On the way home in my driveway, we made out like crazy on that first night. Yes, there was definitely a physical attraction the minute we met, but I was very leery and insistent that I was not going to get serious with anyone, that I was dating other people, and that I had just broken up from a long-term relationship. Jack was not put out by this information. It only seemed to make me more of a challenge. I had no idea he was seeing someone at the time he was dating me. I don't know if it was because I was so different from most of the girls he went out with or that I was older and more mature or the mere fact that I didn't fall all over him and fawn over him like most of the girls he had been seeing. Plus the fact that I was adamant about dating others and not getting serious and I did not pursue him like all the other girls he had gone out with in the past. Because I kept insisting I didn't want to get serious, this seemed to spur his interest even more. That's when Jack would pop over to my house unexpectedly with flowers or jewelry. I tried to give it all back, but he would not accept the gifts back. I think because I kept saying no, Jack fell head over heels from the start. I was, on the other hand, pretty gun-shy. I had been dating Sam for three years—Sam, my first love who I thought I was going to marry. Whom, in the beginning of our relationship, I was looking at houses together for our future together. Who ultimately changed from loving to taking and treated me terribly. It was a horrible relationship. Jack was the polar opposite of Sam. Jack was a tradesman and a painter; Sam was a corporate computer analyst on the rise up the success ladder. Jack was so different from Sam. Sam was successful and affluent. Jack was down-to-earth, a hardworking tradesman, and a sporting nut. Jack would not be put off. He said he was in love with me two months after we were dating.

I, of course, did not say it back. I kept repeating the mantra: "I am dating other people. I don't want to get serious so fast. I like you." That did not deter him. I did date other guys during that three-to-four-month period, but that got old really quick. And after about three months into the relationship, I seriously took a second look at Jack, especially after that wedding scene where he was nonplussed at the fact my ex-boyfriend was in the receiving line. Of course, the fact that he never stopped the strong pursuit and he was totally romancing me and the fact he made me laugh was what made me take a second look at him as relationship material. Plus when I told him I was a virgin, that totally turned him on. So I stopped dating all the other guys. I convinced myself that I was in love with Jack. That was about three months into our relationship. So after going out with similar Sam-type guys, I called Jack up, and at four months, I told Jack I was in love with him. When I look back, I am not sure I really was or if I was just really trying to convince myself to be in love.

Two weeks after I professed that I loved him, it was August 10, we had been dating for four months and two weeks. The tenth was the day of our first date. He had come over to the house, and we were going to order a pizza and watch a VHS movie. I had gotten him a card and a small bottle of his favorite aftershave Pierre Cardin, Polo. He gave me a cute little porcelain trinket box with a card.

I said, "Thank you. That's so sweet." I didn't open the trinket box.

He said, "Open the box."

I was perplexed. I opened it, and inside there was an engagement ring. He got on his knee, and he proposed. I was in utter shock and was completely taken off guard. Out of sheer surprise and being so caught up in the moment, I said, "Is this a proposal?"

He said, "What do you think? It is. Yes, it is." He laughed. He was still on his knees. He said, "Are you going to answer?"

I said, "Yes. Yes, I will marry you."

I was caught up in the excitement of the ring, being proposed to, and being romanced. I ran upstairs and woke my mother up. She said she knew. Jack had come earlier that day and asked her if he could marry me. She said, "If my daughter says yes, then I am happy."

It was a whirlwind of excitement—engagement parties, announcements, and setting the wedding date, which would be September 21, 1985. One year and a month from our engagement. It was an exciting time of fun, parties, and dating. I can honestly say that because of the newness and the excitement in the beginning our relationship, it was good because we both were young and having fun. We partied, drank a lot, and did fun things together. At the time, we had similar interests, and we were very compatible because we had no commitments other than having a good time. I loved his friends, and his friends loved me. I loved his mom and his brothers, and they loved me. It was all going good. I think back now to one of the reasons I said yes. I was feeling pressured at being left out, being the only one of my friends that had not gotten married and that I was still a virgin and wanted to know what I was missing. Part of me was proud of that fact, but the other part was *What the hell am I saving it for?* I felt it was time for me because at least half my friends were married at nineteen, and actually some were already on their second marriages when I was turning twenty-four. I remember one year when I was nineteen, I stood up in ten weddings it cost me a dang fortune. The only recoupment was after that year, I brought all the dresses to a resale shop and sold them for a fraction of the cost to girls going to prom.

So Jack and I had set our wedding date a year from our engagement on September 21, 1985. On the next twelve months, it was all about fun—planning the wedding and the honeymoon, attending parties and wedding showers, going out dancing, and going out and partying after softball games. Fun, fun, fun! I was on a high especially because in my house, my father was out of the picture and I could actually enjoy my home. One thing that I did follow through with was my decision not to have my father walk me down the aisle. We still were estranged, and I wanted absolutely nothing to do with him. I asked my aunt's husband—he was my mom's sister's husband, my uncle by marriage—to walk me down the aisle at my wedding. I did not even want my dad near the wedding. I did not want him as part of my wedding plans. He meant nothing to me. Every binge, every beating, every accident, and every day when I was a little girl begging and pleading day and night for him to stop beating my mom and to stop drinking had taken a toll on any love or affection along with the lewd behavior that started when I was in my teens. I had absolutely written my father out of the picture. I remember my grandmother, my mom's mother, being very upset with me because I was not going to have my father walk me down the aisle at my wedding. See, it was all about tradition. No matter what evil a person did, it was all about how it looks to others. That was what my grandmother was worried about. She was upset that I asked my uncle. She tried to guilt me, saying it was not right that my father was living and that I was not going to have him at the wedding nor walk me down the aisle. I told my grandmother I would be a hypocrite if I did. I would be pretending like we had this loving, wonderful relationship, putting up a front for all my friends and family and guests, who were finally finding out the truth now that the divorce was final. My grandmother was very angry with me. She thought it was wrong. After all, he was my father, and blood is thicker than water. I did not care. I was stubborn, and I was not going to give in. I did not want him to ruin my wedding by getting drunk. Jack who only met him once was okay with whatever I decided to do. He had met him but one time. He somewhat understood from what I told him about my growing up years, which was very little. As I did not want to talk much about it, I wanted to forget all that pain and not think about it. One thing that Jack really didn't understand was why I would not want a relationship with him. See, his father died in a car accident when he was just one year old, leaving behind a young wife with four boys. Jack never knew his dad, but from pictures, Jack was the spitting image of him. I always marveled and was inspired at the strength of Jack's mom, Harriet, who never remarried since Jack senior was the love of her life. How did she do it? Raise four boys, pay a mortgage, and work full-time? I thought she was amazing. See, Jack's dad, Jack Senior, never had any life insurance. He was young, so he did not believe he needed any. How devastatingly hard for her and those boys. When we became engaged, the fact that I was becoming part of her family was a joy to her, another daughter to compliment the other daughter-in-law she already had with her eldest son, Philip. Although he did not understand the dynamics of my father's abuse, he did finally accept how I felt about not having my father there. I think he knew that he was crossing my boundary line by even questioning my decision.

For Jack and I, for the first five years of our marriage, things were smooth sailing. What I didn't realize was that I took over being Jack's mother. There is that codependency trait I inherited. Jack was an overgrown child in a man's body. He was not independent nor self-sufficient. When I married Jack, he didn't know how to even put his paycheck into the bank for a deposit. For years, he was giving his check to his mother to do it for him. Jack lived and breathed his sports: softball, bowling, golf, and floor hockey. He was on many leagues. And that was great when we were first married because I would go and support him at those various events, but I never was a participant. So he was always having fun, and I was just sitting back, watching. Always the enabler. That was okay in the beginning of our relationship to an extent, but it was very selfish and one-sided. Yet I allowed it to keep going on like that because that is what you are supposed to do. Right? Never speak up and say how you feel.

When we started having kids, that routine of a party boy got old really quick. When Jack rebelled when I asked him to give up some of that fun to be a parent, it was a fight. So I just gave in and decided it was not worth the fight. So for twenty-three years, I lived like that, and then there were the high lows of his personality, anger issues, his sexual quirks, his addictions, and my addiction. Because Jack didn't know how to be a parent, it was very difficult for him to be a father. All he wanted to do with our children was play with them, never discipline them, and when they would make mistakes or need some guidance, he would lash out in anger, not knowing how to be a parent. He became verbally abusive and violent. This is where I would come in and have to mediate. See, I was proficient at mediation from all those years with my father. I stepped in and became his mommy and tried to control his violent behavior and irresponsibility at what he would allow the kids to do. He partied all the time, going out and staying out late with the boys. We were the first in his group to have children. It was clear that Jack danced to his own drum of childlike behavior. He also had very strange sexual preferences, and he always wanted me to dress up like a hooker in sleazy negligees and always in heels with makeup in order to make love. Since he was the only man I ever slept with, I thought that was normal. After twenty-three years of marriage, I found out the truth that this was not normal. This was abnormal behavior. Jack had addictions, and Jack was addicted to many things: porn, gaming, and gambling. Jack was cheating on me and probably had been throughout our entire marriage. I didn't ever want to believe it or face it, even though deep down I had probably already known that he had been. I just didn't want to believe it. When it was found out, it was a horrible revelation and realization that I was putting up the same facade that we had the perfect family and family life that my mom had tried to make everyone believe all those years. I had jumped right on the ride and followed her lead.

When my parents finally divorced, my father had made no attempt to establish any relationship with my brother or myself. Therefore, it was easy to not have him at my wedding and basically write him out of my life. However, my brother remained in contact with him. My father—he never could stand on his own two feet. He ended up marrying one of his buddies' sister right after they were divorced so he wouldn't be alone and to prevent her from being committed to a psychiatric hospital. See, Martha had several nervous breakdowns and was not able to take care of herself, so my father, not being able to take care of himself, married her. When I asked him why when I saw him at an event of one of my brother's children, he said it was because he felt sorry for her and figured they could try and take care of each other. They were two peas in a pod. The nerve bomb and the alcoholic—what a great pair. See, my dad could never be by himself. My mom did everything for him. Sound familiar? The apple doesn't fall far from the tree. He was just there, like a mannequin with an illness, who became a different animal when he drank. By the time of the divorce, I considered him no longer my father. He was just this person who provided my mom his sperm to create me. See, after that scene where he almost killed my brother and when the sick lewd behavior started, I could not take it any longer. He was vile, and it was completely clear to me that he had no soul. In all my life, I never saw one ounce of empathy in my father or an ounce of compassion for anyone but himself. He was a heartless, sick bum, who was controlled by booze. And of course, after the way he started behaving toward me then later hearing about and witnessing all the affairs he had had while being married to my mom, she was so lucky she did not get some type of herpes or STD. I know when she first started finding out about them. This scared her. When I was older and an adult, she told me she was tested. Thankfully, those tests came back negative. My father could easily have been considered a pedophile and definitely when drunk was controlled by his penis. His sick behavior as a teenager screwing animals and his lewd behavior when drunk—he had all the attributes. He had *sleazebag* written all over him. It is still beyond my comprehension, and I feel this sick feeling when I think about all those years she stayed with him, knowing all that information and having to sleep with him. It makes me get queasy.

All I know is that my mom felt stuck and felt trapped and that she thought she had no way out, so she decided she was going to make it her project to try and fix my father and prove to everyone that we had this all-American happy family. I think partly this was because she had tried on her own to leave him at one point when we were babies, but my stubborn German-raised grandmother would not allow her to leave him. She told my mom, "Well, you made your bed. Now you just go back and lie in it." Nice, Grandma. Therefore, she had to change, conform, and accept what she had been dealt. So this is where the dysfunction and codependent behavior begins.

At some point when after I had my first child, I had a small tiny change of heart, a ping of guilt that I thought I should make sure my child met her real grandfather so that she never could say to me in the future that I kept her from knowing him. I think part of me was expecting him to somehow be changed. Ha, fat chance. After several attempts to reconnect and get together with him, I clearly remember my two-year-old looking at me and asking the question, "Why does that grandpa not love me?" *Ding, ding, ding!* A two-year-old was more intuitive than me. How can a man that is an empty shell for a brain even have the capacity to show love? He can't, so I made the decision to cut all ties once and for all. I had already made peace and forgiven him for what he did to me, my mom, and brother, but there was no forgiveness for hurting my child. I told my little girl that he moved away; that's why we didn't see him anymore. She never asked again until she was way older, and I started opening up and telling her these stories. "My father was a sick man. He drank so excessively that his brain was so messed up he had absolutely no personality when sober and absolutely no morals while drunk." Hell, when a man fucks an animal in his teen years, how moral is that? That is a crime and animal cruelty. It's no surprise when his body finally left this world that he died from dementia and Alzheimer's brought on by his excessive alcoholism.

You wonder if I am exaggerating his sick pedophile-like behavior. No, I am not. It started heavily when I was around fourteen to fifteen years old. All the years growing up, my father and I had this odd relationship. I loved him as a little girl loves her daddy and worshipped him even through the drunken hazes that as a child, I did not understand. I also knew I was his favorite and I could wield him to my will and get him to do most anything that I asked. He adored me. When I was a little girl, I liked that feeling of power. My mom saw that too. What she could not get him to do, I was the victor. I had the ability to beg and convince him, and most of the time, it would work. This would become that sick ritual I mentioned earlier for years that I completely detested. My love for my father through the years gradually died. Feelings of love and affection slowly ebbed away to feeling nothing except disgust, hate, and anger. At first, I felt guilty, but after what we went through, guilt was replaced by that fear then hate as I got older and more mature. It changed to empathy and feeling sorry for him at his sad existence at the time of his death.

Even though I was fourteen going on fifteen, I had always been scared of his violent behavior before when he was drunk. There was something way more frightening, sick, and sinister that was developing, and I was terrified. His behavior had changed toward me, and there was this underlying sexual tone happening when not drinking; and it became more apparent when he was drinking. When he was drunk, it would start with him trying to hang all over me. Because I was uncomfortable, I would always turn away and turn my back to him for fear he would try and kiss me, but that always seemed to make the situation even worse. He would then wrap himself around me, pressing his front side to my back tightly where I could feel everything, and I mean everything. When I mean everything, I felt him get as hard as a rock, and it scared the crap out of me. I would squirm and attempt to break away, then he would start groping me more and keep trying to hug and kiss my face. This was not a fatherly-like hug. It was more like someone trying to paw and grab something he wasn't supposed to have in such a lewd way. It was gross, creepy, and vile. He smelled and reeked of alcohol, cigarettes, and stale coffee. His breath was sour. His body smelled from lack of hygiene from being on a long bender. I know Mom was beginning to see the light, and she knew that something was very wrong with this picture. She saw firsthand the behavior change, and I think she knew it was not heading in a normal fatherly-daughter way. That is why she never ever left me alone in the house with him. I know deep down she was afraid he would overpower my small five-feet frame and rape me. I was terrified and wanted to vomit just thinking about it and the possibility that he was acting like that to me. How could a father do that to his own daughter? That was when any feelings for him shifted to pure hatred and disgust. In later years when I was an adult and he was removed from any questionable interaction with me, that hatred turned to feeling nothing. The only thing I felt was feeling sorry for his pathetic existence.

One sexually charged incident that I remember was just one of more than a dozen that occurred. This one happened when I was just twenty years old. I had just started working at the corporate company as an analyst. I had graduated cosmetology school, but at that time when I graduated, there were no health insurance benefits offered by most salons. I was at the point in my life I needed health insurance and car insurance. I was a young adult now. Since I did not have a clientele built up and needed money to pay for all that, there was no way I could afford paying a private insurance company for it. I also had a school loan to pay off as well. That's when a friend said they were hiring at this large firm and that they had great benefits. So in my head, I thought I can still do hair on the side either at a shop or from home and then work there if I was hired for the benefits. So I applied for an accounting analyst position, and I was hired as an analyst for this company in the Controller Department. This was kind of funny because I hated working with numbers, and here I was, hired as an analyst working with statistics and financial reporting. At this point, I did not care. I just needed to be able to pay my bills and survive. It happened to be the best fit ever for me as everyone in that department was my age and we became a little network, a family, a support group for one another. They had a softball team. I joined. They had organized outings, and I went—anything to get me out of the house and away from the hell. I made some lifetime friends there, although none of them ever knew what I was living with at home. That part I kept secret. I started in September of 1980. December rolled around, and there was a Christmas Potluck Lunch, which everyone signed up to bring something. I volunteered to bring a nine-layer salad. I had gone out after work to pick up all the ingredients. It was snowing heavily, and the forecast said we were to get at least four to six inches by morning. I was in the kitchen putting the salad together in a huge foil pan. It was just me and my mom living in that house with this madman. My brother, who had always been my avid protector, was no longer living at home. He was practically living at his high school sweetheart's parent's home and didn't come home most nights except to shower and change. He was escaping to his girlfriend's as often as he could and working his brains out so that he could move out. He was twenty-one, almost twenty-two, and was able to purchase his first home and get engaged so that he could escape and run off and marry his high school sweetheart at twenty-two. So for the most part, it was just me and Mom dealing with my father, and it was scary. Because now that I was a grown woman, I knew what could happen, and there was every possibility that at some point, I would not be physically strong enough at five feet, two and 115 pounds to fight off this six feet, two-hundred-pound animal. My father continued to have this creepy, underlying, incestuous behavior toward me every time he came home drunk or sober. At this point in my life, I tried hard to have very little contact with him at all. I had lost all respect for him, and I avoided him like the plague. My father was not human—meaning, he was an empty shell. A man without a soul. In all the years I knew my father, I never saw him possess one ounce of human empathy or kindness. It was my mother who covered for his lack of humanness. He actually did not have a personality. He was dull, and it was probably from the result of overindulgence on alcohol that killed his brain cells. If he did have a humorous personality, it was only when he was inebriated. I truly did not like him as a person. Because he knew that I had lost all affection for him, it was like he became obsessed with trying to get my attention. It made me so creeped out and uncomfortable. My mother saw this too, and she was scared for me.

On this particular night when I was to make the salad for the holiday work party, it was about nine p.m. I had gone out with some of the girls from work for dinner, and then afterward, I stopped at our local grocery store to pick up the ingredients. I started working on the salad about nine thirty-ish. When I pulled into our driveway, I was relieved as he was not home yet. Whew. I could get started and hopefully complete it before he even stumbled in the door, but to my dismay, he staggered in at about 9:45 p.m. I heard the garage door go up, and I heard him stumbling toward the back end of the house where the bathroom was located. After he relieved his bodily functions, I could hear him begin to make his way to the kitchen.

He started slobbering and slurring in that raspy voice. "How's my bbbaby girl?"

My back was to him. I was facing the counter and the ingredients, hurrying as I put the first two layers of the salad into the foil pan. I was trying very hard to ignore him. "I'm fine," I muttered quickly with clenched teeth and a shaky voice. I attempted to ignore his reached-out arms coming at me. I began moving from side to side at the counter to avoid his hands, trying to feign that I didn't see them. I could only do that for so long before he finally grabbed hold of my arm. I forced my front side to face the counter, avoiding turning around to see that horrible face. There he went trying to wrap me in that disgusting hug where I would be able to feel his genitals rubbing against my buttocks. It was becoming increasingly difficult to avoid him touching me at this point. I was like a bunny hopping all over the kitchen. I am sure it looked ridiculous, but he was too drunk to know that was what I was doing. After he had me in that hold, he kept pawing me, rubbing my arm and trying to get me to turn around. I kept working on my salad, and with each attempt of his reach, I would move and avoid him. I could sense his tension and anger building. My heart was racing. I then knew I had to do something, so I mustered up the courage to speak in a soothing tone and say, "Dad, please. I am working on my salad for the Christmas party at work." I was shaking, trying not to sound nervous for fear of agitating him even more. "I can't finish it if you keep interrupting me. I am trying to mix it. Can't you see?" I pleaded. Even though I was pleading, I said it sweetly and in a soothing tone, praying it would work. That he would turn and walk away and go pass out on the couch. Unfortunately, that was not the case this time. My soothing voice didn't work. He then swung me around and wrapped me in a bear-hug grip, which was a lock hold. As he grabbed me, I said as I was turning my face away from him, "Dad, come on. Stop it. I have to finish this for work."

Well, that was all he needed. He snapped like a popcorn kernel popping. He was up against me, and I couldn't move my arms. I tried to squirm, but when I did, I could feel his penis get stiff. OMG, this sick son of a bitch was turned on. I could see out of the corner of my eye that his body got rigid and his eyes were black and evil. I remember I began shaking with fear. I tried elbowing him to break free but could barely move my elbow. His six-feet body had me pin-cushioned against the counter and cabinets. I broke out in a sweat. This was bad.

Then he slurred, "I don't give a fuck about your Christmas party. All I want is a hug and kissssss." Spit splattered everywhere on my cheek as I tried to turn my face. "You're suppppposed to wanna give your daddy a hug and a kiss. What's wrong with a little hug and a kissssssss, you little bitch?" he said, more spit flying through the air.

He had managed to twist me around to face him. Oh my god, he is drooling, and I think I am going to vomit from the vile smell of his breath. I was scared to death because it was the way he said that last sentence, calling me a bitch. It made my skin crawl. I turned white and said nothing, and then out of the corner of my eye, I saw he had grabbed the empty mayonnaise jar I had just emptied and put in the salad. I saw him lifting it in the air high above my head. I squinted, wincing, and closed my eyes, waiting for the crash. I opened them just a little in time to see him slam the glass jar on the countertop. It shattered into little chards of fragmented glass. Mostly all over the counter and the floor, but so close to the large foil pan. It was about a foot away, and to my horror, I saw some fly into my salad. My eyes began to fill with tears. Another thing ruined by this drunken man who I am supposed to call my father.

Tears started streaming down my face. It was already ten p.m. It was snowing like crazy. Of course, it was December, and I lived right outside in a northwest suburb of Chicago. Of course, it would be wicked and snowing. What was I going to do now? I was too tired to go out in the snowstorm and back to the store. And now here he was, this lowlife asshole father of mine who destroyed yet one more thing, and he was still coming at me, trying to kiss me. Something in the atmosphere and the way he was behaving—I knew that on this night, something really bad was going to happen. Something was way off with him mentally. I could tell his advances and innuendos were way more demonstrative than they ever were before. I started yelling for my mom. She was home, but she was in her bedroom with the TV loud, and I knew she probably had fallen asleep and she hadn't even heard him come in the house nor could she hear what was going on.

I vaguely remember him saying, "You little bitch. That's right. Go ahead. Call for your mother." I yelled louder as his big hand slapped me across the face.

Right at that moment, my mom came running into the kitchen. She had been dozing off and with the TV on. She took one look at the scene, and she saw my face as white as a ghost with a red hand mark across my cheekbone, my father holding me inappropriately against the countertop, and the shattered mayonnaise jar. She took it all in, and her eyes widened in anger, fear, and horror.

My father, turning and glaring at her, slurred, "Get the fuck out of here, you rotten fat ass bitch. I was just trying to give my baby girl a kiss, but she is being a bad girl," as he tried holding me tighter. I could feel the beating of my pulse under his fingers' grip. My back arched against the counter. The way he said *bad girl* made my skin crawl.

My mom stepped closer as she turned and grabbed the cast iron skillet that was sitting on the stove. She glanced at me, looked at him straight in the face, and said, "You sick son of a bitch, let go of her right now. You are not going to touch her one more time." He didn't let go of me, and he snickered a sick smile as he looked at her. My mom looked him straight in the eye and said, "This is it. You are done." And *wham*! Down came the skillet on top of his head. She had walloped him right on top of the head. He staggered, and he finally released me. Red-and-blue marks were forming on my arms. "Go. Call the police," my mom told me.

I ran from the kitchen, tears streaming down my face. I believe this was her turning point to finally ending the marriage. It was more than she could handle, watching the possibility of her daughter being raped by this man she called her husband. For all she put up with— all the physical and verbal abuse, all the black-and-blue marks, all the bloody lips, and all the unpaid bills—she had enough, and she had to protect me. She was, after all, my mother, and that is what mothers do: protect their children. I think that night was the cherry on top of the ice cream sundae, and it finally made her realize that there was no way in hell he would ever change or get help. He was not a man. He was an animal. Any man that would go after his daughter sexually was a sick pervert. After twenty-five-plus years of living in this hell, she was finally at a crossroad. It dawned on her, and she finally had the strength to see that there was a light at the end of her tunnel. And it was getting brighter. Because of the earlier divorce-proceedings situation, she was a little wiser and smarter.

I had not realized that Mom had already started legal proceedings for an order of protection and that the divorce papers were just waiting on that paperwork both to be served at the same time. So when this evening's nightmare happened, even though he had not yet been served, it was still in process. I am not sure why my dad did not get up off the ground. But my mom's whack on the head had made him stop, his eyes still glazed with the pain of being clobbered, and he had a look of semi-defeat. *Thank God*, I thought as he stopped coming toward me. Relief flooded through me, yet I was still shaken to the core of what could have happened had my mom not intervened. Yet the horror was short-lived as always, and the night of terror was not over by far.

As I started walking toward Mom, I glanced over and took one look at my father's face. It had this evil, menacing look. His face was as red as his bloodshot eyes, and they were full of rage. He started lunging toward my mother. "You fucking cunt." He said, "You're nothing but a piece of trash. I should have dumped you years ago."

He threw her into the refrigerator, knocking the magnets and papers off that were on it. My mom yelled at me to go call the police again. I ran shaking and trembling to the phone and called the police for the second time. Thankfully, 911 was in place by then; so they could hear his mouth rambling a slew of abusive, offensive obscenities, and they could hear the beating just as clearly as I was watching it. "Oh, please get here as fast as you can," I said, my voice ragged through sobs. "It looks as though he is going to kill my mother."

The police, who were regulars at our house by that time, got there within five minutes. They took one look at the mess, took one look at me with the red handprint on my cheek and tearstained face, and then took one look at my mother, whose bruises were already forming. They grabbed my father, took him outside, threw him in a six-feet drift of snow, and told him to cool down or they were going to cuff and arrest him. That finally seemed to subdue him. Since he had already been in jail several times, I guess he did not want to go back. When the police came back inside, they asked my mom what happened. She went through the scene. The officers had this look like they had heard it all before, and they had. I felt such shame and embarrassment. They asked if she wanted to press charges. She shook her head. She saw the pity in their eyes, and she quickly told them about the pending restraining order that was going to be served next week. It was almost as if they didn't believe her because they had heard this all before. It was like a rerun on TV. Before they left, they told her that she should call 911 at any time should we feel that we were in danger again. They finished with their report about twenty minutes later. My dad had been sitting in the snow all that time. By the time they went outside and my dad was pretty subdued, the knock on the head along with the snow had cooled him off. He, I am sure, was almost hypothermic and almost about to pass out.

The two policemen yanked him up and brought his sorry ass to his feet and brought him inside and threw him on the couch where he moaned. His head fell back and hit the sidearm of the couch and eventually passed out. The police looked at us sadly. I could see in their eyes pity and disgust. It was so humiliating. I felt such shame. I just wanted to curl up and crawl in a hole. Why my mom didn't feel the same is beyond me, but deep down, maybe she did but was too beat down to care anymore. Why did I feel shame when it was my father who should feel shame and remorse for the pain and hurt he caused us? But looking at him, all I saw was a bum, and for that bum, all he felt was the drool slipping out the side of his mouth. The officer with the brown eyes, who had such empathy in them, told my mom, "Please call us, Mrs. Stewart, if you need us again." She nodded. She followed them out and locked the double orange doors, and once again, they left us alone with that animal. Along with the drool, he was already snoring like a pig, and he smelled horrendous. Yet again, we had survived one more brutal attack.

I slowly dragged my feet back to the kitchen, and there I was, standing at the kitchen counter, crying, and my mom trying to help pick the first layer of the salad off because that was where the pieces of glass landed. She looked at me and said, "Honey, I think we can salvage this salad." She worked tediously, inspecting the salad as she spoke in a soothing tone that it was going to be okay. "Just hang tight for the next two weeks. Everything is going to change, I promise." After about a half hour, my mom said, "I think we got all the pieces. It should be okay, honey." During the salvaging of my salad, here is where the hysteria comes in. My mom, trying to make me laugh, said, "We should have left him outside and let him turn into a popsicle, and we could have decorated him as a stiff snowman." Both of us, out of sheer exhaustion and stress, started a fit of giggling at my mom's remark. Once our fit of giggles ended, the reality was that we had to go on living in that hell for two more weeks until the papers were served and my mom could change the locks. Two more weeks of walking on eggshells, two more weeks of hoping he came home at five p.m. I was thoroughly exhausted. By the time we were done in the kitchen, it was one a.m. My mom hugged me tight, not letting me go, and she said, "I will never let him touch you, ever. I promise you it's going to be okay." I hugged her but was unsure that what she said was true because several years earlier, she had tried to divorce him but ended up reconciling with him. I was eighteen at the time and never understood why and was really angry with her for a long time because she gave me no solid explanation why she did it. It was until later years I found out why she did what she did and understood why. I nodded, my shoulders sagging, and she said, "Katie, I mean it. This is never going to happen again. You have to believe me." She then said, "Try and get some sleep and try to smile and enjoy your holiday work party tomorrow."

In my head, all I kept thinking was, if only the officers could have just left him outside and let him die of hypothermia. Whose loss would it have been? He was a detriment to society. A terror on the roads waiting to kill some innocent victim, a terror to us, his family. Who would miss him? Let him turn into a frozen stiff. The world would have been better off. I know that sounds harsh and cruel, but our lives would have been so much easier. My mom would have been released. I wouldn't have to fear being raped by my own father. Of course, in America, that would have been cruel and be considered murder. That would be a crime even though he had broken so many laws since I could remember, yet we would have been the guilty ones, not him. Why is it that the victims are the ones who are punished? How could that be fair? How could someone who had inflicted so much pain and suffering, who violated so many legalities, get away with them? It's called the cover-up. The very next day after that horrific night, I did take that salad to work. I could not even take a serving of it. I did not touch it, nor did I have one bite of it. I was sick to my stomach and was nauseous watching every person I worked with take a serving full on their plate. All I did was watch with anxiety and worry that one of my coworkers would take a bite and get cut by a piece of glass and have blood spewing out of their gums. Thankfully, they did not, but my stomach was in knots all day. I threw the whole remaining salad in the garbage before I left the office that day, filled with an insane relief.

Sometimes I sit back in utter amazement and wonder how our family managed to survive that hell. How did we manage to laugh and make the best of those horrendous situations? Basically because we were a threesome family unit. We stuck closely together, protecting one another from the big bad wolf. You could call us the three musketeers or the Three Little Piggys. In any case, we were a tight threesome. In our family, we took the good with the bad. The bad memories, however, were beginning to start outweighing the good memories. All that hard work of trying to make some semblance of happier times and memories were beginning to take a toll on our outward persona. The stress of trying to put on a front and hide our secret took its toll on all three of us, impacting us in different ways and ultimately leading us on the path of how we would handle future relationships. It would greatly impact me in my relationships with men. I was always trying to please them. I had no voice on what I wanted or how I felt. I would cower when I did something that was not the normal expectation of me, expecting the worst and usually getting it by abuse in some form. It was the same ride that I watched my mom got on to ride for years with my father and then ultimately with the person she is with today. She is on the same merry-go-ride. She never got off. The same ride my brother was on. It's the only thing we ever saw and ever learned. It is a cycle of dysfunction, and I am very afraid my two children are on the ride and won't be able to fall off of it like I did. I tried for so many years but could not get off the constantly spiraling circle. I would try and convince myself that I was doing something different, choosing someone different, but see, a wolf is sly and can change disguises and hide the truth until the wolf devours your soul, your spirit. My dad did for years, both my ex-husbands did, my brother's ex-wife did, as well as my mother's current significant other, whom she has stayed glued to for twenty-six years and endured abuse and belittling. She went from the frying pan to the fire.

I was so naive and could never see the wolf in people. I always looked for the best in them basically because I was so eager to find someone to love me, something I lacked so badly growing up from my father, that I would excitedly jump right in any relationship where someone on the surface treated me good and said they loved and cared about me. All the while, I would be thinking they aren't going to be like Dad. They were going to be different. I would try so hard to envision what a healthy relationship was or should be. I would sit and fantasize about Ozzie and Harriet or the loving Brady Bunch family. I wanted that kind of love. See, the sad thing is that when you are a rabbit, every wolf is able to detect that you are the prey, the target. They immediately prey on your weaknesses. The wolf is the taker, and the rabbit is the giver. The wolf takes what the rabbit gives. Being the rabbit, my self-worth was so low I didn't love myself enough to wait and heal and even try and bother to really learn what real love was in a healthy relationship. Therefore, the dysfunctional ride continued, and I never got off the merry-go-round. I hopped from horse to horse or unicorn to unicorn until I finally got here to where I am today and where I have finally fallen off. See, growing up dysfunctional, I never felt good enough, never felt worthy, and never felt I had the right to voice my opinion, that I deserved better. I thought sickly that it was always somehow my fault. My fault my dad drank and acted the way he did. My fault that my ex-husbands acted the way they did. I would ask myself, What did I do to cause it? What did I do wrong to encourage their choices and bad behavior? I felt that I failed. No matter how I tried, I could not stop the circle. I could not stop the drinking, the beatings, the yelling, and the cruelty. It seemed the more I tried to control, the more I lost control. So when I got married, I landed up on the same damn merry-go-round without even trying to stop it. I didn't know any better. I was following a pattern I was used to and the only one I knew. That being said, I am just the result of a dysfunctional upbringing; but I had no choice in choosing to be in that cycle, nor did I choose to want to be on that constant merry-go-round of insanity. I was just thrown on it.

By the time I was old enough to realize what ride I was on, I was too scared to jump off, so I continued to ride the ride. Until one day, I decided to change, to alter the pattern, to set boundaries, to pull the plug, and to fall off and ride my horse or, rather, my magic unicorn away into the sunset where light and love live. It has taken years to do this, and the impact of doing so is going to unbalance the ride and upset some of those who still choose to stay on it, those who won't understand why I fell off or rather rode off. See, facing the past even though it is painful, it is growth. It doesn't mean you are reliving it over and over again, never to move forward. It means you are recognizing patterns and seeing firsthand why you repeat them and how you can stop repeating them. It's about setting healthy boundaries even with the people whom you love dearly and not feeling guilty about doing so. It is most likely that the people you love are still on the ride, and they may or may not ever get off of it. This doesn't mean that you have to stop loving them. It just means you have to walk away when you know that your integrity is being compromised or questioned. It's about not feeling sorry for yourself. It's about looking inside of yourself and learning to love the spiritual being you are. It's about forgiveness. Forgiving yourself foremost firstly because you had no choice that you were on that ride for so many years and never made the attempt to get off sooner. It also means you can forgive those who still are dysfunctional and sick and who don't like the stance you are taking to move forward to a healthier existence. You can forgive them, but you do not have to accept where they are at in life. And you certainly do not have to accept their bad behavior. Remember, dysfunctional people love confrontation. They love the fight because it brings you right back to their level, their high, and puts you right back on the ride. Dysfunction merry-go-round 101. There is one thing I have come to realize: you just cannot go back and change the reality of what happened, nor can you erase it. No matter how you pretend it did not happen or pretend it has not affected you, you would be a phony. Because what you lived and what you learned is evident in all your decisions and defines your core character and has affected you both personally and externally. The only thing that has not affected you is your ability to make a choice to stay on the horse or to fall off of it and not let it control you. Yes, that merry-go-round ride defined my family, including me, and it has had the trickle-down effect to everyone in my immediate circle. Once you have been born into it, it becomes the dysfunctional circle. It's like an inherited heritage, much like what you've been born into. One important thing that I have realized through this whole process of healing is that even if the ill person has left your inner circle, it does not mean the dysfunction disappears. See, dysfunction once bred continues to breed. All of us are molded by the events we were exposed to as infants, childhood, and adulthood that went way beyond our control—molded by others and influenced by their past beliefs and behavior. Those have been inbred in us the minute we were born, developed, and programmed early on during our child-hood from our parents, grandparents, mentors, teachers, and peers. Because of that influence and that programming, it has defined us into the people we have become. See, our paths were mapped out as soon as we were an embryo in the womb. That pathway was designed and influenced by others, and we did not have a choice. If our her-itage of relatives were always dysfunctional, then so would we be. That would be our life. It was not our fault that our guidelines and life choices were the result of dysfunction and pre-programming. Yet if you can see the unhealthy pathway, you can stop the cycle. You can fall off. You don't have to get back up on the horse or get back on the ride. You can set boundaries, react a different way, and begin doing things differently. Everyone in my family—well, we all are on the ride or have been on the ride. All of us are battling some sort of dysfunctional inner demon in ourselves. For me, I have fallen off, but I am always teetering on the brink of falling back on it; and I am still trying to learn how to survive—to grow, to evolve, and to learn how to break the spiraling circle—because it does become an endless revolving circle that never stops. It's so easy to give up and just stay dizzy and fuzzy. After all, who wants to feel pain or actually have to face the fact that you are flawed not by choice but by heredity? I battle this on a daily basis. I coped and coped with it in numerous ways. Sometimes I did it alone with my best buddy, the 1.5-liter bottle of wine, harboring that secret escape and staying silent. I pretended all is perfect to the outside world. I was embarrassed, ashamed, and alone.

I felt completely lost, not wanting to face reality; and many times, I wanted to escape, and I chose escape at various periods in my life. It is way easier to run away, to keep secrets rather than speak the truth and tell your story. If we don't tell our stories, we aren't authentic. If we keep them hidden, they end up going around and around. It becomes the never-ending merry-go-round circle. We end up disappearing. We fall into depression and loneliness, and we become isolated. We run away from telling our secret. Some of us fall into the addictive coping, a form of escaping through alcohol and drugs. Alcohol was my vice, my escape. Some of us become robots of shallowness because that is way easier than showing the truth and being vulnerable. I did both for a period of time, and it made things all the worse. When we escape through other avenues, it's just an easy way out, a quick temporary numbing, but in the end, the pain is still there, revolving around and around. There are so many different ways to escape the truth—so many addictions or addictive behaviors whether it be codependency, enabling, drugs, sex, alcohol, prescriptions, gambling, video games, food, sugar, and shopping. The list is vast and extensive because there are so many things that we can use to escape truth and reality. Addictions are abundant in this new-age world. There are those of us who decide to be angry all the time and let hatred take over, becoming bitter and holding resentments toward everyone and everything that happens to them in life. Or better yet, we extinguish ourselves by choosing suicide as the only way out. Instead of looking inside ourselves, we decide to blame everyone else for our misfortunes and yet not seeing it clearly that it's the way we react to those circumstances, however dysfunctional they may be, not realizing we do have a choice. We do have a voice. We have the choice on which path to take, negative or positive, harmful or healthy. The choice is ultimately ours once we become adults. We do not have to become a clone of what influenced us since birth. We can choose our destiny as we become adults and become our own person. Unfortunately, we don't have that luxury as infants and children. We have to follow the rules and guidance of other adults and mentors' programming, which was the programming that they received. As I said earlier, it is the trickle-down effect. We are guided by and influenced by those people and what they believe no matter if they may be pointing us in the wrong direction. Once we become adults, if we happen to end up on the dysfunctional merry-go-round, we don't know how to get off; and we go in circles, choosing to bury our heads in the sand, and follow the same patterns over and over again. The same learned programming. We don't believe there is any other way, and we are scared. We let fear play a big role—fear of falling off or fear of feeling pain if we do. We avoid thinking that there is something very wrong, and we don't want to face those inner thoughts and feelings and demons. And so we make the same continuous bad choices in our work, personal life, and relationships, repeating the cycle and the ride over and over again. That cycle would include accepting abusive behavior and treatment from others and not speaking up for ourselves because we hate confrontation or we think somehow we deserve it. Losing ourselves in other people's agenda or getting on someone else's ride. We become experts at enabling, making excuses and becoming major people pleasers to compensate that lack of fulfillment, love, and peace. In the mind of the dysfunctional, we feel we provoked it, and we accept someone else's abusive bad behavior. We make excuses and condone it as being okay, stating that's just the way they are, so we accept it as normal, that it's okay for people to behave in a misogynistic manner. The definition of *misogynistic* is a person who has a hatred of woman, someone who has a narcissistic personality. That's an illness. That's what I lived with growing up. If you don't stand up and say no and put a stop to the misogynistic person, set up a boundary, stop enabling the enabler and the abuser—then the merry-go-round never will stop, and you will never be in a healthy relationship or be treated with respect. Time to shut it down. Time to end the relationship. If you know there is no hope of recovery, you need to distance yourself from the abuser, the negative lifestyle, and get off the dizzy ride and stand tall for yourself. It's not right that we think we deserve it to live in hell, that we keep thinking it will get better. I know because that's what I witnessed growing up. It is the way I thought relationships were. I became an enabler like my mother. I kept thinking if I act this way or if I do it this way or say this, maybe my daddy wouldn't go out and get drunk. And so the ritualistic behavior gets passed on generation to generation. Well, I am writing this so it will stop in my family, that this may help others stop the insanity in their family.

This acceptance of misogynistic, narcissistic behavior became virtually the way I went through my adult years in my various failed unhealthy relationships. I would think, well, if I wore the right heels, dressed the right way, wore the sexy negligee, and let him play all his little-boy sports, maybe he wouldn't treat me so badly. Or if I gave up this and did this for him, maybe be wouldn't be mean to me. Maybe he would love me. I just would comply with everything that was expected of me because I was afraid and hated dealing with any type of confrontation, fighting, or discord. When obviously I could never change the behavior pattern, I used other outlets of escape from my unhappiness. Dipping into the numbing effect of alcohol to take away the pain I was feeling, I became a full-blown alcoholic. This is how I was programmed and how so many people who grew up in a dysfunctional family think. It is what we are used to, and that is how we have always lived. It's a pattern and program we were taught early on. So we think it's acceptable. We continue to allow it. Our family was definitely the epitome of a family riddled with that kind of tolerance, acceptance, that kind of illness, and dysfunction, including the big one: the disease of alcoholism. That was my ride, my merry-go-round, the one I was on. But now at the age of fifty-four, I am jumping off of it. I might fall and get scraped, but I am falling off the ride. I'm running and jumping off the horse now before it's too late. I no longer fear speaking the truth and sharing my authentic self because I love who I have become. A stronger, better version of me—someone who can survive, thrive, learn new things, set boundaries, and still have the ability to be empathetic and love unconditionally.

Yes, this is my story—the fact that my father was an alcoholic and that I let myself fall down the same rabbit hole. He's totally dysfunctional, and his entire side of the family being dysfunctional and riddled with a long list of alcoholics is only the tip of the iceberg. I never wanted to end up like him, yet I did. I detested him in the end, so why would I want to end up like him? I almost did, and that scared the shit out of me. I thought I was escaping, but I was going down a road of self-destruction. That scared the shit out of me, it consumed me, left me powerless, and out of control. Therefore, when people say that it isn't hereditary, the disease of alcoholism, I totally disagree to a certain extent. I think the genetics are there in all of us and that we all are prone to cross that line of addictive behavior in some form or another. Whether it's with food, alcoholic drinking, illegal drugs, prescription drug abuse, smoking, gambling, enabling behavior, porn, codependency, video games, sugar addiction, and shopping—whatever the fix is to get us to that state of escape, that quick little adrenaline high. All these provide temporary mood alterations, and with those chemical alterations, it changes the way we feel. Sometimes it makes us feel euphoric, on top of the world, and unstoppable. Sometimes it provides the numbing because we are trying to escape from feeling any physical and emotional pain. Sometimes it happens just out of clear habit or programming. That euphoric feeling, although it's temporary, can be the escape we crave or just do because it's a way of life or it's what we were exposed to as children. Once we figure out these escape hatches, that's where it can get scary because if you come from a family lineage of addictive behaviors, that line can easily get crossed. I know from firsthand experience how easy it is to cross the line. I used alcohol as a numbing escape, crossing over to alcoholism and addiction for five years.

I went from social drinking to excessive from the age of thirty-four years to thirty-nine. I was married to a misogynistic, selfish man. I was so unhappy and felt worthless as a wife. I felt I couldn't do enough. I felt inadequate as a mother. I allowed him to make me feel unworthy—making me feel I was not a good enough daughter, sister, friend, and social planner and that I became the perfect people pleaser to all the people in my life except for myself. It became a way of life, a survival technique, and an escape from the pain—something that I began to have a hard time controlling—and we tend to keep going back for more and more, repeating the patterns of abuse. That would include all those addictions I listed and one more: it would also include the enabling behavior of accepting abusiveness toward ourselves. That euphoric numbing of substance abuse was my only means of escaping the madness. That precarious line of what society considers normal social drinking can easily turn to addictive usage and abuse.

One never knows when that line is crossed or when it happens. Does it happen due to heredity because you were born into a family of alcoholics? Does it happen when you are depressed or when you have been so traumatized you need to escape reality? And then you begin to like and crave that escape? Does it happen because you enjoy the euphoric state of mind so much you think it's too fun to stop? Does it happen because you have watched it and lived through patterns and programming of watching family members do it and you just follow along in their footsteps? Medical doctors, therapists, and scientific studies cannot determine why it happens, nor can they determine when it can happen. It happened to me. It was no longer fun and lightweight. It became a need to survive. For each individual, it is a different set of circumstances, a different situation when that precarious line is crossed. Because no matter how you try to convince yourself that you can be healthy, when you come from a dysfunctional family, in the reality of life, that is a rarity. Anyone living in the actuality of that kind of environment is exposed to the cycle and the illnesses caused from it. You can spend an entire lifetime trying to pretend and convince yourself that it does not and that it did not affect you, but you would just be lying to yourself and hiding from facing the truth. Because no matter how you try to run away from the reality, you grew up in dysfunction, surrounded by illness, and were programmed early on from the get-go. It takes courage to look deep within and to quit pretending, quit hiding, do some soul searching, and constructively recognize the patterns of abuse and dysfunction. Dysfunction is an illness, just like alcoholism is a virus and that virus has spores that create diseases of various kinds within the dysfunction. That being said, I am telling this story because I had both viruses. I still do. One thankfully is dormant and has been for years; the other I still drag around with me, and I am still trying to make peace with it. That would be surviving the behaviors of dysfunction. I was born into a dysfunctional family of alcoholics and abuse and am surrounded by enablers. It's like having shingles. If you have chicken pox, you still carry the virus.

Both my mother and father had this illness because they were born into a dysfunctional family. My father was worse off. He had alcoholism, dysfunction, and misogynistic genetics on his side. That's where my beginning and story starts, not just with the horrific scenes I've described about my father. It starts with both my father and mother. Yes, it goes way back to their birth and my grandparents on both sides. So to begin with, let's start with my dad. You heard some of the stories earlier, so you will realize that is where my painful experiences mostly lie. I really cannot tell you when my dad became an alcoholic because he came from such a long line of alcoholics it may have been in his blood and veins when he was in utero. Basically, he possibly could have been bottle-fed booze from the time he was an infant. I know that is a funny thing to say, but it really could be the truth as I know that back in the day, which was 1928, when he came into this world. Alcohol and smoking were the norm and were very prevalent in men and women. There was no raised awareness that drinking or smoking while pregnant would affect or harm your baby. So saying he may have been drunk in utero is an understatement. Basically, he may have had no choice from the time he was created on where his path would lead. I only heard bits and pieces of the family history about his parents and siblings from my mother. She had told me that he was born into a heavy-drinking, chain-smoking family. I only remember meeting my grandfather one time, and he was with his second wife. And I remember looking at both their arms, and both had wrinkles and brown spots everywhere—not birthmarks but big blotchy brown-and-purple spots. When I asked my mom what they were, she told me that they were liver spots from liver disease, liver disease from alcoholism. They were scary looking. They looked a hundred years old to me as a child, but in reality, they were only in their early sixties.

My dad was born near Wild Rose, Wisconsin, a big drinking town where all they did was drink and smoke sometimes morning, noon, and night because there was nothing better to do and literally nothing else to do. Small town life in a hick town. Drink, smoke, go out, and screw the farm animals. So in his case, it was probably totally genetic, and he really did not have any control over alcoholism happening in his life as he was surrounded by boozers. His father, his birth mother, most of his brother and sisters, and even his stepmother were alcoholics.

Needless to say, when I was growing up, my mom tried her best to make sure we did not see that side of the family too often. That being said, I can tell you for a fact that our family survived solely and only because of my mother. She made sure that not all the situations that my brother and I remembered were bad, and although she came from a dysfunctional family herself, she used all her strength and survival techniques to help me and my brother, always doing her best to try and compensate in the dysfunctional madness. Her pretending we had the perfect family was the only way she thought would help us get through the horrific moments. Yes, it could be considered a form of enabling, but it was the only way we could survive through it. It's quite ironic though on the outside. People looking at our family through the years would never ever realize there was any stitch of horror going on. Most people, when my parents finally got divorced, did not believe us when we told them why—that my dad was an alcoholic and used to beat the living shit out of us, that he was in jail numerous times, and that the reason we had so many new cars was because he totaled them. They were incredulous. "No way," they would say. "Not Kevin." Even my best childhood friend who recently told me she never knew what we had lived through and she lived right across the street from us. Yes, gosh, we kept good secrets in our family. If you were to look back through the many photo albums my mother created, the happy family memories that she tried to create, and you saw those pictures, you would think we had the happiest, healthiest family ever. That everything we did together created the best times ever growing up in our household. That we were the epitome of the all-American suburban family. Pictures, however, do not tell the truth. They never reveal what's hidden deep within the soul of those smiling individuals who are looking back at you in the photographs. Those are only moments in time. They don't depict the other dates and times where you were covered in bruises or the black eyes, nor could you see the red blotchy bloodshot eyes from crying. Those pictures and moments never made it into the photo albums. The pictures smiling out on the pages mask the true reality. They show no feelings, nor do they reveal what really did happen behind closed doors. See, the old saying that "A picture can tell a thousand words"—well, that is a pile of bullshit. Pictures are beautiful ways to remember the happier times, but they are so artificial and superficial. They depict only surface memories of some happy times. Those pictures only show smiles and beauty, not frowns, tears, or bruises. They don't tell the truth, nor do they tell the stories that are locked behind the faces in the photographs. And they don't tell the story that happens behind the closed doors of home.

Back to sharing with you is the story behind the photographs. The story of the true picture of our family, not the picture-perfect pictures in those albums but the truth of how we all became the individuals we are today. What amazes me the most is how my dad managed to live till he was eighty-seven because he drank so heavily, smoked like a chain-smoker, and ate horribly. He was one of the most unhealthy persons ever. I cannot count nor can I tell you how many cars my dad totaled, how many accidents he had, and how many arrests he had in different counties for DUIs all over the Chicago land area. I do have corresponding documentation on some of those arrests. Not all of them. I could only dig up a few court documents. Those agencies that processed the paperwork never connected the dots because there were no computer systems back then. I also cannot tell you how many times the phone would ring, and it would be the police notifying my mom that he was in jail or the hospital calling and telling her that he was brought in injured from an accident or a kind restaurant owner who felt terrible for our family and wanted to help by telling us where he was because they knew our family and he was in their establishment in a drunken stupor. Those calls were the most frightening because our biggest fear was that he hurt someone or killed someone. It was never fear or worry about what happened to him because somehow, he always managed to survive. Because there were no computers back then, he got away for years drinking and driving, getting DUI after DUI, and having his license revoked and still driving without one under the influence of alcohol. He played Russian roulette, and he didn't care. I think it was divine intervention that had a hand in making sure no one was hurt mortally or wounded by him. Maybe because I don't think as a family we would have been able to handle it. Finally, after many years, Cook County, McHenry County, and Boone County came into the computer age. And lo and behold, everything was being entered into the computer, and the legal system and law enforcement finally began connecting the dots. I have documentation on one of his many driver's license suspensions and arrest info in McHenry County and also info on the overnight jail stay in 1977 in the Wheeling Jail, our neighboring town. Once all the counties were computerized, there was a warrant out for my dad's arrest, and he went to prison. That happened after my parents' divorce. I think he was incarcerated for about three to five in a federal prison, according to my mom, and forced in prison to do a twelve-step program. Not that it did him any good. You can't teach an old dog new tricks, and my dad was an old, sorry, sad dog. Once he got out, he continued to break the law and drink and drive with no license. His drinking slowed down to an extent, but nonetheless, he continued to drink until his alcohol-ridden brain no longer worked and he had to be put into an assisted living home because he was diagnosed with a form of Alzheimer's that was induced by his excessive abuse of alcohol.

These stories, although heart-wrenching and sad, are riveting because they speak the truth of what a family goes through in the pit of dysfunction and alcoholism and the continuous ride on the dysfunctional merry-go-round that the entire family is on. It has been pivotal for me as the victim because it has taken me fifty-four years to authentically tell it, to write it all out, and to share my experience. I became motivated when I was unpacking a box in my closet, I found journals, letters, and writings some from when I was sixteen and seventeen years old, which was a very difficult time in my life when I contemplated suicide. Journal entries from when I first hit rock bottom when I finally admitted I was an alcoholic at the age of thirty-nine. I included these at the end of my story. I feel it is so important to share those early months of my sobriety. Those beginning journal entries depict the anxiety, fear, and pain to stay sober. I knew I had to change my life and live a sober life. I also found homework assignments written when I was seventeen; thus, becoming a pivotal year for me. I had signed up for a Marriage and Family as an elective in high school. This class, which I had no idea about, would finally force me to expose our family secret. The same year, and this is very corny, my mom planned a summer family trip to Nashville to make up for all the horrific times we had endured during the year. See, that was what my mom did. She would plan these little family outings and camping trips and excursions to try and salvage some normalcy in our life since throughout the year, there was none. It was during those family trips that our family actually seemed halfway normal because our dad did not drink on those trips. On this particular family vacation, we went on a trip to Nashville to the Grand Ole Opry. We were somewhere in Nashville at a museum of Jonny Cash memorabilia where his book *I Walked the Line* was displayed, and my mom bought it. I was an avid reader, and I was the first to read it from cover to cover. I was riveted, and it made me want to so badly speak to Mr. Cash to tell him about our family, to share our history, and to let him know that he was not alone. I felt so ironically close to Mr. Cash and his family. So like a starstruck teenager, I wrote and mailed a letter to Johnny Cash. This was in 1980. I have the original because I mailed him a copy of it. It is located at the back of this book. You can see how there is not much difference from what a seventeen-year-old was experiencing to what I as an adult experienced. I highly doubt the letter ever got to him. I am sure it probably only got as far as the fan club head, but for a seventeen-year-old begging to be heard, it was healing to write. After rereading it now, I wonder if whoever read it could feel the pain of a family on a downward spiral of destruction. I never did get a response back.

This would be the first time that writing truly sparked my interest. My mind thinks so fast that when I write, it just seems the words flow from my mind to the typewriter faster than I can type. Mr. Cash's story about his addiction to alcohol was so significant it made me realize even the rich and famous are affected by this disease. No one is immune. No one is safe from its destructive clutches. Once it has its ugly arms wrapped around you, even fame nor fortune has the ability to prevent the cunning hold of this addiction and its dysfunctional traits. Sometimes there is so much in my brain it is hard to get all the puzzle pieces into sequence. For me, it became so much easier in life to write my feelings than to be able to verbally express them. At times, I hid behind my words. I felt so much bolder when I wrote, and I can be so bluntly honest on paper than I can face to face. I don't know if that is because I feared confrontation so much after having lived through so many confrontational scenes in my family. In me, there was such a lack of self-worth and lack of self-confidence to profess anything I felt strongly about for fear of standing out. This may be considered part of the people-pleasing syndrome that goes hand in hand with the dysfunction. It's the old adage: "Don't rock the boat. Don't tip the boat over. Just go along with whomever you are with wants you to feel because, God forbid, you speak up and really say how you feel. And they may not like what you say, or for that matter, they may not like you." All part of the dysfunction, always worrying what everyone else thinks. Living in fear that if you did speak up or speak the truth, you may be judged. So just keep your mouth shut and don't vocalize. Otherwise, you won't be accepted. Keep those thoughts and feelings hidden and a secret. That is what I did to avoid any type of conflict. I stopped being true to me or being honest. This is how I lived my childhood and handled my relationships with men.

It was another form of people-pleasing everyone else but myself, and it would become a staple of how I would deal with many relationships in my life. If the going got too tough or uncomfortable and if I had gotten lost because I just went along with the flow of the ride, I would hightail it out of there with a letter of goodbye. I became a master of articulation through writing—pretty much a cop-out form of communicating face to face for fear of being shot down, interrupted, of being vulnerable, and admitting how you feel. It's the easiest way to avoid conflict. I was so proficient at writing my thoughts and feelings on paper I was like a speed writer. I used to when I was in high school. Wait till an hour before a book report or a big written project was due; I would actually sit down and write a full-blown report several pages long on paper, turn it in, and end up getting an A+ on the paper. Writing and telling stories has always come naturally for me. Some of them make me laugh, some make me cry, and then there are some like these that reliving them just totally drains my psyche. I consider all of them a form of healthy purging. I have learned to live through them all. Guess what? I am still here, and I survived. Wait a minute, I should say I am still trying to survive. I am a work in progress, still ever evolving. The only way to learn from the past is to purge it and continue to make conscious decisions to face the demons—to be open-minded, to keep learning why the same things keep repeating themselves, and to keep searching for the truth. To be observant at the repetitive patterns and to stop the ride from making another revolutionary circle. Am I not right? It is like the old saying or quote: "When life gives you lemons, make lemonade." They truly are not kidding because I had a whole orchard of lemons. I could have opened my own lemonade factory, and God bless my mom; she owned the orchard.

However dysfunctional she may be, she is an absolutely amazing lady. What I have found in life is that many dysfunctional souls are truly amazing people. They have just been going in circles. Mom—well, she did her best to create for my brother and myself some sense of normalcy in the insanity, and I truly mean craziness because at times, it simply was insanity, what we did to survive. Each day I am alive, when I catch myself thinking back through some of those memories that I described earlier, I shake myself and do my best to move forward and to not keep reliving them. It does happen, and those are usually my darkest days. I pride myself in the fact that I strive to be positive in a negative world, and although I am on a merry-go-round of dysfunction, I chose to fall off and not get back on. I try every day to make the best of what life deals me. I am sober because, believe it or not, I did it for me and not my father, even though now I realize he never wanted that luxury of recovery. Many times there are people like me walking around with slumped shoulders, who walk around with a grimace or who are grumpy and just plain miserable. They walk around with a negative attitude about everything, which makes almost anything you face worse. Those people are people you don't want to be around because their karma is dark. As an enabler and codependent, I realize that I have become the analyzer, the people-pleasing fixer of everyone else except myself. Sometimes this trait can be a good thing, but many times, it is not such a wonderful trait. I inherited this trait from the programming my mom bestowed on me. She always said we never know what that person is going through. Really, she was referring to our family and my brother and me. "You are absolutely right. For years, no one knew about what went on behind the closed doors of our home. Even my closest friends. There were so many times that I wondered how in the heck did they not know. How the heck did we get out of that situation unscathed or killed?" Emotionally scarred, yes, we were. The bruises heal, but the emotional scars stay. We really worked hard at hiding it, and damn it, that was a full-time job for all three of us. So many incidents, so many stories—it is hard to actually remember them all, but here is yet one more of them.

I remember my mom getting a call from the owner of our favorite town pizzeria called Pit-n-Pub. I think maybe I was fourteen and my brother thirteen at the time. That pizzeria place held many happy memories for my brother and I as we grew up. We went so often that my mom befriended the owner. My mom had many events there for Boy Scouts and E-Harts, which was a local girls club created by Bertha E-hart who was from Mount Prospect, Illinois, the neighboring town in which we lived. E-Harts girls' club was very similar to Girl Scouts. I belonged to it all the way until I was a senior in high school from second grade onward. Mom—well, she was our den mom for all of them. The owner of the pizzeria, Dick—well, he would let us go back where the pizzas were made, and we were able to have make our own pizza parties. We had many events there. Later, as I was a young adult, we would go there after our park district coed volleyball games. Dick figured out that my dad was an alcoholic. See, toward the end of my parents' marriage, my dad was really bad. He would still hold it somewhat together for gatherings, but in public away from us, he was not hiding his drinking. Dick was always very supportive of my mom, me, and my brother. He became very protective of our family. He had very little respect for my father. He saw it upfront how he became when he drank. So he knew the brutal truth. So toward the middle of my high school years when my dad decided he was not going to try to attempt to control his binging and as the dynamics in our family life were changing and my father saw that none of us really cared to beg him to stop anymore, he started binging way more often and way closer to home. In the past, his bar hangouts were closer to where he worked. Now they were way closer to our home. Pit-n-Pub was just one of the places he started letting loose at, and Dick, the owner and our friend, had seen this. One evening, when none of us were with him he was there pounding beer after beer and becoming more verbally loud and belligerent, Dick finally told him he had enough to drink and that he needed to go home. My dad became very angry and belligerent with him. Well, Dick was smart. He had seen my father's keys laying on the table, so he took them when he was not looking and locked them in the cash register. He watched my dad groping and searching the table for his keys and watched him get super angry when he could not find his keys. Because there were patrons that had young children—after all, it was a family place—Dick warned him he'd better go outside or he was going to call the police. This put a little fear in him as he had just had a run in with the Wheeling police months before. He proceeded to reluctantly stagger outside. See, my dad could not afford one more offense. He was on a thin thread with law enforcement as it was with all the DUIs and accidents, not to mention that his license had just been reinstated. There were no cell phones, so he could not call us. So by the time Dick phoned us, he had stumbled off into the dark and was nowhere in sight. Dick explained to my mom and told her he had been there pounding beers and that he had taken and locked his car keys in the cash register so that he would not drive away drunk. Dick told her that he asked him to leave and that when he did, he became angry and stumbled outside. He said he did not want to cause us any more trouble, so he refrained from calling the police. I remember listening to my mom thank him, her face bright red with embarrassment once again. In my head, I was like *Great. Here were go again.* We threw our jackets on, and following the same routine as always, we were going out to search for my father so he didn't get into more trouble. We all hopped into the car, hoping he would not be far from the establishment. The drunk stumbled away before Dick got a chance to see which direction he went. Mom decided to go directly to the pizzeria and then take a route back that she thought he might be walking on. We drove the main drag where we thought he could have walked. He was nowhere to be found. So where was his drunken ass? It was frigid cold out with snow on the ground. We were in the Chicago suburban town of Arlington Heights in the middle of winter in the freezing cold. We must have been driving for at least forty-five minutes. My heart was racing. I am not sure if it was panic or excitement that we might find him dead. I watched my mom as she was getting a bit frantic, not sure if it was out of embarrassment that someone else would find him first before we did or fear that he might hurt someone and do something that would put our family in yet another precarious situation. We drove down Old Willow Road by the slough or duck pond, as we used to call it, and lo and behold, right before we got to the pond, we found him facedown in a snow-filled ditch five blocks from our house. If he would have stumbled and gone yet another one hundred feet, he would have fallen in the slough or duck pond and probably drowned as it was not yet completely frozen over. How he did not die from hypothermia or drowning is beyond me because there was at least an inch of freezing water in the ditch with the snow. His face was sideways, missing the ditch-filled water. He got lucky again. The SOB always managed to live through these things. He was damn lucky that he was passed out facedown. Otherwise, I am so sure he would have drowned. I remember it took all three of us to haul his ass up and put him in the back seat. After all, he was six-feet tall and about 220 pounds. That man survived so many near-death situations and accidents where he was passed out in frigid weather, and he never died. I cannot even count how many bar brawls there were where he got beat up by other bar thugs and came home beat up to a pulp.

I know one thing: what my mom was so afraid of was getting a sexually-transmitted disease when she found out how many bar floozies he was sleeping with throughout the years. Back then, there was no talk of HIV yet nor HPV. However, that did not stop her fear because there were other STDs she may have gotten because of his many liaisons. He was always so stoned that he never even remembered who he hooked up with. The reason I know that for a fact is that one such floozy had the nerve to show up in our driveway one night. Her name was Gloria, with bleached-out, frizzy blonde hair, a trampy-looking woman with bright-red lipsticks, yellow teeth, and tits so big they were balloons about to explode. The son of a bitch had given out our home address and made her all these grandiose promises, boasting of bucks. The bimbo thought she had her meal ticket and sugar daddy with my dad. The nerve of that dumb bitch when she pulled up in our driveway acting all entitled and looking for him because he promised her all these things. My father pretended he didn't know her, that he had no memory of her, and my mom and brother escorted her or rather—should I say—dragged her sorry ass back to her dumpy car and told her if she ever stepped foot on our property again, we would have her arrested. I remember my brother grabbing her trashy hair as she was rolling up the window and saying that to her.

"Lenny promised me!" she wailed. Good God, he didn't even give her his real name. I think my brother, by grabbing her hair, scared the living daylights out of her because her face had turned white and her blood-red lipstick was sickly smeared across her left cheekbone. "Stop it," she said. "Lenny promised he was going to marry me."

My brother, who really never lost his cool, screamed, "You dumb ass bitch. He was drunk when he told you that, and *Lenny* isn't even his real name. Now get the fuck off our property, you trashy whore. You better never think to step foot on this property again." We never saw her again, which was surprising because I am sure she was a frequent flyer of one of my dad's hangouts. I have no doubt he saw her again and made up some story. Thankfully, we just never heard about it or saw her again.

During my grammar school days, it was always very difficult to have friends over on the weekends because we never knew what Friday night would lead to if Dad went on a bender. Mostly had to do after-school playdates or enjoy the two clubs my mom was the leader and organizer for, the E-Harts girls club and the Cub Scouts. Those were safe venues because they happened during the weekday. Dad was usually always a good boy during the weekdays. The day of the week when we would need to worry was on Fridays. We did, however, try the few times with the Friday-night friend sleepover. I remember that if he was on a bender on the Friday night when one of my friends was over, I would be sick to my stomach with worry that he would come home and make a scene. Most of the time, as it creeped toward the 5:30 p.m. mark and my dad was nowhere to be seen, my mom would drive the friend home before he came home, pretending that one of us was sick. If a friend would come over on a Saturday and he was passed out on the couch from the bender the night before, we would just tell our friends he worked the late shift and that's why he was still sleeping. I was always so embarrassed seeing him on the couch snoring and smelling sour and nasty. I pretended that was normal, but deep down inside, I was so ashamed. They would ask, "Why is your dad still in his work clothes, and how come he is always laying on the couch sleeping?" I would make up some sort of "Oh, he didn't want to disturb my mom, and he had to work overtime or he was on the night shift." They would kind of shrug and not say another word. It was so humiliating watching their reactions because I just knew they must smell that my dad reeked of alcohol and cigarettes and BO. When we didn't have friends over me and my brother would wake up and creep out to the family room, as he laid snoring away a hangover out on the family room couch, we tried not to gag from the smell. We would find the Lysol spray my mom kept in the laundry room. It smelled so horrid that my brother and I had to cover our noses and hold our breaths and, for fear of waking the raging bull up, just spritz here and there to get that sour vomit-like smell out of the air. It was so disgusting. He was such a dirty, unsanitary man. He had no hygiene skills whatsoever. What he learned about hygiene was from my mother. I think if she was not around, he would wear his underwear and socks for a week. Gross. Just knowing from my mom that when she met him, half his teeth were rotting out of his gums. I guess because he was so strikingly handsome on the outer appearance that she chose to overlook what was on the inside and the rotten-teeth situation. He was the epitome of tall, dark, and handsome. You can see from his pictures what a handsome man he was in his younger years before he ravaged his body with alcohol. He was even more dashing when my mom had him get his teeth fixed. My brother is the spitting image of him, as is my brother's son. I often wondered what my mom's reaction was when she first met him and he finally opened his mouth and she saw his rotting teeth. The mere thought of it turns my stomach. Yuck, what the heck was she thinking? When you look at the glossy black-and-white photos of my father before he was with my mother, you can see that he never smiled a toothy smile. It was always a closed-mouth smile. That was how he hid the truth from my mom. I am sure that was short-lived when he actually started talking to her. For some reason, there was something that sparked her interest, and she was willing to overlook that flaw. From any angle that I looked at it, I thought it was gross. I remember my mom telling me that before they actually married, my mom made him pull those teeth and get dentures. Uppers and lowers. Yep, typical fix-it mode. See, Mom never figured out that you can't change a bum into a stud. She thought she could, and she desperately wanted to prove that to my grandparents. After all the years of beatings, we learned great tactics on fighting back, enough to at least protect ourselves from not being killed by one of his drunken rampage rages and binges. Like that one time I described before where he was on one of his beating rampages and my Mom grabbed the big wrought iron skillet in the kitchen and hit my dad over the head with that big ass cast iron frying pan. Fearing for our lives and the constant problem of his lewd behavior as I started developing and moving from daddy's little princess to a teenage girl with breasts. That was so fricking gross and scary. When I was younger, I adored my dad, and like all adoring children, I would hang all over my dad for attention. Now all I wanted to do was push him away as he tried pawing all over me with his red ruddy face and that glass eyeball, which would be draining gunk out of it, as he would try to hug and kiss me. When he would attempt to grab hold of me, I would be able to smell his vile breath. He would be so close to my face that when I was turning my head, I would get a whiff of it, and it would make me want to vomit. Then he started spitting and slurring words. "Come here, baby girl, and give your big daddy a kiss." It was the way it sounded and the tone of his voice each time that made my skin crawl. My mom was terrified by those scenes because her friend across the street had told her that her father had raped her at age thirteen when he was drunk. That was why Mom never ever left me alone if she knew he was out drinking. When my mom had whacked him with the skillet, she thought she had killed him, but she didn't. Another time, I punched him so hard in the right eye my mom was freaking out. I remember her saying, "I hope you punched him in the bad eye, not the good eye. I don't want to end up taking care of a blind drunk." LOL. Funny and scary all at the same time. There were several other times when we fought back hard. Particularly, this one time, we actually knocked him out because he went down hard and did not move for an hour; but we saw his body moving up and down, so we knew he was still breathing. He woke up the next day laying in that same exact spot on the dining room floor, clueless to why he had a big headache. "Dang," my mom said. "I thought I killed him that time." The three of us rolled in a fit of hysterical laughter. You just had to laugh at the insanity of those wicked scenes that were like from a movie. We were definitely the three musketeers in my eyes, the three of us. My mom learned very early on in her life that she had to be the fixer. All she ever did was try and fix our family, and of course, that fix-it or enabling codependent behavior got passed down to me and my brother and so on and so on, generation by generation. It's that merry-go-round again that never stops revolving till you unplug it or take the horse and ride away or fall off like what I am doing.

One day, but not always, one of the riders realizes what they are doing, and the rider tries very hard to get off the ride and fall off and take a different route. As a family, we did many things to try and escape the madness of our home life, but each one of us is on a never-ending merry-go-round of learned behaviors and programming. All of us are traveling various different destructive roads with addictive behaviors and relationships. My brother at twenty-two was trying to escape when he married his high school sweetheart. He left our dysfunctional house to end up on a controlling, toxic, abusive ride with his first wife—who, after several years, was verbally abusive and physically abusive and had an affair and got impregnated by her employer. When my brother found this out the hard way, he filed for divorce. During the divorce proceedings, he helped her get an abortion so that she didn't go to a crackpot doctor and get botched. She begged my brother not to say anything to her family. My, brother who was so utterly honorable, did not. He tried to be so diplomatic and fair, yet when you are dealing with an evil individual, you cannot. It just enables them to be more abusive. Evil is greed, jealousy, and animosity; and that girl was all that and more when, at the divorce trial, she tried to weasel profits from his house that he purchased long before they were married. Then she even tried to claim my mother was to take her on a vacation to Hawaii but did not because of the divorce, and she tried to convince the judge she wanted payment for the trip she felt she deserved. The girl was nuts. My brother was such a trusting nice guy. He never even changed the locks when the divorce papers were filed. Overtrusting and believing people have integrity, which, in this situation, was such a flaw. One day when he was at work, she came with her family in tow and a U-Haul and cleared out the entire house of furniture. My brother pulled up just as they were taking off, calling the police and calling me in a panic. That evil witch left him with nothing but his mattress. The police could do nothing as my ex-sister-in-law was no longer on his property. Once gone, he had no way of getting his possessions back. Just another situation where evil grabs onto goodness. At the trial, the only winners were the lawyers. When she tried to slander his good name, his lawyer said, "I have to bring up the abortion because of the way she was manipulating and painting the picture that she was the victim" to the judge. At first, the judge was falling for it because she was a great little liar and actress. My brother's lawyer said, "Time to come out with the truth. Let the cat out of the bag." That is exactly what happened. I remember her family, who had no clue about her infidelity and the pregnancy, gasped when the truth came out about the abortion and stormed out of the courtroom. The look of shock and anger on her face was priceless. In the end, my brother did end up with the house, and that was it. The lawyers got the rest. The only thing that was salvaged was the house and his reputation. He was emotionally damaged after that relationship; and thankfully, his spirit was healing when he met his current wife, my sister-in-law, and had 3 beautiful children with her, two girls and a boy. I really have no idea and don't know what demons my brother has dealt with emotionally all these years as we don't talk much about the past with each other. Nor have we really talked about the bad choices we have made in our relationships. What we do talk about is we ask ourselves why our mom has repeated the cycle.

My mom is a wonderful, intelligent, smart woman, but a woman who has no self-worth or appreciation and love for herself. She escaped her abusive upbringing with her father by marrying my father, who was an alcoholic and abusive verbally and physically, and put up with it for years to finally divorce him and then repeat the cycle once again by choosing a man very similar: controlling, verbally abusive, and has issues with his drinking. A man that has alienated her from all the people that love her, yet she chooses him over friends and family. I don't know what it is in our inner personalities as women that we seem to think we deserve it, that we do not deserve love. I did pretty much the same thing in my life. Mom—well, she went on to date a few good men, several who were very, very good to her, but she was not turned on by them. She was attracted to the taker, the one that faked who he really was, the one that reeled her in and acted like he cared and loved her when she was giving her all. And then when the dynamics of their relationship changed financially due to the economy and she was forced to live on a fixed income, his true persona came out. He became mean, abusive, verbally controlling, and a racist. Friends and family began to slip away because they could not stand to be around his toxic personality, yet she has still held on for the past twenty-six years and endured his abuse. Her famous enabling comment is "Just ignore his behavior. I do. He wants to rile you up because he is a pot stirrer, like his mother. He wants a fight. So just walk away." Abuse is abuse any way you look at it. Accepting bad behavior is enabling and codependent and demoralizing. The only difference between my father and him was and is that he doesn't regularly binge drink, nor does he beat her. He lashes out with verbal abusive comments, along with controlling and manipulative behavior. Like all newbie relationships, in the beginning, the relationship first started out as seemingly decent, but it was all superficial. In the beginning, he seemed caring and loving. That was when the money was rolling in. See, he is fourteen years younger than my mom, so he was a kept man. My mom was and is incredibly generous with him. She took him on trips to Hawaii, took him motor homing all over the United States, and even took him to Alaska several times. She had him quit his Wisconsin job and move to Illinois. She got him a maintenance job where she worked. During this whole time, he never contributed a dime to their relationship. He was and is fully supported by her. My mom doesn't know what a healthy relationship is. She has never been in one. Tom—well, he was as sweet as Cheshire Cat in the beginning. Then Mom got breast cancer and had to have treatment and support, and her life changed drastically. The company she worked for ended up being sold. The money was not rolling in, and she was now on a fixed income. The dynamics changed, and Tom was cut off from the fancy things and vacations and lifestyle he was used to living. Something he was not used to dealing with, he now had to be frugal and on a fixed income. His behavior through the years has become hateful. He is controlling, verbally abusive, and at times, when he drinks, does become violent. Yet my mother still continues to enable him, and deep down inside herself, she thinks she deserves it. She doesn't know any other way of living, so she ignores it and puts up with it. She is afraid of being alone, so she continues accepting the abuse, thinking that she is setting boundaries because she thinks she speaks her mind and puts her foot down when she has had enough. She has lost so many loving and good people in her life because they refuse to put up with his toxic behavior and rudeness. So instead of being with people who are loving, healthy, and nurturing, she continues to be with a negative animal. And just when she is at the end of her rope and he knows it, he behaves just a little bit better, keeping her merry-go-round ride a little slower until he recharges his battery and then the cycle repeats itself.

It truly is sad, and it breaks my heart. During the past twenty-plus years, I have watched him beat this vibrant woman down, much like my father, by verbally abusing her, controlling her every move, and trying to alienate her children, my children, and her friends. I tolerated his behavior for my mother's sake for years, but once I started getting healthy myself and learning my enabling triggers and dug deep within me to learn putting someone down to make yourself feel better is toxic, his antics did not work with me anymore. I won't allow it. Before I worked on myself, I kept quiet per my mom's request not to cause havoc and ignore him and his behavior. But as he has worsened and friends and family refuse to come to events, parties, and celebrations because of his toxic, cruel verbal abuse; I have stepped up and told my mother that it is not acceptable. I love her dearly. She is seventy-nine years old and does not know what it is to be healthy and not an enabler or codependent. Unfortunately, although I have finally set boundaries, he has won. He got what he wanted: for me to stay away from my mom when he is around and her friends to stay away from her because of him. So who is the winner here? She feels she cannot be alone, yet she is more alone than she ever has been in her entire life walking on eggshells, being treated horribly, and being a servant and a slave in her own home. I refuse to stay on the ride that my mom has been on and the one merry-go-round of programming she put me on when she raised me. I am falling off. He is a sick individual. I tell him off, and I walk away from him when he is out of line and when his toxic energy tries to suck me dry. The saddest thing about that is that he ends up being the winner either way. It's exactly how he wants it, and my mom loses, seeing the loved ones that love her because of it. She says she understands, yet she doesn't walk away. She doesn't get help and doesn't do anything about it. She just repeats the same cycle and tells him she is at the end of her rope with his behavior that it is unacceptable, yet the funny thing is, she has already accepted it as normal. He listens to her blah, blah, blah, her broken-record cow tows and pretends to be contrite and sorry and acts like a whimpering puppy and is all fake and simpering sweet for a brief period and then returns back to the same hateful human being he always has been. My mother once told me he raped her when he was in a drunken rage. I was appalled at hearing this information. Apparently, he is identical in so many ways like my father and her father and all the men in her life that she is used to; and he, too, cannot control his alcohol binging, and it, too, turns him into a raving lunatic. That would explain why I rarely see a drink in his hand. It is just a matter of time before the physical abuse will start to happen again because the verbal abuse won't be control enough for him. He wants to snuff the life out of my mother, and he is doing a damn good job of it. I see this happening, and there is absolutely nothing I can do. I am completely helpless to help her get off the circulatory ride. The saddest thing is that both my children see it, and they see the cycle repeating itself. He's the only grandpa they have ever known, and I hate thinking that they are going to envision this to be a loving relationship. They certainly did not see it with me and their father, and the relationship he is currently in. They didn't see it with me and Arnie. They won't know healthy unless it hit them over the head. At seventy-nine years old, she spent three weeks in a trailer writing pages and pages of the abuse she has endured while he was off having a grand old time panning for gold in Alaska because she is so afraid that when she dies, he is going to steal everything she owns, and she wants it to go her children and grandchildren. What the hell kind of quality life is that? She could have had three weeks of wonderful visits with friends and family in Illinois and spent quality time with them, but she was more worried about getting it typed and done so that it was all documented before he came back from his fun time. So sick and so sad—the things we do because we think we are protecting our loved ones, but really, we are enabling the abuser to have total control over our lives. Totally dysfunctional.

I know this because I lived it myself. I know how brainwashing it can be when someone is abusive. How you begin to think it is your fault, that you are causing the men in your life to treat you like dirt. I am living proof of what programming and growing up dysfunctional does to you and how I chose two men who were just like my father and the man my mother is with in so many ways. We all know that verbal abuse is just as bad, if not more harmful emotionally, than physical abuse. Words hurt—words you can never take back. Words damage your soul. Bruises heal, but hurtful, hateful words do not. As you have now read, our family has yet to jump off the merry-go-round and land in a field of daisies. As I said earlier, I, too, married two abusive men—first, Jack, and then Arnie. I went through the similar rituals that I have watched and continue to watch my mother go through. I am here to tell you I want out. I want off the ride. I want the cycle to end. I already watched my daughter get on the ride and choose an unhealthy, physically and verbally abusive relationship with a man she was convinced she could fix but who was already, at seventeen, a felon. I remember finding out who she was dating from my boss who knew everyone at the school. She said, "Katie, get in here. That boy has been kicked off campus for threatening a faculty member's life." I went white. And here was my daughter dating him. I remember eleven months later, I painfully picked her up at the hospital with a black eye and stitches in her forehead, yet she continued to go back for more. She didn't know any better than I did on what a healthy relationship should be. I obviously was not a good role model in the relationship arena, neither was her grandmother. So she thought what she experienced as her first love relationship was normal.

To give you some insight, in my first marriage, I was naive, young, and sexually inexperienced. I didn't know what love was, nor did I know what healthy love felt like. I just wanted to be married and wanted out of the house. So I convinced myself I was in love. In the beginning, I am not going to lie, our life was one big party.

Partying, staying out late, drinking, hanging with friends, bar hopping, softball games, and vacations—it was fun. During that interim, there were just a handful of times the Dr. Jekyl would come out of Jack, and I would just pooh-pooh it to a hangover. Later, I would find out about five years into my marriage to Jack about his serious and frightening anger issues, which would be screaming and violent at times, always yelling and throwing things. He had temper tantrums, and each time, it would become worse. The anger and rage would become more directed toward me, and I just took it and accepted it. I did not want anyone to know, so I pretended everything was fine. It was terrifying. It got worse when we had kids. Then the lying, the evading the truth, and storytelling became his standard everyday personality. In the early years of our marriage, he kept those behavior issues at bay, but then his true persona came out. He would fly off the handle at the littlest thing, and he was extremely negative. He had major, major anger issues. He could not control the temper tantrums, and he had no patience whatsoever. He was verbally abusive and condescending. He wanted me to always dress like a hooker and wear makeup and heels to have sex. I allowed him to make me feel inadequate. These behaviors ultimately destroyed our marriage, along with the cheating and various addictions he had such as porn and gaming. Before kids, I never saw any of that because life was one big party. After we were married for five years and had two children, a boy and a girl two years apart, then his anger issues began to escalate as his patience with the children became very thin. He would throw physical abusive temper tantrums, such as throwing things and yelling and screaming like he was insane. I would be the mediator, always intervening and trying to protect the kids. His family would judge me as being a pushover when it came to discipline, yet they did not live the violence and verbal abuse that we lived. I remember one of my nieces defending my ex-husband as being this wonderful hands-on father. Well, yes. In the public eye, he was. He looked picture-perfect as a coach, at the daddy-daughter dance, and at the Cub Scout campouts, yet those were temporary times where he could control his anger in front of others. In the end though, some people began to see that side of him as it worsened through the years. I contemplated leaving him several times but ultimately stayed because of the kids and because I was afraid to be alone. I demanded he attend anger management classes and see a psychiatrist as it had gotten so bad. Jack's nature was so addictive. He had issues with online gaming, and one major one was his addiction to porn on the computer. That and along with his quirky sex fetish of always wanting me to dress up in skanky negligees and heels in hooker-type fashion. That was the only way we made love, so obviously, I continued throughout our marriage to comply with this since I did not know that was not normal. I remember he came home one day with these red hooker heels all excited and so turned on by them. Since I was a virgin when we got married, he was the first man I ever made love to, so I thought it was what wives did. I enabled it and allowed it. I also decided it was my duty to let him do all his little-boy fun things such as play on three softball leagues, two bowling leagues, a basketball league, a golf league, a floor hockey league, and then go out with the boys after each one of those games. All the while, I was at home taking care of the kids and their activities. I did that thinking that was what wives did, to sacrifice their fun for their husband's pleasure. I lived that way for fourteen years, and then I couldn't take it anymore. I was going through a very dark period. I was so unhappy, so depressed. My kids were three and five, and I had sunk into the abyss of depression and unhappiness. So I started numbing myself. I started doing the very thing that I abhorred seeing my father do: drink. I started numbing my unhappiness with alcohol and also supplementing it by shopping for material things, living beyond our means and spending money we did not have on vacations and on activities for the kids and the house. Around that same time, my aunt, my mom's sister, had become very sick with brain cancer, and that made me sink deeper into depression. I was devastated. She was such a beautiful person, and I loved her dearly. I would try and go to the hospital as much as I could after work to sit with her. When I got home, the kids were asleep and in bed.

At this point in time, I was miserable. I was in such a depression. My marriage was awful. I was constantly walking on eggshells. I put on this front that everything was always perfect for friends, for the kids, and for family, just like what my mother did all the years I was growing up. My escape started with a few glasses of wine every night when I would come home from visiting my aunt at the hospital after working a full day at work. I continued to convince myself it was just to unwind, but deep down inside, I knew it was because I could not face the pain I was feeling. That couple glasses of wine eventually led to a bottle of wine every night. When that didn't work, I would chase it with a shot of vodka. Then a year later, that bottle was not enough to take away the pain, nor did it help me sleep. It did, however, help me when I had to make love to my husband, which was becoming exceedingly difficult. I knew I was crossing the line I never wanted to cross. I had watched my dad battle with this disease and addiction in his entire pathetic life, and yet here I was, going on the same merry-go-round ride he was on and never got off. After four years of closet drinking, wine and a few shots of vodka were not enough. Then it was half a liter of vodka. Then I would hide the fact of how much I was consuming by hiding the empty bottles, filling the vodka bottles with water. I woke up every day feeling pain in my back and stomach, my head pounding. I just tried to get through the day, working and getting the kids to where they needed to be and doing what I needed to do to just function so I could repeat the cycle all over again at night. I was in so much emotional pain. Soon with all addictions, my body had begun to crave and need alcohol. I would manage to control myself, which was a major challenge, and to refrain and wait and only do it after the kids went to bed and fell asleep. I wasn't always successful and would be tipsy-turvy in front of them on more than one occasion. Jack and I had major fights about my drinking. Instead of helping me, it gave him the ammunition to verbally abuse me even further. I no longer wanted to feel anything. I just wanted to be numb. This would go on for four years before I came to the realization I had done the very same thing that I hated my father for all his life and I had crossed the line to alcoholism. I mastered closet drinking and graduated into a functional alcoholic. I would be fine during the day, the busy time where I would be working and taking care of the kids and the activities and people-pleasing everyone but me and pretending everything was fine. Then when it came time at night after they were asleep and where I had to think about how miserable and unhappy I was in my life, I just could not hack the thinking and the unhappiness of how I was living. I guess you would call that a functioning alcoholic. So my dad was the functioning binge alcoholic; now I was a chip off the old block. Now I was the daughter and a functioning closet alcoholic. This made me feel incredibly worthless and such a failure. Everything that I did not want to be, I was becoming. It made me incredibly guilty that I was abusing alcohol just like my father for totally different reasons. Nonetheless, it was destructive. It was as if I had jumped on a runaway Segway and couldn't jump off. Except the only difference was, I was trying so hard to be perfect in every way. I could go, go, go—be the great wife, mother, employee, best friend, daughter, and great hostess to the outside world—but on the inside, I was dying and in so much pain. Hmm, sound familiar? Like mother, like daughter. No one knew the fine line I was crossing except for Jack and my mom. I hid it well for a long time, closet drinking, but then it became more and more difficult to hide it. And because they were too close to me, they saw the path of destruction I was taking. Like I said earlier, instead of being loving, supportive, and trying to help me, Jack used this knowledge against me to be even more verbally abusive. He relished in making me feel awful. He made me feel worthless. Yes, I allowed myself to be treated that way. I was the enabler of my ex-husband's bad behavior. I was so guilty about my addiction that I took it because I thought I deserved it. See, I could not stop the merry-go-round. I just accepted it; I had a problem, and that I deserved to be treated this way. I would make excuses for his condescending attitude, his belittling, his anger, and his narcissistic abuse toward me and then toward our children. It was a very flawed relationship. In the end, I am not even sure I loved Jack because it had never been a loving and equal partnership. He was always taking something from me: my self-worth, my kindness, and my giving nature. He was never supportive of me when I was sinking into the abyss of depression. He continued to use it against me, to abuse, and to hurt me even more, telling anyone who would listen—especially his family—horrible things about me, which would later come out at our divorce.

One night, I hit rock bottom. I finally realized I needed help. I felt so ill, so low. I reached out to my mom for help. She was battling her own battle scars, trying to survive the ride, but she was scared for me. She saw that I was on that sinking ship, and she found a great doctor who specialized in addictions. I went to him for a year. I joined a twelve-step women's group. I got healthy and substance-free. I was thirty-nine. But boy, was it not easy. I craved alcohol, and it was everywhere, surrounding me at parties, at friends' and families' houses. It was incredibly difficult in the beginning to be around people that drank socially and who were not alcoholic. Ultimately, I weighed and measured my options: self-destruct and continue to kill myself while my children watch or face my demons. I decided to get healthy for me. No one else but me. See, I knew a lot about addiction and addictive behaviors. For years, I had gone to Alateen while growing up. Why I chose the path of alcohol as my escape when I knew it was destructive and could possibly kill me, I will never know. I made a conscious decision to stay and focused on my two children and to try and do everything for them and to help them avoid the same pain. That, too, is addiction. You have to let your loved ones live life no matter if you see them buying the same ticket and getting on the same merry-go-round. You cannot control them, fix them, or stop their own ride. The only thing you can do is control how you react and control yourself and your destiny and stop enabling. Going through that addictive merry-go-round actually was an epiphany for me. I became a much stronger person, living without numbing. During that period, I remember the therapist telling me, "Now that you are physically healthy, you have to decide if you want to remain in this unhealthy relationship, if you really love your husband enough to forgive him and stay married to him." I remember pondering that thought, and my personality was not that of a quitter. Plus I was constantly fixing things that my husband would break. I am not talking furniture. I am talking about doing things like using company equipment for side jobs and then having an accident and getting caught and getting sued and then ultimately a pay cut and demotion from a company he worked at for twenty years. Then my cousin who knew that he was floundering offered him a job at his environmental company. My husband accepted. It was his escape from the humiliation of getting fired from the family company. In the end, his gradually downward spiral to unethical behavior made him screw that one up as well. His paperwork and organizational skills were terrible, and he did not log hours in correctly. And then he would come home during the day and sleep, letting the water samples thaw out in the cooler, which were environmental samples to be tested, and then he would have to go back and waste more time to get new samples. Yes, it was a full-time job for me and a constant battle to make sure he did the right thing, not the inappropriate, and I was trying to protect his image to my children, friends, and family. Yes, I enabled his bad behavior and his verbal abusiveness. I don't know why. It is the vicious cycle of dysfunction and addictive enabling behaviors, that merry-go-round, that I just couldn't escape or allow myself to get off. I convinced myself it was not that bad, but it was. I was miserable.

The ultimate, craziest decisions happened when things really were out of control. My daughter had been in a major accident with my mother in Wisconsin when she was sixteen. She had PTS badly, and so did my mother, both refusing to get help. My daughter was angry and becoming out of control. I felt helpless. My husband was on a sinking ship, grasping to hold onto a job, and financially, we had been living way above our means for quite some time and sinking into the abyss of debt. At that point, my daughter started dappling in minor addictive behavior, doing things teenagers do: sneaking out a window and hanging with a not-so-savory crowd. Her grades started to fall. I tried to get her to open up to a therapist. Her anger was as tall as a mountain. At the suggestion of the high school counselor, he suggested putting her into a forced therapeutic school where she could get therapy. We could have family therapy. She could go to school and work with animals. Our family was a mess, yet thankfully, I was still sober but emotionally a mess and with no support from my husband on what to do to help her. I was so scared for her. I felt like a single parent as my husband was off doing his fun and games as always. I researched schools and found one in Arizona. We had gone there for vacations, so we applied for a student loan. My husband and I took her there. It was the hardest thing I ever had to do because we told her we were checking out schools. She was all excited about it until she realized we were leaving her there. I had been collecting all the things she needed—mattress, pillows, her clothes, all the necessities, her favorite books, and her stuffed animals—and shipped them up there without her knowledge. The look on her face after she toured the girls school and found out she was not coming back with us was one I shall never forget. She looked at me like I was a traitor, that I betrayed her, and yet with all the love in my heart, I had to leave her. I wanted her to get help, to get the tools she needed so that she was not forced on the same ride as her mother and her grandmother. I thought I was doing the right thing by her. The guilt I felt reliving that look of horror and fear on her face, that we were deserting her, I will forever live with it.

My husband and I left, and we tried to grapple with family therapy sessions and visits, none of which focused on the abusive family dynamics of our family but of what she went through during the accident and what she felt like when I was numbing my pain with alcohol for those four years from the time she was five to nine years old. We never revealed the destructive behavior of her father. We just schmoozed and glossed over his anger issues and his unethical, perpetual childlike behaviors and choices. I just let the blame fall on me, and that was because of the incredible guilt, remorse, and shame of my alcoholism. I blamed myself for where my daughter was at emotionally at that point in her life. So when it came time to make a decision to begin anew, our house in Illinois was already more than we could handle, and Jack was in way over his head at my cousin's company. He started dappling into his quest to become a police officer, something he had always wanted to do. I was so eager to have him focus in something else that I encouraged him to start applying every time we went to visit our daughter. It was then that we made the decision to sell the house in Illinois and to purchase a house in Maricopa, Arizona, a growing town outside of Chandler. The goal was a fresh start for all of us. So I took out my profit sharing. We had my mom cosign on the house, and we purchased it. He got out of my cousin's company in the nick of time. We decided that he go to Arizona and get the new house ready and get a job at Home Depot and start trying out for the various local police positions. That meant heavy-duty training. Jack became addicted to running and working late. I was at home packing up the house and getting my son through baseball season. We knew my daughter was ready to graduate from therapy school. The plan was a fresh start in August for us all. It was a difficult decision as I was leaving my friends and family, my entire support system, to go to the desert, but I thought it was the only way to move on. The therapeutic school said that a change of scenery for the whole family could be a new beginning, and I thought also it would get Jack back on track. So I told the kids we all needed a fresh start and that we needed to support their dad in his new career goals. I didn't tell them the truth that it was because we were sinking, that Jack's behavior was ultimately making this decision for us all, and that I was enabling him even more by letting him get his way and do what I always did: just keep on doing everything for him so as to not rock the boat. The kids blamed me as the culprit for the move, and I let them continue to hero-worship their dad and protected him. Forever hiding the truth—that's what I did.

Once we moved in August, I felt so isolated, and Jack started working late nights at Home Depot. And when he was home, he immediately would go out running. He was, all of a sudden, this crazy addicted runner. Our sex life, even though odd and quirky, had never been a problem, but now all of a sudden, he couldn't get it up. I remember telling him maybe he needed to see someone, such as a doctor. That maybe he was going through some midlife male menopause. Hello, earth to me. Hmmm, penis not working for me. It is definitely working for someone else. Of course, I had my blinders up because I chose not to see the warning signs, pretending that they weren't there. Jack, at this point, was in his self-absorbed world. He almost missed getting into the Chandler Police Department by a hair and lost out to someone from the military. One of the sergeants running the tryouts suggested to him to go apply to be a Police Detention officer, which I encouraged him. See I, was grappling just to survive as the kids were not doing well. My son especially who had been outgoing at home, who loved sports, all of a sudden did not want to do anything. He was going to be a freshman. He had a learning disability with reading, and I worked tirelessly with the Special Ed department of the high school, getting him into the right teachers and trying to involve him in his favorite sport: baseball. My husband was oblivious to the kids, and when my son started sinking into depression and chose not to participate in baseball, my husband verbally berated him, even killing his spirit more. The more that happened, the more I encouraged him to focus on his career and leave the kids to me to protect them from his verbal rampages. He did finally get into the Maricopa Police Detention Officer program, and for eight weeks, we supported his studying and late nights at Home Depot.

I remember my daughter coming to me and asking me very curiously, "Mom, do you think Dad is really working this late at Home Depot?"

I said, "Of course. He would have no reason to lie to me. We trust each other." I was saying that with a grain of salt because I really did not trust him. He had lied to me so often throughout our marriage that I just accepted it.

Well, I did not realize till later that she had seen his phone text messages, and the messages she saw were romantic innuendos; and they were not from me. She was subtly trying to tell me. At that point in time, I was just in survival mode, trying to make the kids happy with the move, trying to find a job, trying not to pick up a bottle and drink my anxiety away, and not worrying about where and who his penis was visiting. I had finally secured a position with the school district as the administrative assistant to the director of curriculum. It was a great position because it helped me be closely involved in the education and needs of my kids and monitor it in a close manner plus keep close tabs on both them. Unfortunately, my relationship with Jack was going downhill fast. We were fighting more, his money was secretly disappearing as fast as his paycheck came in, and I was starting to question why. Then the big explosion. I got a hysterical phone call one afternoon while at my desk, which was right outside my boss's office. Here my seventeen-year-old daughter caught her father jacking off to porn on the computer in the middle of the family room of our home. She was hysterical. Of course, I had to play it down because I was at work and certainly could not talk about it with my boss sitting four feet away from me. I told her to lock herself in her room and we would address it when I got home. My mind was spinning. What else had he been doing all these months? He was acting very shady. I got home, and he denied everything, I knew he was lying, and my daughter had no reason to make it up as she idolized her father, although she was starting to see a side of him that was quite unsavory. I started investigating telephone numbers and found one popping up quite a bit. It was a Washington Exchange. Things were beginning to click. I kept saying to myself, *Let me just get to August. That's when the kids leave for Wisconsin for a week with their grandma.* It already had been a year of transition, stress, and health issues for me and the kids. We got there in August. In December, I had to have a partial hysterectomy due to a huge grapefruit-size cyst in my uterus, and then I had a cyst in the gland of my left breast that had to be surgically removed in April. Then with all the depression and things going on with my son, on top of that, I found out that my daughter was starting to hang out with a boy that was scary trouble. See, even therapeutic school did not stop her from taking a destructive path and make destructive choices in relationships. I could not even deal with that yet. I was treading water and was precariously on the verge of falling off the wagon from the stress of it all, and now I had to deal with the fact that I knew something had been majorly not right with my marriage for a long time.

Once the kids left for Wisconsin to my mom's, I decided to face the fire. I emailed him at the jail that I knew something was not right, and what the heck is going on? I expected to have him come home and talk his way out of his behavior, but instead, he shocked me by calling me up on the phone and stating that he was not in love with me anymore. He was in love with someone else, and he wanted a divorce to be with her. The Washington Exchange number, and her name was Elsa. I immediately thought, *Oh, he is flinging with Elsie the Borden Cow.* Somehow the joke of that softened the bitter blow and made it kind of comical. So after twenty-three years of marriage and devotedness and protecting his ass, his penis ran off with the other woman. I don't know why I felt so betrayed. Our marriage had been far from happy for so long. It still hit me hard. It was a blow to my ego, and I was hysterical. All that kept running through my brain was, How long has this been going on? I decided to investigate and took the phone records way back, and it had been going on since before I even left Illinois. Why the hell did he not have the balls to end our marriage the right way? Be a man, not a coward, and end it in Illinois, not have me move my children worlds away from everything they ever have known. What a selfish son of a bitch. We would have sold the house and divided the money, and I would have kept the kids in Illinois. Now that the cat was out of the bag, he decided la-de-da, I can leave and use this house as a revolving door. I remember crying hysterically when he first told me. I went and grabbed all the jewelry I could in my jewelry box to pawn. I checked our bank balance and saw that his paycheck had not been deposited. I called the bank, and they said he had cancelled his direct deposit. My heart clenched with fear. I got into my car and started driving down the highway to the I10, weaving and crying when a cop pulled me over. I hysterically cried, "My husband left me and the kids after twenty-three years. He is having an affair, and he took his paycheck. And I have no money to pay the bills. I need to pawn my jewelry so that I can pay some bills." The officer thankfully did not give me a ticket as I rambled through my snot and tears about what had happened. He said, "I am not going to give you a ticket. I want you to turn the car around, and I am going to follow you back to your house. And you are to promise me you are not going to leave it till Monday." I agreed, rubbing the dried snot from my nose and black mascara from the back of my hand on my pants.

So I sat alone in this house, that I had sunk all that I had into it with the hopes of saving our family, but our family was not savable. What was I going to do? I had no money to pay the mortgage. I was in panic mode, then the anger kicked in. I went online, and I went on to our cell phone account and figured out how to block the bimbo's number. See, I payed the bills. No way in hell was I going to pay to enable him to talk to this home-wrecking bitch. I waited to put the block on until the evening we left for the airport on a red-eye flight to Wisconsin to meet up with the kids. I didn't want him to know until after we landed and I had gone over all the papers the lawyer had gone over with me. He was a horrible person, doing that to me and the kids, and I considered her to know better. Yet who knows what lies he filled her head with about me and the kids? I have always been a decent, fair-minded person, always doing the right thing and never hurting or cheating anyone. Yet here was this man I had been married to for twenty-three years, being spiteful, selfish, and stooping to the level of evil. What I could not fathom—yes, do it to me, but not your children. He didn't care. He was thinking with his penis. I was all alone in the desert by myself. All my family and friends were all in Wisconsin, where we were later meeting up during the middle of the week for our annual trip to Christmas Mountain resort. My mind was racing. How could I possibly face them all? We had airline tickets already. What was he thinking? Was he thinking we would go and pretend nothing was wrong? No way in hell. I called my mom and told her what happened. The kids were with her. I remember my mom saying, "That selfish bastard," forgetting that the kids were there. She was so worried about my welfare mentally she had to admit to them what happened. They were so upset. She tried to calm them after finding out that their dad was cheating on their mom. Very hard to swallow. Although my daughter suspected, she had done the very thing I did all my life about my father: kept it a secret. Our family was always revolving on the merry-go-round of the dysfunctional cycle—great at secret keeping, great at hiding, and great at protecting and enabling.

On Monday, I looked like hell and went into the office like a walking zombie going through the motions of getting through my job. My boss, who was a kindred spirit, picked up that something was not right. After asking me several times if I was okay, I broke down and told her the truth. She relayed a similar, almost identical experience and gave me the name of her lawyer and told me to call him immediately for advice. I am so thankful for her support. I was walking in a clouded sphere, not knowing what to do. I spoke with him, and his advice left me shaken. He said that I should get on the plane, be amicable to him, be sweet, be fair, not to act with emotion or anger, type everything up (dividing everything evenly), and have him sign off on it and make him agree to it. Then go to a bank notary in Wisconsin and have them notarize the document. If I could do that without going through two lawyers and a divorce trial, I would save so much money, and it could be over within a couple of months. I wanted to vomit. All I could think about was, I had to be civil to this man who was an addictive, abusive pig who cheated on me and violated me? What the hell kind of disease did he give me? Is this the first cheating? Or have there been multiple? I absolutely was numb and nauseous, and oh, how I wanted a drink so bad. I was craving the escape. I wanted to disappear and not feel a thing, but doing so would have been another living hell, worse than what I already was in. How dare he leave me with no money to pay the bills and leave me with the mortgage and joint credit card debt? I notified all the creditors immediately. None of them really cared, but I wanted it on the record about what happened to buy me time on trying to get out of this mess. I had no love left for him, just disgust and anger.

When I finally got a hold of him (because the minute he had admitted to the affair, that was free reign to him to not come home—bastard), I asked if he was coming back to the house to take the limo that we hired to the airport. He said yes like it was a done deal. He was going on vacation. I was incredulous. Really? Get a penis fix from your girlfriend and then go on vacation with your wife. WTF? I got on that plane feeling like I was going to puke. I had typed up everything and adjusted it accordingly, trying to keep emotion out of it all. I think he was a bit shocked that I was being so calm and cold. I went over everything as calmly as I could in front of the strangers sitting around me. It was overwhelming and nerve-wracking to sit there and not be angry and to keep emotions at bay. He looked it over. I was so detailed and so fair at writing everything out that I think he was relieved to just sign off on it all. We went to a bank when we got into Madison, Wisconsin, and had the paper notarized. I made him a copy. Once that was done, as we were driving to Christmas Mountain about to face our children; in the coldest, harshest voice,

I told him that he drop me off, get into the rental car, turn his little butt around, and drive to Illinois for the week and stay with his mother and brother. That under no circumstances was he staying at Christmas Mountain, that I wanted no part of him, and that our family and friends did not either. He was shocked and looked like a pathetic puppy who was left out in the cold.

He said, "Can I at least say goodbye to the kids and tell them this is not their fault?"

I said, "They are young adults. Of course, you can."

He went in and hugged the kids with that woe-is-me look, but they were angry, very angry. They were accusatory and said they hated him for what he did. He left with his tail between his legs. Then later when he got to his mom's house, he called me super angry because he realized that he could not call his bimbo girlfriend from his cell phone on the drive to his mom's house. That is because I went online fifteen minutes before the limo picked us up and blocked her number on his phone. The only way he could call her is from his mother's landline. Boo hoo.

He was like "Don't you think that is immature, blocking her number?"

I said, "Absolutely not. If you want to call her, you can get your own personal cell phone and pay for it."

He said, "You're being the biggest bitch."

I said, "Oh well."

When the week was over and we flew back to Arizona, the atmosphere was awful. The kids did not want anything to do with him, and of course, he started accusing me of turning them against him. I never talked poorly about their father. I always spoke fairly. They made their own conclusions. They were adults. Meanwhile, I was dividing everything evenly, trying to work with the credit card companies to make a settlement and call Countrywide, which had our balloon mortgage. I fairly gave him half of everything, half the Christmas decorations, half the furniture, half our paintings, and half the pots and pans. I gave him every picture of his family. I even told him I did not want the bedroom set. It brought too many bad memories for me. Here I was being good and fair to an ass because instead of being grateful, he took it to the next hurtful, vindictive level. I don't know what lies he told all his family through the years about me and the kids, but they were all hateful. My kids were devastated because all those years, I had always treated his family with respect and love.

They, however were hateful and wrote horrible letters to me and to my daughter. My daughter was so hurt and so angry that she fired nasty letters back, speaking the truth and telling the secrets we had kept hidden. It didn't help. Because we all know that when you do such a good job of pretending and enabling and keeping secrets, no one seems to believe you when you speak the truth. The truth is, no one really knows what goes on behind closed doors, and we choose to see what we want to see. So they only saw the surface Jack, the fun-loving Jack at parties and gatherings. They only saw what ideas Jack had put into their heads. That's what they chose to see. When they wrote horrible letters to my kids and me, when all we ever did was treat them right and treat them with respect and love, that was hurtful. I could see how they could turn on me, but the kids were innocent victims. I had to respond back. I wrote them heartfelt painful letters, all the truth. In the end, his mother and brother both apologized to me when they saw the path and pattern of destruction his life took.

My ex-husband turned into such a hateful person to me and to his children, especially when he decided to accuse me that I was hiding money in a secret hiding place. He had the gall to subpoena my mother's bank records. Really? What the hell? Do you think honestly that I would hide money? And let my kids go homeless when the house we moved and fell into foreclosure? And let my mom suffer that loss because she had cosigned on the loan? Because through all that haggling, his lawyer requested me to copy every paper and receipt and tax return for the last ten years? Don't you think if I could come up with the sixty thousand dollars to buy him out to keep us from losing the house, I would? In the end, the lawyers won the most money. So dumb. While he was off shining his penis, I was trying to stay afloat, put food on the table, and haggle with creditors while working.

I was also trying to stop my daughter in making a grave mistake and choice. She was still hanging out with the bad boy who, as told by my boss, was kicked out of the school district and thrown into juvenile detention center. My daughter defended him and went to his rescue, stating we didn't know the real story. He was a smooth-talking thug who could schmooze the pants off you if you let him. He had her bamboozled, and there was nothing I could do to stop it. He was scary with his temper. I tried to convince her, but she was already encroached into his life and he had her so brainwashed she would believe and do anything he said. I heard them fighting physically one time, yelling and screaming, and I thought, *Oh no, she is in an abusive downward spiral.* I tried to forbid him to come to the house and got a restraining order, but she smartly told me to take care of my own life and that when she was eighteen, nothing was going to stop her. She was right. As much as I got her all the help, gave her all the therapy, and gave her all the love, she was raised in a dysfunctional family, and she was following the programming she was taught. There was nothing I could do to stop her from hopping on the same merry-go-round that we can't seem to get off. She accused me of being a racist because he was black. Race had nothing to do with me wanting her to see Brent for the conniving, lying, wicked, abusive, scary thug he was. If she had brought home a nice, respectful, caring boy—black, white, or yellow—someone who treated her like gold, then I would have been so happy because then I would have succeeded in breaking the abusive cycle. She was eighteen now, and I had gotten her into a trade school and into apartment housing. I had to since by May, we were going to be officially evicted since the house was foreclosing. Her father could care less about any of what was going on with his daughter and with his son, who was so depressed and sunk into the abyss of Xbox addiction to escape. Their father was in Elsa's realm and world, and all he cared about was her and his penis. He didn't try and contact the kids for months. I knew there was little I could do to stop Brent from seeing Amanda. She was on her own. He was a high school dropout and a felon mooching off her. All I could do was pray.

As the days got longer, my mother came out to help me. She gradually had yard sales and sold everything off, from my wedding dress to the china. I remember coming home and saying, "What happened to the refrigerator?"

"Oh, I sold that today."

She then supplied us with a little, tiny fridge where Stephen and I kept hot dogs and lunch meat. I tried to make the best of the situation and told Stephen, "Think of it as camping." I remember the people at the Christian church I had started taking the kids to during the divorce helped us move several times, no questions asked. I had decided to contact a realtor and rented a house in Maricopa on the other side of town right before Christmas to try and give the kids a good Christmas and feel settled, only to be told by the realtor that the people who owned the house I was renting had let it go into foreclosure, just like what the majority of people did when the market crashed. He was like "You have to be out by January 1." Two weeks before Christmas, I explained to the pastor what happened, and they moved us back into our original house, the house that was foreclosing. We had Christmas there. We decided to stay to the bitter end. And finally, I found a two-bedroom apartment in the neighboring town, Casa Grande; but it was not ready until the second week in June, and we had to be out by June 1. Here we go. The church moved us once again this time all the way to Casa Grande, to the garage of my boss. I promised them I would ask the help of my boss's husband and friends to move us into the apartment. Stephen and I had to stay in the Holiday Inn with the two dogs for two weeks. Finally, in the middle of all that chaos, Jack came to his senses when he had no money to pay his lawyer that he was losing. He signed off on everything, and the divorce became final in April. He was ordered to pay child support for Stephen, a pittance that helped pay for his food and clothing, and Stephen was falling deeper into the clutches of online game addiction. Tour of Duty was what it was. I am sorry to say I let him. I didn't feel I could take one more thing away from him and devastate his life with loss once more, so I allowed it. I tried to get him to go to a counselor. He refused. I did get him a job through my boss's father at the local grocery food store chain, but it was very difficult because we only had one car and now we lived thirty minutes from work.

By this time, I was mentally and physically exhausted and so alone. I felt so worthless, so helpless. When my daughter helped me with an online profile on a major dating website, I let her. I can tell you honestly I did not know how to act or be. I had not been on a date for twenty-four years. I didn't know the protocol—what was considered acting overboard or overzealous or needy. I remember having a guy I had talked to several times over to the house for dinner. I wanted it to be romantic. I wanted to make him feel special. Actually, I just wanted him to like me, to impress him, and to wow him so he would think I was special. I don't mean sleep with him. I was just so excited to have someone over I had candles everywhere. I had a sunken bathtub, so I told him to go take a bath while I was getting dinner. I had candles and wine surrounding the entire bathtub. I had the CD player set up with romantic, classic jazz music. I had a men's bathrobe laid out by the ensconced bathtub. The look on his face was incredulous, and I immediately was embarrassed and felt insecure. Candles all over the outside by the pool. Keep in mind, this was a first meeting and first date. I made my favorite dish and dessert, and, don't cringe, I had a candlelit table set up in the master bedroom. The bed was already gone. Jack took it, and I had my folded-up cot stored in the closet. We then went swimming and made out. It was freezing in the water because it was winter in Arizona. I could feel his hard-on pressed against me in the pool, and that was, I admit, exciting and reassuring that I still was attractive. I walked him to his car and kissed him good night, and he thanked me for everything. It was awkward. Hell, we didn't even know each other, and here I put together this romantic, intimate date. I remember the very next day, he emailed me, telling me this was the best date he had ever been on and that my husband must be a complete idiot or asshole. That I was one of the nicest people he had ever met. I didn't know what to say, except to ask if it was too over the top. He said yes, but he loved every bit of it. He said he liked me a lot, but I really lived to far from him, which was true. He lived an hour away. He said there was some guy that would snatch me up in a heartbeat. It inflated my ego that I still was likable. I could feel myself blushing with embarrassment when I thought back to the whole evening. I truly had no clue and was clueless what was too much in the dating protocol and what was too little. I had no single friends to hang out with, and I could not put Amanda and Stephen in the middle of my singleness after what they already had to deal with. Stephen hardly talked anymore. He was always sleeping or playing his Xbox. The only thing that got him out of the house was school and his job. I was beginning to feel more worthless and lonely. Of course, that's when there is a beacon on your head that says, "She is the one that will do anything and everything for me. She is an enabler and a giver. And right now, she is very vulnerable, so she is ripe and ready for the picking."

Needless to say, I was way too trusting, and not being a very good judge of character, I was a beacon for the narcissist, the broken, and the needy type of man. I met Arnie on the dating website, and he fed me everything I needed to hear. And I was so vulnerable and gullible I believed every syrupy thing he said. In the beginning, Arnie seemed to be the polar opposite of my ex. He said he was a former drummer in a band. He was working at a production company, and he had a house but it was lost by a storm. He had a car. I believed everything he said. On our first date, he brought me flowers. He romanced me. I was vulnerable and lost, a beaten-down version of who I used to be, and I trusted and believed everything he said. I let him woo me to the max because I needed to feel love. It was a whirlwind. I met him in September. By November, I moved him into my apartment. Stephen could not stand him, and Arnie knew it; gradually, the tension grew. November came, and all of a sudden, I get a yelling and screaming phone call from Arnie that his car was towed and that I needed to leave work and come pick him up immediately. It scared me because he was so demanding and angry, but what did I do? I jumped in the car and drove for forty minutes to pick him up. My stomach was in knots. I picked him up, and he made up some story that they didn't receive his car payment. Really? After investigating, I found out that he got his car from one of those fly-by-night car companies and missed two payments. Well, they came and took it back. It was reported. So now here I was, getting up an hour earlier at 4:30 a.m., driving him forty minutes to work and then driving to the school district where I went with a pillow and laid on the floor of my boss's office for an hour, setting my phone alarm. Then I was getting up, brushing myself off, splashing water on my face, and then sitting at my desk. What had I gotten myself into? I had thought. Yet I still let Arnie manipulate me into asking me to marry him. See, he knew a sucker when he saw one. He knew it was my nature to want to fix the broken. My self-esteem and worth were in the dumpster. I was mentally broken myself and sick. So I agreed. In the meantime, I found out that Stephen needed more help in school and the Special Ed department where I worked was not cutting it. They had gone through a staff change, and they could not provide what he needed. My boss suggested the Tempe school district. I knew that the tension was escalating between Stephen and Arnie. I was torn. The thought of asking Jack to have Stephen move in with him turned my stomach sour. Jack lived in Tempe right by the school. I thought if I got him to Jack's and he could walk to school and if I could get him a transfer to that area's grocery store, which also was a walking distance from Jack's condo, that would be great. He could finish his senior year in a good program. The only downfall was that he had to live with Jack, who was living in bachelor-style mode, not a good role model as his morals had gone directly to his penis. His condo was a revolving door of one-night stands. Elsa had dumped Jack months before, and he had become a womanizer. It seemed like the perfect solution for Stephen's education as far as school and his job, but the living arrangement stunk. But the other option of living with me and Arnie was not good either.

Arnie made no bones that he felt that we should have our alone time. He wanted to control me and everything I did with friends, with the kids, online, and on Facebook. It was really scary. He would go into these jealous rages, major red flags and warning indicators, yet I chose not to see them. That was December. Stephen was not happy about the change. He thought I was abandoning him. I was, to an extent, but I wasn't at the same time. I was an emotional mess. I let myself be manipulated and controlled. I chose to ignore all the warning bells. That January, I got a phone call from my daughter she was in the hospital, beat up by the thug. He left her lying in a pool of blood by her car in Mesa with a black eye and a cracked-open forehead. I was sick. I remember going to get her at the hospital. Here my beautiful daughter was going down the road of letting a man physically abuse her. I remember telling the Mesa police officer he was a felon, but he only shook his head and said, "Unless Amanda is willing to press charges, there is nothing we can do." He said on the side to me, "I see this happen all the time, where the girlfriend protects the abuser." Like mother, like grandmother, there she was, following in our footsteps. She ultimately was forced into filing a restraining order and press charges in order to break her lease. It broke my heart to watch this. I was completely helpless to show her the light. I was doing the same thing myself all over again and got involved with a controlling, abusive man again. Both kids could see it. Both kids did not like the way Arnie treated me, but what could I say? I was already in too deep. I don't seriously know what I was doing. I just went through the motions of trying to survive. People I had made friends at work with were happy for me that I was with Arnie. They knew what happened with Jack. One friend even lent us the use of her minivan until we could afford another car. I was too embarrassed to tell her the truth as to why we were down to only my car.

Then in January, two weeks before the wedding date in February, Arnie got laid off from work. He also got a notice that he owed child support, which he had lied about, stating he had paid it all, yet there was no record. Then the tax evasion letters began to come in the mail. By then, it was too late. I was married to him. I found out he had not done his taxes for six years. I was panic-stricken. He began drinking heavily and smoking lots of pot, flying off the handle if I was five minutes late getting home. I would get home from working all day while he spent the day watching TV and smoking weed to no dinner on the table, him expecting me to make it and serve him— which I did because if I didn't, he started yelling at me. I knew I was in way over my head, and I had made a big mistake. He had no job, and we were trying to live on my salary. Here I was enabling again. I was filling out online applications all night long for him, while he sat home all day, sleeping and watching TV. Ever the enabler. I convinced myself I was helping. He finally had an interview at the

Frito-Lay plant. Thank you to my enabling by filling out the long, long online application. The interview was for a production inspector. Well, that went well, except for the glitch of the drug testing. He had me order this fake pee test and convinced me that it was fine. People do it all the time. That the weed he smoked was for his back problems. Ha ha. He got to the drug test, and lo and behold, they did not do it with pee; they did it with a hair sample. He was caught. No job offer. He was still unemployed.

It was the beginning of fall. We had been married nine months. I was under so much stress, worrying about Stephen and praying that he was okay and feeling guilty that I had to throw him to the wolf in Tempe just to get away from the coyote I was living with. It was insane. I didn't want to admit to both kids that I had made a big second mistake. I didn't want to burden them, and I didn't want to hear, "I told you so, Mom." They were both getting dizzy on their own merry-go-round. In the beginning of fall, I had the sinking gut feeling something was not right with my daughter. I knew she had been secretly back together with Brent. Then the phone call. She called me, hysterical. She was five weeks pregnant, and she did not know what to do. She was scared. She was alone. Brent was there on again, off again. I told her I would support her in whatever decision she decided. I was sick to my stomach. It was what I dreaded, and there was really nothing I could do. She made the decision to go to the Planned Parenthood office and terminate the pregnancy. The day of the appointment was a nightmare. Arnie, who was increasingly jealous of the connections with my children, would not let me go without him. I was heartsick enough and then had to deal with his condescending, abusive, controlling lecture the whole way from Casa Grande to Mesa. We got to her apartment an hour before the appointment.

I was knocking on the door. She would not answer. I knocked and pounded for ten minutes, stating, "Amanda, it's Mom. I'm here for the appointment." She was always a heavy sleeper, but I think she just was avoiding answering the door and pretending she didn't hear me.

Arnie was in the car, yelling, "This is fucking ridiculous. Bitch, get your ass back in the car! Let's go."

I was shaking. After fifteen minutes, I reluctantly got back in the driver's seat. I started to drive away, and I pulled into a gas station to call her and text her. By this time, Arnie was livid and screaming at me at the top of his lungs. I could not concentrate.

"Your daughter needs to figure this bullshit out herself." He got out of the car and slammed the door. He was yelling so loud people were looking at us in the parking lot.

I finally snapped. I said, "Get the fuck away from this car," and I slammed the gas pedal down to the floor, backed up fast, and hit the lock buttons on the car doors as he started pounding on the window.

He said, "Open this fucking door, bitch. Now."

I said no, and I slammed on the gas and turned right out of the parking lot. We were a mile away from my daughter's apartment.

Now I was shaking, my heart racing. I knew he was going to be pissed as all hell. I didn't care. All I kept thinking was I had to get away and help my baby girl. Little did I know that some passersby had called 911 and reported an altercation between us and police had arrived at the gas station then drove down and stopped Arnie, who was walking on the sidewalk because someone pointed him out as the person involved. He told the police, "Oh, it was just me and my wife having a little disagreement. She left me here to cool off, Officer, while she went to go pick up her daughter." I found that out after I found him waiting in the grocery store parking lot across the street. His face was beet red. He was pissed. I dreaded picking him up. I did, and he said in a menacing voice, "Don't you ever do that to me again, or I will beat the shit out of you."

His face and his demeanor scared the crap out of me because I knew he meant every word of what he said. "I couldn't think while you were yelling at me. I needed to call my daughter," I said in a small voice. "I don't care what you think. She is my daughter, and I am not leaving until I help her or get her through this situation."

He said, "Fine," with gritted teeth and got in the car and slammed the door. It was then that I found out about the good Samaritans that called the police. *I could hug those people*, I thought. They probably saved me from a worse situation, more than they ever realized.

Amanda finally answered the door. I told her the appointment was made at Planned Parenthood and she can either go or cancel it. She finally reluctantly answered the door and slowly shuffled down the stairs with me to the waiting car. Arnie was waiting there, and all he said to her was "You are doing the right thing. You cannot support a baby." I looked at him with disgust.

We drove silently to the clinic. Arnie dropped us off in my car. He said he would be back in an hour to get us. We got out and went inside the clinic. I could not offer to pay the three-hundred-dollar fee that Planned Parenthood needed. So Amanda's grandmother, my mother, came to the rescue and paid for the three-hundred-dollar office visit by phone with her credit card. My only job was to go with her. My heart heavy and my emotions torn, I knew that she was in no position to have a baby. The thought of terminating a life created made me literally sick. I am not against abortion, but I myself would choose a different option such as adoption. I never told that to Amanda. I tried not to say anything but to give her every option to choose from because I did not want to sway her decision. I wanted it to be hers. I know Amanda felt the same guilt and pain, and she was scared. We got there, and I silently watched her fill out the paperwork. The office was packed with couples. I kept thinking that all these people had unwanted pregnancies that they were ending. How utterly sad. There were so many people who could not have a baby, and yet here were all these babies wishing to be born. When they prep you before they give you the medicine to terminate and give you the D and C, they show you a sonogram picture. They print it out and give you a copy of it. I remember Amanda showed it to me with tears sliding down her cheeks, pain and anguish in her eyes, and I remember feeling cold and clammy. After it was all over, the nurse walked her toward me and said she needed to rest and lay down and gave me the instruction sheet in the event she ran a fever or had heavy bleeding.

I remember walking Amanda in the hallway, and then she turned and looked at me straight in the eye and held out the picture and said, "You and Grandma made me do this. This was my baby. I'll never forgive you."

I felt a pain in my heart like I was stabbed as her words stung me like a bee sting. I felt as cold as ice. "Amanda, I didn't make you do anything," I said in a shocked, anguished voice. "I encouraged you from the start that I would support you in whatever choice you would make. I gave you all the options. Planned Parenthood information on terminating a pregnancy, adoption, and raising the baby on your own. Your grandmother and I—all we did was she offer to pay for it and that I would be there to help you through it. It was ultimately your decision."

She said, "I wouldn't have done it if you and Grandma hadn't kept pressing me and pushing me that direction. I just want you to know that I am going to get pregnant again and have a baby, and there is nothing you can do to stop me."

It was threat. I shook my head incredulously, completely hurt. No matter how much love and support I give, I still was the bad guy. "All we were doing was trying to help you," I choked out. She did not answer as I walked her slowly down to the car.

Arnie looked like the Cheshire Cat. I could tell he was thrilled at the outcome. She was angry with me, and the situation caused a rift. Just what he wanted. At that moment, I literally hated him. After we got Amanda safely back to her apartment, she avoided me like the plague for the next couple of weeks. No matter how many times I tried to call her and check on her and tell her I love her, her responses were short and curt and cold. I was waiting to tell her that I was planning on leaving right after Christmas to Florida. She had moved into a new apartment, and she was finally gradually warming up to me not hating me from that ordeal. I wanted to show her some happiness and fill her world with magic like I did all the years she was growing up. I always made holidays magical for the kids. It is one of the happiest memories they could hold on to. I was thrilled that she wanted to see me. I was so hoping I could extricate myself from having to bring Arnie, but he was glued to me at the hip. I couldn't go anywhere without him always monitoring me. I did not care. I tried my best to ignore him because I knew it was going to be so hard this Christmas telling both Stephen and Amanda I was moving to Florida. I knew that they were going to be upset, another parent deserting them. Yet I wasn't deserting them. I was trying to get them far away from danger, and I needed help. I needed to be in a safe zone because I was scared. Arnie was getting worse every day. I just had to get through Christmas and try and make it special with no conflict with the kids.

In the beginning of December, I went to the Dollar Tree and picked up some decorations in Amanda's favorite colors, blue, and went through the many boxes I had saved for her through the years of Christmas decorations and picked out some special ornaments. We went to her new apartment to decorate and break the news. I could tell Arnie just about practically had a hard-on. He was so excited to burst her bubble and tell her we were leaving. I told him to please let me do it. We got there with dinner, and I started decorating and making it look festive with lights and garlands.

When I was all done, I said, "Amanda, I have to tell you that on January 15, I am moving to Florida to live in the house Grandma has that is not rented and to help her through her hip surgery."

She looked shocked. Her face turned gray, and big tears filled her eyes. "So you are deserting me when I need you most," she said.

I said, "I am not deserting you. I will always be here for you."

She said bluntly, "I am pregnant. And I am due in August, and I am keeping this baby."

My eyes widened with shock. She had made good on her threat. "Is it Brent's?" I asked her.

She said, "Yes, and he is excited like me. He is going to help me." I gasped. She said, "I know what you think, but he is here for me, not like you. And now you are going to miss it all."

I said, "Amanda, I cannot stop you. You have to do what is right for you. If this is what you want, then I am happy for you. Remember, people don't change. Brent put you in the hospital six months ago, left you in a pool a blood. He still is the same person he was then as he is now."

She shook her head defiantly. "He loves me. We want this baby. You can't stop me now."

119

"Amanda," I said, my heart sinking. "I never stopped you before. I know you don't believe that, but the choice was always yours."

"So you really are going to leave me and Stephen?"

I lied and said yes. "I need to help Grandma." I did not want to tell her the truth that I was scared to death of the crazy man standing next to me.

Arnie said firmly, "Katie, it's time to go. We have to let the dogs out."

I hugged her tight and said, "I love you, Amanda. I want you to be safe, loved, and happy."

She pouted and said, "I am. I can't believe you're leaving." She threw one more jab at me.

My heart was sick. Next, we picked up Stephen and took him out to dinner, and I told him I was moving.

He said, "So it's true, what Amanda just texted me. You are deserting me too. Dad's never home, and when he is, he is screwing a different bimbo. Last week, I walked in on him doing it on the couch."

"OMG, I am so sorry, Stephen. You should not have to see that from your father." Inside, I was seething. That sick son of a bitch can't even have the morals to go in the bedroom?

Stephen wailed, "I have no one."

I said, "Yes, you do. You have me, and I will call you, email you, skype with you. And I will be back in May to see you graduate."

My heart was breaking. I just wanted to fix everything, part of my codependency and enabling and fixing the broken. How could I tell them I was terrified, and I didn't know what to do so I was running to my mom for help? I had to admit to someone the hell I was living. In the beginning, things were still in the newbie stage when Arnie was campaigning for my heart and being as sweet as pie and taking advantage of my vulnerability and inexperience. He played on them so well. I had only been with one other man, my husband, so when Arnie and I made love eight times in one day, I thought I had hit the mother lode. I remember that day clearly. I was both enthralled that I could excite a man that much, but I also was exhausted. How could a man get that sexually aroused that quick with no breaks in between? I was in wonderment and sore as hell. Later, I would find the bottle of Viagra that was hidden in his clothes. As the months went by, that simmered down and slowed. He had me then, and he knew it. I was married to him. I was so dumb. Here I get out of one abusive marriage in April of 2008—broken, no healing time, and no soul searching to try and pull the plug on the merry-go-round and stop the continuing cycle of dysfunction. No, I go and meet someone in September and believe every word he told me. I have him move in with me in November because I was so lonely and afraid to be alone. I get manipulated and talked into marrying him in February 2009. Even though those red flags were there, my programming said, "It will be okay. He didn't mean it. He said he was sorry." Now I was married to him and stuck. Every day, I woke in fear. We took a trip to San Diego on Memorial Day. We went with no money. I thought my check was going to be in the bank the day we checked into a cheap motel. It wasn't, and Arnie started screaming obscenities at me in the parking lot of a shopping center, calling me a dumb bitch. I spoke with the hotel proprietor and begged him to let us stay and that the next day, I would be able to pay with my debit card as my check was direct deposited. He was a nice man, and I could tell he felt sorry for me. I was able to calm Arnie down with a blow job. I was seemingly getting to be an expert at blow jobs as it prevented me from having to endure sex. Thankfully, Arnie loved them so much he didn't figure out that's what I was doing. By the time we left in January, every passing day was becoming more verbally abusive—yelling, screaming, demanding sex, pushing and shoving me around. He had gained fifty-plus pounds and was close to 290. He was six feet, three and 290 pounds to my five feet, two and 130 pounds. When we had sex, I literally would feel like I was being crushed and suffocated. One time, he collapsed on top of me, and I could not breathe. I was beginning to panic, trying to get him to roll off me and get his wicked dick out of me. I couldn't move him. He thought that was comical, seeing my face and seeing me panic and squirm in fear. The ultimate control.

In order to move to Florida, I had to cash out my retirement through the school district to pay the five thousand dollars for the moving truck. I was literally broke. We had five hundred dollars to our name and my crummy Elantra. We loaded it up with his Alaskan malamute dog, which was like a German shepherd, Sammy. He had no business owning that dog. He did not take care of him. That dog had a cyst the size of a volleyball that he carried around for a year. The dog never was on heartworm and never had vaccines until he met me. The dog cowered around him, and I was constantly protecting him from spanking him.

We had Sammy and my little Schnoodle loaded up with minimal necessities and started the long drive from Arizona to Florida. We could not afford to stay in a motel except for one night because we had to survive on that five hundred dollars until both of us found jobs. On the way there, I began noticing blood in my urine. I thought, *Oh no, I have a urinary tract infection and no insurance.* I remember halfway there, we were in North Carolina, and it was cold. We were in a rest stop trying to sleep, the windows frosted with the two dogs, and we were freezing. We turned on the car every hour to warm it up, but it would only stay heated for a short time. We had to endure it because we had no choice. Once we got to Florida, my mom could sense things were amiss and strained between the two of us, but he never left us alone so that I could talk to her. It was almost like he knew I wanted to talk to her and tell her something, so he never let me out of his sight. It was sickening. My mom shrugged the bad feeling she had and began showing us all she had done to furnish the duplex. She said that she was still going to keep it on the market while we lived there. She was beaming at my reaction. She had done a beautiful job, and she even had done a matching mini Christmas tree to match the furniture she had gotten at an estate sale. I loved it and was so grateful. That was the Thursday prior to Super Bowl Sunday. Mom had gotten a call that a realtor wanted to show the place.

I laughingly said, "Mom, you did such a good job decorating it, it's going to sell in a heartbeat."

She said, "No, it's been on the market for a year with no bites."

Well, I jinxed it because the couple that came and looked made an offer, and it sold the very next day. And we were homeless as the moving truck pulled up. Arnie was an ass. The first thing he said was

"Great. You get me down here, and now we have no place to live." I ignored him because I had more things to worry about. I needed to see a doctor so I could take care of this blood in my urine.

I applied for unemployment but was denied because I had quit my job voluntary. I was not laid off. Arnie, on the other hand, could apply for unemployment still. I filed for assistance and got emergency aid because I told the women I had a medical problem. I went immediately to the doctor, and they started treating me for a UTI. Here is the horrifying truth, the UTI was not going away I was still having blood in my urine and pain. I was sent to a Urologist, specialist, and he told me I had a Bladder tumor and he thought it could be cancerous and I needed surgery as soon as possible to remove it and possibly then followed by radiation treatments. OMG, I thought. How much more suffering do I have to endure? An abusive second husband and now surgery, with the possibility of it being cancer? I was in despair. How could God do this to me? I so wanted to drown my sorrows and toss my sobriety towel in. I was at the bottom. I felt defeated. I felt there was no light at the end of this nightmare I was living in, that I had gotten myself into, yet I still had to put on a face and go on like I was fine. Inside I was in absolute fear. The surgery was scheduled, and the tumor was removed. All through this Arnie was zero support, had no empathy, and acted like I was inconveniencing him by this health scare. Thankfully the pathology report came back benign, the tumor was not cancer. My prayers were answered. I think God knew I was at the end of my rope.

Thankfully, that kept Arnie at bay with his sexual advances. That was a relief. I don't think I could have dealt with that as well. I was trying so hard to keep it all together. Shortly after that, I found employment at a local animal hospital. We only had one car, so I had to beg my mom to help me out with a loan to buy a second car, a used one, so that Arnie could use it to find work. He didn't flinch in taking other people's hard-earned money. I felt horrible. He finally secured work at a factory for Tervis Tumblers in Sarasota. I was relieved he had a far drive.

Things were relatively smooth at first, but then Arnie's ugliness started to come out. See, he and my mom's significant other,

Tom, butted heads. They both were abusive narcissists. Of course, they would. I barely could stomach being around both of them. One night when my aunt and uncle were in town, we were at my mom's for dinner. Arnie was having me serve him mixed drinks from the bar when Tom said, "I think Arnie has had enough," when he saw me go over and make him another.

That set him off, and Arnie said, "Don't you talk to my wife or order her around. Who the hell are you, telling me I can't have a drink? This isn't even your house." I felt my face turn beet red. I broke out in a sweat. The atmosphere was charged. Everyone felt uncomfortable. Then Arnie said, "That's it. We're out of here." I quickly hugged my aunt and uncle and my mom. I walked right by Tom, ignoring him. I had decided long ago that Tom was just using my mom. I looked out of the corner of my eye, and I saw my aunt and uncle shaking their heads in disbelief. Arnie started slurring as we walked to the car, "That son of a bitch. I'll beat the shit out of him before I let him order you around like that again."

I called my mom the next day and apologized. She said, "Katie, what have you gotten yourself into? You went to the pot to the frying pan."

I knew she was right, but it ruffled my feathers. I said sarcastically, "Mom, I love you, but you have no room to talk. I will come over and talk to you if I can get away."

Three weeks earlier, I endured another brutal incident, and I was determined I had to end things before I was found dead. We had gone to the Ribfest in Saint Petersburg. Styx was playing after two country bands. I was looking forward to actually doing something, and watching a concert outside by the water, I was hoping it would lift my spirits. That was not what my world consisted of: peacefulness. See, Arnie could not go anywhere without alcohol, and since we were piss poor, he decided to smuggle mini-liquor bottles inside his tube socks, knowing that my backpack would be searched. There was no arguing with him about not doing it. Rather than fight it, I fueled it and enabled it more by putting some in my socks when he could not fit them all in his. I cannot believe that I did not just throw in my sobriety towel and join him, but I never succumbed. I just knew

I could not fall off the wagon. I was in hell already. That would be the inferno. He had been drinking all afternoon and was starting to become obstinate and belligerent.

He said, "I am going to the bathroom. Are you coming?"

I said, "No, I don't have to go." I was relieved to be free of him even if it was brief. It was hot, and I had my hair put up in a ponytail.

I was making conversation with the older lady next to me when all of a sudden, I hear this voice yell, "Take a piece of this, motherfucker!" I looked up to see Arnie grabbing his crotch, yelling, "What, you piece of shit? You want a piece of this, fucker?"

I looked over to the group of two guys and a girl yelling back to him, and then I see security coming over. I said, "Arnie, what's going on?"

He said, "That motherfucker spilled a beer all over me." I started to get up to grab his arm and tell him it's not worth it when he shoved me down in my fold-up chair and said, "Shut the fuck up, bitch."

I could see the horrified look on the woman next to me. I snapped. I popped up and said, "I'm done."

He said, "What the fuck is that supposed to mean? Where do you think you are going? Sit your sorry ass back down."

I continued to ignore him, my heart racing and my hands shaking as I folded up my chair, and said, "I am out of here." I turned away from him and glanced at the woman next to me. I saw pity and disgust in her eyes. I was humiliated. I started pushing my way through the crowd of chairs all lined up waiting for Styx to come out to the stage.

He started yelling at the back of my head, "Get the fuck back here, bitch." I kept walking as fast as I could. The next thing I knew, my neck snapped back as the back of my pony tail was yanked hard. It was Arnie. He had caught up to me. He pulled me against him and said in a seething voice right below my ear, "Don't you ever walk away from me again. You hear that, bitch?"

We were in the middle of a huge crowd, sandwiched in between a wall of people most of whom were under the influence and oblivious to what was happening. I said, "Let go of me, or I will call the police."

He laughed and then growled, "Go right ahead. Call the police."

My mind raced through all the possible scenarios if I did. He knew I wouldn't. Because the truth was, I knew that if I called the police and had him arrested, one of his cronies at his work who believed his made-up stories would bail him out, and he would come back to the house and beat the shit out of me or kill me. It was like a flashback to when I was five years old watching my mother. He snickered. "Yep, I thought so. Smart girlie."

He yanked me by the arm, dragging me back to the car. He was squeezing the back of my arm so hard I was wincing. We got to the car, and he threw the keys at my face. "Get in and drive." He couldn't drive because he was toasted. By this time, my stomach was in knots. I was shaking. All I wanted to do was cry and run away. I felt so stuck, so trapped. Part of me actually wanted to drive off the Saint Pete Bridge to end the madness. The only thing holding me back from doing so was the fact that I could not leave my kids. They would not be able to survive one more loss. Arnie slurred, "Get us home, bitch." My stomach wanted to lurch. I looked at him and shook my head. How was I even remotely attracted to him? He was vile and condescending. He was not even good-looking. The thought of going home and having to deal with his sour breath breathing down my neck made me want to vomit. I could taste the bile in the back of my throat.

As I drove the forty-minute drive, I just prayed. *Please let him pass out so I can get us home without an accident.* Thankfully, my prayer was answered fifteen minutes later when I looked over and saw him slumped over and slouched in the seat, snoring with drool coming out of the corner of his mouth. Being outside in the heat, humidity, and sun, you can just imagine how the car reeked of alcohol and BO. OMG, how I did not miss that smell? Remembering my father, remembering my alcoholic self, I cracked my window in order to breathe and so I would not vomit. We pulled into the garage. He was still slumped over when I decided to leave him there while I attended to the dogs. It would be so much more peaceful for them since all he would do was yell at them and then both of them would cower in fear. After I took them both out, I went to go look at my right arm, which was super sore. Investigating his handiwork in the mirror. I saw blue and purple fingerprints on the back of my white arm. Ugly. My skin began to crawl when I heard him coughing and sputtering. I dreaded him waking up from his stupor. That meant that now I had to endure his disgusting attempt at lovemaking.

"Where are you?" I heard him yell from the bedroom in a raspy voice. "Get your ass over here and give me some head."

I wanted to gag. I don't know what was worse: forcing myself to suck his tiny penis or letting him attempt to get on top of me to try to find the entryway to attempt to fuck me with his limp alcohol-induced dick. Either way, both were horrible options. In the end, he got bored with me sucking him, and he demanded that I flip over and let him get on top of me. He did, and he spent the next hour trying to harden his soft penis to no avail. He was on top of me. I could hardly breathe. It was sixty minutes of hell, his slobber all over my face and his breath sour. I had to envision myself in a peaceful sphere of water and that I was underwater, being bathed and cleansed, in order to suffer through it. When he finally released himself, he collapsed on top of me like a dead whale and passed out. I tried to wiggle and move, to no avail. I was beginning to panic because it felt as though I was being suffocated. I could feel myself breaking out in a sweat of panic. I tried to bring my hands up and tried with all my might to push him sideways off of me. Finally, it worked. I gasped for fresh air. I felt sick. I immediately wanted to get in the shower and clean myself. I went to the couch and laid down. I was mentally and physically exhausted. It was late, and I had to get up early for my new job as the front office receptionist. It was literally down the street and five minutes away. I still had the job at the animal hospital, the place I first gained employment when I first moved down to Florida, but now I only worked on Saturdays. This was good because I was able to give Sammy, Arnie's beautiful neglected dog, the proper care he needed. Such as that huge cyst—I had it removed, and when I did, the doctor was like "I cannot believe this poor dog has been walking around with this for over a year." It was the size of a volleyball, and it was filled with fluid and dead rotten tissue. It weighed five pounds.

I was trying so hard to keep it together at my new job, but I was failing and messing up. My normal jovial behavior was not there. I was exhausted and had circles under my eyes. I was jumpy. My nerves were shot. My boss noticed this change and asked me what was wrong. She said, "Is everything okay at home?" She saw the bruises on my arm. They were too big to hide. My voice cracked, and I croaked, "No." Then I broke down in tears as she ushered me into her office. I told her everything. I told her I had asked my mom to help me make an appointment for a lawyer that specializes in abusive cases. She said, "Do what you need to do to be safe." I said thank you. I was grateful for the support.

I finally had gone to my mother's the day after the Ribfest and broke down and told her the truth. She suspected it. I was ashamed and embarrassed and disappointed in myself. Shortly after leaving work, Mom called me and said she was able to get an afternoon appointment with a lawyer in Tampa for a consultation on Wednesday. I had been writing out everything that had happened in chronological order. It was a form of therapy. As I was writing it, I kept asking myself the question, "Is it that bad? Am I overexaggerating? I left as if I was going for work that Wednesday but went and picked up my mother. We drove down to the lawyer's office. I met with his assistant and gave her all the paperwork I had written. She said to give her half an hour while she went through it all. We waited in the lobby. My stomach was gurgling with nerves.

She came out and ushered my mom and I into the office. She said, "This is serious, and it is escalating. This is not going to get better. The violence is increasing, and you need to get out now before you become a statistic." She then said, "In order to save money, you can go down to the courthouse and file the restraining order and order of protection, and I can give you the number of a state aid attorney to assist you with the process. He is good, and he will walk you through the steps. Then at the order of protection hearing, our office can handle serving him the divorce papers."

It was all happening so fast I was scared. I said to her, "So you think I am not imagining it? It is bad?"

She said yes. "The one thing you need to do is to get your car away from him as it's in your name."

I left the office numb. My mother said, "Let's go do it."

I said, "Mom, I can't."

She said, "What do you mean you can't?"

I said, "I have to do it my way. I can do it tomorrow and then serve him on Friday, but I need to have him served in Sarasota, where he works by that police department. I need to open a storage locker up and get a kennel for his dog. And as soon as he leaves for work on Friday, I need you to come over with your car, and I will load my car up with all his crap and his dog. I will go drop his dog off, and we can make several trips to the storage locker and get rid of all the stuff we accumulated while we were married, such as camping equipment, the gas grill, etc."

My mom was like "Why are you doing all that for him? He doesn't deserve it. He is an evil, abusive narcissist, and you don't owe him anything. He used you."

"Mom," I said, "I do not want him coming back saying I cheated him from anything, nor do I want him to think his stuff is here at the house."

"Really? He doesn't deserve all of that or anything for what he has been doing to you," my mom said angrily.

I said, "Mom, I cannot for fear that he will come back for something. If he does, he will kill me. I know it."

She went pasty white. I felt awful putting my seventy-seven-year-old mother through that turmoil. She had just had hip surgery; and the other hip was causing her great discomfort, and she had a hard time maneuvering. Yet here she was, doing her best to help in any way she could to help me out of this scary mess. I came home from the lawyer's, and that night, I reached out to a long-time friend and broke down. I had known her for years, and she, too, had many rough experiences with the men in her life in wickedly abusive relationships. I never understood why because she was a person who is so sweet and kind, and yet she seemed to attract the needy and the men who were phonies. She had the beacon on her just like me that said: "Giver. Looking for a taker. My heart is open for abuse and crushing." She said she came to a realization the night she and her kids had to leave literally with the shirt on their backs and nothing else that she needed to change her way of thinking. She told me about a book that her therapist recommended to her, which saved her life. It was called *Why Does He Do That?: Inside the Minds of Angry and Controlling Men.* This book was instrumental in my healing. It showed me I not only was an enabler but that I also was a victim, that my dysfunctional upbringing had much to do with the way I handled men and my relationships.

After coming home from the lawyer's, I had a few hours before Arnie arrived home where I could secure the kennel and the storage locker and put a plan into action. The next day, Thursday, I worked a half day and told my boss the plan. I said I was going for the order of protection at lunch; that I needed Friday off because I was going to have him served; that as soon as he left for work, I was bringing all his possessions and everything we had accumulated while married to the storage locker; that I was having him served, delivering the envelope with the letter I had written saying goodbye and all the info where his dog and possessions were; and that I was going to hop in my other car that Arnie had been using, which was at his place of employment, and drive off. Sounded quite easy, but it was not. I went and filed the order of protection, waited for over an hour and a half for the judge to issue the temporary order, and secure a court date for the hearing. I was a nervous wreck because it was getting close to 3 p.m., and I still had to make it home before Arnie so he would not suspect. It was 3:30 when I received the temporary order to be served. I took it as I needed the Sarasota Sheriff's Department to serve it as it was in a different county. I made it home five minutes before he arrived home. The back of my neck was wet with sweat. I remember standing in the kitchen with my back to him while I was making a sandwich for dinner and him coming up to the side of my face, picking up a steak knife and holding it an inch from my left eye. I could see the point of the knife from the corner of my eye.

He said in a dark voice, "What is up with you? You are acting different, all cold and jumpy. You better not be doing anything."

I laughed a nervous laugh. I said, "What are you talking about? I'm just making dinner."

"You are acting weird," he said.

I turned and forced myself to be as sweet as I could muster in the state of fear I felt. I reached up and put my arms around him and shut my eyes and slammed my tongue in his mouth in a frenzy attack to change his inquisition to lust. It worked, but I was the loser because I had to give head and I thought I was going to throw up when he released himself inside my mouth. I had to swallow so fast so as to not gag.

The next morning while he was in the shower, I snuck to his key chain and removed his house key from his key chain. I then had told him I was running to the pharmacy to pick up some Pepcid for his acid reflux, and I ran to the cash station to take out the cash that was my paycheck. I had transferred my check the day before to go into a new account. We had been using the temporary money debit card for direct deposit, so it was easy to do. I got back as soon as he was grabbing his lunch. I gave him his Pepcid and kissed him quickly good-bye, my heart racing. As soon as he left, I started running around the condo, grabbing everything of his and throwing it in a box or bag and shoving it in the car. I called Mom and her significant other. They came as quickly as they could. We made three trips back and forth to the storage facility. I had paid for three months up-front. On the third trip, I took his dog, Sammy, and God bless him. He was a nervous nelly, and he took a crap in my front seat. Thankfully, it was in his blanket and not on the seat. My heart broke when I left him at the facility. I told the kennel that it would be at least a week before he would be picked up. That was a lie because I really had no idea when he would be picked up. I did not put any of my contact info on the sheet, only Arnie's info and cell number so I would never know. I then went to a place where you could open a mailbox up and filled out the forwarding information, having my mom's significant other pose as Arnie. I had a copy of his driver's license, and although both Arnie and Tom had beards and brown hair, they really did not look alike. But the lady at the mailbox rental did not question it. I had to cut all ties so he could not have the excuse to come back to the house for anything. I was scared to death of him. It was only eleven by the time we went to the sheriff's office to give them the document to serve. My poor mom was holding up okay even though I knew she was in a lot of pain. She was such a trooper. As I came out to the car, there in front of me was my mom in the passenger seat of my Ford Focus, and there was steam coming from the engine. Oh my god. What now? I got in the car, and the engine smelled like smoke. I could barely see out of the window.

My mom said, "I don't know what happened. It just started smoking. I think you need to pull over to a gas station and call Triple A."

I said, "How could this be happening?"

I called Triple A, hysterically insisting that they send someone as fast as they could. All I kept thinking was I have to get to Arnie's work before he was served to grab my other car he was driving before he got served and decided to drive off with my car looking for me. It was an hour before the Triple A tow man came. I was a basket case and rambled hysterically to the driver my whole story. His name tag said Steve.

Steve said, "I'll help you." He said, "I mean it. I had a bad relationship too, so I know what you are going through."

I said, "Thank you, but just get this car to the repair shop."

Meanwhile, all of a sudden, my phone started blowing up. It was my two kids. Arnie had been served, and he started calling them, asking if they knew. They had no idea what was going on, and both were mad because they were clueless. And here I was, trying to protect them and shield them from the violence and worry, and now they were being bamboozled by Arnie stating I had gone off the deep end. It was crazy. I was trying to tell them what was happening and filled the gap of the two years of hell I was living in a five-minute phone conversation, trying to get my car to the repair shop. Dear God, I wanted a drink so bad. My nerves were shot. Reflecting back, I knew that was the wrong escape hatch, but oh, the euphoric numbing would have been heavenly only if the aftereffects would not be deadly. All the while, I was in a panic about my other car disappearing now that Arnie had been served. He started violating the restraining order immediately by calling my cell, then my mother's cell.

In a split second, it came to me. I told my mom, "I am going to text him that I am coming to his office in ten minutes so he won't leave." By this time, we had dropped the other car off at the repair shop, and I was now in my mom's car driving toward his place of employment. "In your car, I will jump out, and you two can hand him the envelope while I go get in the other car and drive away so I will have no contact with him. You just hand him the brown envelope."

My mom was shaking. "Okay, if you think that will work." I prayed that it would.

The voice mail on my phone said, "Don't do this. I love you. We can work it out. I am sorry I have been so mean lately. I promise I will get better." I deleted it. It made me sick.

The ten-minute drive to his facility seemed like it took forever. Once I calmed both kids down and told them I was okay and told them not to answer his phone calls, they still were upset because I had left them in the dark. I reassured both of them I was going to be okay and that they shouldn't be fooled or talk to him about anything, and I told my daughter to please unfriend him on Facebook. I sent Arnie a text that I was there, and I saw him being walked out by a female coworker. This six foot, 3,290-pound man was leaning on her like he could barely walk. It made me sick since the night before when he had been holding a steak knife to my face and threatening me. I quickly saw my little Elantra and hopped out of the back seat and ran to it. My mom's significant other got out of the car and walked toward him with the brown envelope and handed it to him. I started the car and pressed the gas pedal and backed up and slammed the gas down and drove off, my hands shaking, and I was not looking back.

He said, "What is this?"

My mom's significant other said, "Read it," and turned and walked away.

I already was on the road. My stomach was in knots. I was a nervous wreck. After I arrived home, my mom made sure I was safe.

I locked all the doors and stayed on the couch with the dog jumping at every outside noise I heard. The next four weeks, I was scared of everything. I walked around in a daze as I never slept more than a couple of hours because I was so afraid to not be on guard. Arnie had violated the order of protection several times by emailing me, by putting messages on Facebook, and by trying to contact my daughter on Facebook. Because he was so manipulative, he practically had my daughter convinced it was all a lie and that I had made all of it up. That was until I sent her the paperwork I had shown the lawyer of the events that had led up to the order. He was ordered by the lawyer that if he violated the order of protection one more time, charges would be pressed.

A week before the hearing with the judge, a state-appointed attorney called me to go over what would happen in court. The state-appointed attorney said normally, he just goes over the procedures on what to expect and what will happen. Yet when I told him the entire scenario and sequence of events, he said, "I am not just going to go over this with you. I will go with you to the hearing. I am not liking what I am hearing, and it sounds as though he doesn't follow legal rules and that his behavior is unsteady." I was both relieved and more terrified. Obviously, I was not exaggerating the circumstances, and if all the legal field felt it was imperative I have protection, then this was serious. On the day of the hearing, my mom came with me. I was so shaken, and my stomach again was a bundle of nerves. The attorney got there and met with both my mom and me and briefed us on to what may or may not happen with the judge.

When the time frame came, he said, "It appears he is a no-show."

I said in a shaky voice, "No, he is here. He is sitting right across from me with someone, and they are staring me down."

The attorney was like "What? He is not supposed to be on this side. He is already breaking rules, and he didn't even check in with the court bailiff."

The police officer at the desk called Arnie and his crony over. He got up, his eyes never leaving me, and walked over to the desk. Five minutes later, our case was called into the courtroom. The judge came in to the courtroom. I was shaking. Mom sat behind me. I know this was so hard on her. Here she was, struggling with her walker into the courtroom.

The judge looked at me and stated, "Ms. Stein, why is it you want an order of protection against Mr. Arnie Emmett? And how long do you want it for?"

I said to the judge, "Permanently as I am terrified of him." I stated, "He threatens me with his physical presence. He is abusive and scares me, and the night before, he just had a steak knife to my face."

The judge looked at Arnie. "Mr. Emmett, is that true?"

Arnie said, his head lowered and trying to look forlorn, "I don't remember." He mumbled, "Judge, I wasn't well. I have been in the hospital and being treated for anxiety and depression." He then piped up in a defiant voice, "Judge, do you know what she did to me?"

The judge looked at him. "No."

"She took all my things and put them in a storage locker and took my dog and put him in a kennel."

The judge looked incredulous. He said, "Ms. Stein? Did you do that?"

I said, "Yes, Judge. I wanted to make sure that he had access to all of his personal possessions and his dog, and I gave him all the items we had gotten since we were married. I wanted to be fair, and I did not want him saying I kept anything."

Complete silence in the courtroom. Then the judge threw back his head and started laughing. "I cannot believe you did that, Ms. Stein. In all my days as a judge, I have never heard anything or anyone doing such a thing." He said, "Mr. Emmett, you should be thanking her for not throwing everything you own in the street."

I looked over at Arnie, and his face was beet red. He mumbled, "Yeah."

The judge then looked over at me and said, "I want to commend you for your ethics. I would like to put your name and face and what you did on my wall. You should be my poster person for ethics when it comes to doing the right thing in ending relationships."

I blushed. "Thank you, Judge."

He said, "Now the order of protection. If I do it for over a year, this will permanently affect Mr. Emmett's record. Mr. Emmett, I expect you to honor the order."

He said, "I don't want it, Judge. I love her. I was messed up and in depression, that's why I was doing crazy things and so violent."

The judge said, "Mr. Emmett, I am glad you are seeking the help you need. Regardless, you are to still be under the order of protection to stay away from Ms. Stein. If you violate that order, you will be under arrest. It will be in effect for ninety days from today. Ms. Stein, is that agreeable to you?"

I said, "Judge, I would like it longer than ninety days."

The judge said, "I am going to do it for ninety days since Mr. Emmett is seeking appropriate medical treatment. If I do it for the full year, it will harm Mr. Emmett's opportunities for employment as it will be on his record." My heart sank. *The system is protecting the abuser once again*, I thought. "Do you understand, Ms. Stein?"

"Yes, Judge."

"The order is in place and will be in force until May 1. Again, Ms. Stein, I commend you for being honorable and ethical. I wish all the people who came before me would adhere to what you did."

I said thank you. The attorney who was with me said, "Thank you, Judge." He bent over and said, "That's a first. I never have heard this judge commend or compliment anyone."

As he was saying this, I saw out of the corner of my eye a process server go up to Arnie and ask, "Are you Arnie Emmett?" He said yes. The server handed him an envelope and said, "You have been served."

The divorce papers. A look of anger flashed in Arnie's eyes, and he looked right at me and said nastily, "So this is how it's going to be. Throw me away like a piece of garbage."

The court-appointed attorney said, "Do not respond. Wait here for fifteen to twenty minutes with your mom to ensure he exits first."

I so knew the judge was wrong when he only gave him ninety days to stay away from me. I knew he was not going to leave me alone. It was not going to be that easy. After that hearing, Arnie sent me scary emails saying, "I saw you the other day. You are still as cute as ever. I never stopped loving you, Katie." His email was rambling and incoherent. This panicked me. It made me so afraid to leave the house. When I did leave, I felt like a teenager having to call my mom and tell her I was leaving for the store, then calling her when I returned. I no longer slept in my bed. I was too scared that I may not hear the door being broken into and wanted to be close to the phone. After violating the order several times by sending emails and posting mean messages on Facebook and trying to message my daughter, all of which I forwarded to the state-appointed attorney, he was told he would go to jail if it continued. That threat was the only thing that finally stopped them. Now the only thing I had to wait for was the court hearing on the divorce. That date was set for April. That would be the next time I would have to see his face in person.

That April came, and again my dear mother, who was now seventy-eight, came with me, hobbling along in her walker as her hip was still healing from surgery. Arnie was there, and when the judge came in and heard the case, Arnie got belligerent and loud and said, "Judge, I do not want the divorce."

The judge stopped him and said, "I have looked through the case and the order of protection that is still in effect and about to expire on May 1. Mr. Emmett, it is evident to me that Ms. Stein is not wanting a reconciliation. Isn't that true, Ms. Stein?"

"Yes, Your Honor." Arnie pounded his fist on the table.

She said, "Mr. Emmett, I advise you to adhere to the order. I hereby grant the motion to end the marriage as there are no assets or monies involved."

Arnie's face turned red. He got up and slammed his chair against the table. "Well, you got what you wanted." And he slammed the door.

Relief flooded through me. I was shaken. It was over, yet fear still resided in me because now the order of protection was about to expire on May 1. Was I safe? Would I always be looking over my shoulder? Would I ever be able to sleep in my bed?

Before the judge left the courtroom, she did state, "You know, Ms. Stein, you can file for an extension on the order of protection."

I nodded to the judge and said thank you. I waited thirty minutes before I felt safe leaving the courtroom with Mom and her walker. We made it to the car without incident. My two-year nightmare was over, and I thank God I never picked up that one drink to escape the horror. I think that scared me just as much as that two-year nightmare relationship.

During that whole last year in Florida dealing with Arnie, it was so heart-wrenching and difficult to know that my daughter was going to have a baby without me present and without me giving her my full attention and support. I couldn't do so because he had been constantly monitoring my every move. I was not happy that she chose to get pregnant again by Brent after all the beatings and violent behavior she endured in the last four years by him. I had no choice but to support her decision to keep the baby and try to be tolerant of him when he was around. She had Bobby in early August. I could not be there. Brent was there and seemed to be excitedly happy when he learned it was a boy. At first, he was a hands-on new daddy, but that got old quick. I went out there despite Arnie giving me a hard time and spent a week with her three weeks after the baby was born. Brent was in and out of the apartment, and she never knew where he was going. I had a mother's intuition that something was not quite right. She was doing more and more—caregiving, working, and supporting both him and the baby. He was so damn lazy it made me sick. He was doing less and less.

When Bobby was less than a year old, I remember she called me hysterically and said it was over with Brent. She had caught him with another woman, and he had a two-year-old daughter with her. So he had hidden another baby mama all that time from her. She was pretty darn devastated. Even though he was playing both women, he still wanted control over Amanda. He was obsessive. He stalked her. He would make repeated calls and text messages to her cell phone. He would show up where she worked and follow her. He would show up at the same places she was at with her friends. He picked fights with the guys that were in her group of friends because of his insane jealousy. She was scared he would go off and do something bad to her or Bobby. He was known to be violent. He had a felony conviction.

She had a child now, and now she realized she had to protect him. So she changed her phone number and her address and blocked him on social media. She had to do this several times. I was still in Florida, and I felt sick to my stomach knowing she was going through a violent situation without me just as I was going through one and I was all the way in Florida. Even if I predicted it and saw it, I couldn't stop her from the same ride I was on, just as she and my son could not prevent me from going and marrying Arnie when all the red flags were there in front of me. It has been four years since she has had any contact with Brent, and for that, I am so grateful. She has a hard life. She works three jobs as a single mom. She does not get child support because that would mean he would have rights to see Bobby, and she knew he would be a job jumper to avoid getting his wages garnished. Not worth the risk of putting your son in danger. It's been four years for me as well. We both survived our ordeals, but we both are scarred.

Now jumping back to us three musketeers: my brother, Mother, and I. We made some doozey choices in our lives that we are still trying to move past. All of us have been in the relentless fix-it-mode for years, and all three of us, especially me, tried so hard all those years to fix these unfixable people or unfixable situations in our lives. Like my father. Funny thing is, my father never asked to be fixed. Never asked for help. So why did we even bother? How dumb were we? We cannot fix anyone but us! Why did we think we could fix him. He was unfixable because he never saw that he had a problem. We needed Enablers Anonymous, not Ala-non or Ala-teen. In all twenty-five years plus, my father never admitted he was an alcoholic and never wanted to fix himself, and when he thought he saw us at our ropes' ending point, he would placate us and attempt to pretend to want help. I remember when my mom finally demanded him to go to AA or she would divorce him. I remember she dropped him off at the meetings and watched him walk in to attend. When she would go back and pick him up, he would have a big smile on his face and a bunch of pamphlets—of course, making my mom feel very hopeful and in control. On one of those AA nights, she dropped him off, but she didn't leave right away for some reason. She was parked at the end of the parking lot. I'm not sure why she did that, but I think it was because she sensed things were going way too easy. She was right because five minutes after he walked into the building, he came walking out with some brochures and walked to the cafe at the corner. She waited the hour, and sure enough, she watched him walk back into that building; and at the time the meeting was to end, he walked out to her waiting car that she had pulled up in, pretending totally that he had attended the meeting. She called him out on it and never took him again, and he never went again. I only remember in my whole time growing up that for one entire year, my dad did not take a drink. That year was the year that showed us little glimpses of what our lives could have been like if he remained sober. He had turned into a different person, an actual human being. Someone who had a personality. Someone who could actually carry on a conversation with you, who had a sense of humor and who seemed like a nice person. Of course, that was it, one brief year. The rest is history. I think that was the same year when he fell off the wagon. He got into a bad car accident, hitting a tree, and when he got out and stumbled out of the car, his fake eye popped out onto the asphalt. The police and ambulance were already there, and they got on their hands and knees looking for the glass eyeball so that they could bring it with him to the hospital. That sounds like a circus scene, and I am so sure that it looked like that as well.

Let's get one fact straight: being a fixer-enabler of someone who is tightly wound into your inner circle is a full-time, bloodsucking job, and it does not pay well. It's a no-salary position. There is absolutely no gratification, no satisfying result. Because usually the person you are trying to help or fix doesn't want to be helped and resents you for even trying and treats you like crap for doing so. All those years of attempting to fix my dad's problem was the dysfunctional lifestyle we led. The disease itself, alcoholism, is a lonely, deadly disease that spirals out of control and affects everyone in the family who is in close proximity to the alcoholic. I know. I have lived with an alcoholic, and I became an alcoholic. It affects everyone in the family. Everyone has the illness. There is no getting away from it because it is like a virus. It's contagious, and no one in the family is safe from it. The family becomes victims to stress, anxiety, pain, anguish, and ultimately, insanity. I learned that hard reality when I finally was bold enough in my later teen years, around seventeen to eighteen years of age, to go crazy. I finally did things to shock my mother and ultimately tell my mom I was going insane and needed help. That all cumulated to me going into a hysterical fit of sobbing and rage and me taking a women's shaver and making baby cuts on my wrist to scare my mom into thinking I was going to kill myself. The result scared her into getting me to Ala-teen and to start seeing a psychiatrist. I never got completely healed because I stopped going when I thought I was okay. But with the reality of living in a dysfunctional lifestyle and growing up with an alcoholic, unless you continue to work on you, the healing stops and the disease continues in some way, shape, or form—either with behavior, addictions, depression, etc. The most disgusting thing that resulted after that was that my mom finally filed a restraining order against my father and filed for divorce. I was eighteen. She got some milk-toast lawyer who was not strong enough to go against and fight the lawyer that paid off the Cook County judge that my father's work drinking buddies got him. She was going to lose everything she ever worked so hard for, like the house she built, to that rotten bastard. That bastard had the balls to do the ultimate unforgivable thing as to have his lawyer subpoena my psychiatrist during the trial to say I was lying about everything and making it all up: all the beatings, all the sexual advances, and all the alcoholic verbal and physical abuse. So here I was in a courtroom, mortified, ashamed, and embarrassed because under oath, that psychiatrist told my personal history. I remember the judge looking me straight in the eye, asking me if it was all true and if I was scared of my father. My face, a sick bright-red mass of teenage embarrassment, fear, and shame. I said yes. He granted the restraining order, but everything got put on hold when my mom's lawyer told her something dirty was going on. So my mom dropped the divorce proceedings and attempted a reconciliation with my father. I remember I was so angry with her for doing that. I had just turned eighteen. I had to get away, so I called my friend in California. And I told Mom I was going to California to visit her for a month. I remember her telling me, "You don't understand why, but there is a reason." Well, she was right. I did not understand how she could take that sorry man back into her life and try to coexist with him. Later after finding out what she would have lost had she not done that, I understood. My mom, I think, was relieved I was going to California so she did not have to worry about me being in the same house as my father. My brother was practically living at his girlfriend's parent's house and working two jobs. I think she realized I was safer there than living at home with the drunk. I do have to say that going to Ala-teen though did show me that I was not alone and that there were so many young people going through the same insane turmoil and feeling the same way, and that did make me feel better.

I wish my brother would have gone with me, but he was too stubborn and did not think he needed any of that important infor-mation and the unified bonding of people who were living the same type of hell. See, being a girl and more dramatic, I was grasping for straws of survival. I was seventeen when all that came down. That was when some divine intervention happened that led me to take a class in my senior year called Marriage and Family. I only took it because the description sounded romantic to me. You get assigned someone to marry in class, have a fake marriage, and raise a real egg baby. LOL. A hard-boiled egg that you had to make sure did not crack. Yep, an egg baby. The class was a lot of journaling and writing. What was I thinking? It never occurred to me that I would have to speak about my family. I thought it was going to be about marriage and learning to become a family. It was the marriage, love, and fantasy that intrigued me to take the class. It didn't even occur to me at all that I would be asked core questions about my family. I was just thinking about the fun part of getting married and having an egg baby. I had no clue that the "family" part of the class would delve deep into my core of vulnerability and open wounds up that I did not want to expose or feel. That in order to pass the class, I would have to open up and tell the hidden family secret, or fail the class. I actually found those journal writings in a box with my sobriety journals. That class was the catalyst in getting me to speak the truth. I cannot believe I actually kept the notebooks. There are some very poignant writings in there. I re-read those journals when I began writing this book. Reading them really reminded me how deeply at seventeen-year-old's point of view the impact of living in alcoholic environment affected both myself and my family. It is very uncanny and ironic that those writings are so closely intertwined to how I feel today. This particular assignment, which was a defining one, was on "How does the past affect your life?" Oh no. First, you had to do a family tree or chart that was worth twenty points, then you had to do research on those family members, which was worth forty points, and the remaining forty points for the grade was you had to write how the past affected your life. I was so torn because if I spoke the truth. then RL Mason, the teacher, would see the real me. That teacher would play a major impact of helping our family and helping my brother immensely. He saw in my brother's vulnerability, he saw how guarded and how he internalized and kept things inside. Once I opened up to RL, there was no holding me back, but my brother kept his feelings in check and totally locked up. I am forever grateful for his wisdom, kindness, and his willingness to go the extra mile to help a family in desperate need. Once I opened up, the first door of journaling throughout that class was the catalyst to my writing. Even though it was the immature writings of a seventeen-year-old, it none-theless was my way of channeling the pain.

I also remember around that same time, I was beginning to test my sexuality, and I had started dating boys. That was very difficult because of my confusion of only seeing the kind of intimate rela-tionship my parents shared, which was a very sick, sordid relation-ship, not loving and not affectionate. Plus, of course, I was a good Catholic girl who went to eight years of kindergarten through eighth grade before I went to a public high school. It was inbred in me that sex was forbidden until you got married, that it was a sacred gift. I actually did believe that to be true. I did not want to give myself to anyone unless I knew for sure it was the real deal—only in love and if I was married. I wanted to be a virgin. It was not so much as adhering and believing that principle. It became almost like an exciting chal-lenge for me too and also a way for me to escape my fear of trying to be sensual or intimate with anyone. So needless to say, I adhered to that sacredness basically because I was totally terrified after seeing how my mom responded to my dad's sexual advances, which only happened when he was trashed. At least that is what I remember. She only gave into that kind of intimacy when it was forced upon her by my father after he was inebriated.

My first serious boyfriend was at sixteen, and he really was a nice guy. But I was totally freaking scared of being intimate with him, so I was pretty much a nice girl tease, as what you would call me, or PT. Kiss, make out, get the guy all hot and bothered, then it was like a button I turned on and off. I would shut down emotionally and physically when it got too heated. It was like I was numb. I forced myself not to feel, and if I did start to feel tingly good, I stopped abruptly. If the boy got too serious, I would take the easy way out and break up with them. I remember my boyfriend Ron Thomas. He was really nice, but he was head over heels. And I remember my mom freaking out one day when he was over to go swimming and I had just come in from outside where we had been making out by the pool, and there was Ron laying on the redwood picnic table in his black speedo with a woody. My mom was like "You are not going back out there for twenty minutes." Of course, I was so embarrassed that my mom saw that and of course, me seeing it through the kitchen window. So I broke up the next week with Ron over the phone, with a written breakup I read to him because I was too chicken to talk to him in person. I remember how flustered I was because he kept trying to interrupt me while I was reading it. Hey, did he not get the memo? I had this written out there will be no interruptions allowed. Every time he asked why I was breaking up with him, I had no answer. I kept going back to what I wrote. "I am not ready for a serious relationship." Blah, blah. Anyhow, I remember how unbelievably shocked I was when his mom and dad called my mom and asked what Ron had done to me to have me break up with him, that they liked me so much and that he was devastated and that they wanted to know what they could do to fix it. My mom was a bit flustered and said, "She is only sixteen. She should not be dating just one guy." I did remain friends with Ron, and I actually asked him to my senior prom as I was not dating anyone. He was already a sophomore in college. We had kept in touch. It was like a deja vu date since I had gone to his junior prom at our rival high school.

The sad thing was that all those guys I dated and dumped were really nice guys. They didn't deserve that, and the majority of them fell head over heels in love with me, which made my guilt even worse to handle when I would break it off because I was so scared at not knowing what expectations were in the physical sense of a relationship. I only thought I cannot be like how my mom was with sex. It was degrading. I watched her for years do things she did not want to do just to placate my father so as to not cause a scene or a beating. So sexual encounters with a boyfriend scared the crap out of me because all I saw with my mom and dad's intimacy was only happening when he had a few too many, and then it was the sounds from the bedroom that were like a *wham bam*, jump on and off, and pray that alcohol intake was not to the point where he got violent and beat the crap out of her or pass out on top of her and suffocate her. Oh, dear God, I just had a déjà vu! That was me with Jack and Arnie. Round and round we go, and there the cycle repeats and it became very clear to me that the woman had to do the pleasing, you did what the man wanted, not what you wanted. It was all about pleasing him, to not cause flack or disharmony, or confrontation. That is how I viewed intimacy, and that scared the shit out of me. So staying a virgin became kind of like a high or an exciting challenge and big achievement and actually a safety net for me since half the girls I knew already had sex and gave it up already. I felt in control and like I won the award. Yes, I am the girl that held out and can hold out forever. I was raised as a good Catholic girl, the nice girl you take home to Mom and Dad, the rule follower, not the rule breaker. The one who was flirty fun with a big heart, kind, and had a great sense of humor. Kiss the boy, make the boy fall in love with you, but then break it off because intimacy was too scary. Bottom line: sexual intimacy was difficult for me. Even while married, I would have to have a few cocktails under my belt to feel like being the amorous way my husband wanted me to be, dressed up like some hooker slut. As a teen, I learned early on that alcohol could make you feel comfortable and have confidence. So like all teens, I started experimenting with alcohol to try and give myself the escape to feeling on top of the game and confident.

We had a bar in our family room with lots of wine and hard liquor. It was beyond me why my mom had it right there. Flaunting it in front of my father, the alcoholic, was just so weird because it was like leaving milk out for a thirsty cat and expecting the cat not to drink it. The odd thing is that my dad didn't. He never drank at home. He would be on his best behavior at home, and in his dry drunk stage, then he would go out on binges and come home drunk and blasted. I never ever saw him with an alcoholic beverage at home in front of me and my brother. So I really think my mom always did that for show, having that bar out in the middle of our family room, and to test my father. To see if he could refrain from touching the family bar, which amazed me that he did. That is another fact why people who hung around our family never believed me, my brother, or my mom when we told them the truth—that my dad was an alcoholic and had been for years, beating us and was verbally abusive. In front of the neighbors, family, or friends, he would only drink coffee or soda, which was the reason why no one really believed us when the truth came out about the beating and binge drinking.

About that time when I started dating, I remember I was curious and wanted to see why my dad liked drinking so much. I remember I started sneaking gulps of liquor before I would go out on dates to boost my confidence. Yes, there it is again, the sign of a possible genetic disorder. Yes, that euphoric feeling did the trick. It worked. I felt confident. I felt more sexually attractive. Finally, after watering down the alcohol, my mom figured it out, and I got into a big shit-load of trouble from her. It shocked her, and I know it scared her. She stopped stocking the bar. It was around that teenage time of sixteen to seventeen, and I already was heading toward insanity. My mind and emotions were a mess. My parents at that point were getting to the end of the marriage. There was really nothing left. My dad was getting worse and worse with the binging. Car accidents were almost an every-other-month routine—mortifying times for two teenagers trying to hide the family secret. It is so funny to say that I actually still kept the family secret going from my closest friends but chose to open up to strangers such as Mr. Mason, the Marriage and Family teacher, and then the people I met at Ala-teen. I never even really told the serious boyfriends. I had one whom I had for my entire senior year, and he never knew about my dad. I was really good at hiding. I became a master at it. So did our entire family. Hiding is bad behavior, pretty much the same as how I hid my first husband's bad abusive behavior and my second husband's abuse, which was even more abusive and pretty much how my mom's second relationship with the man she is with today like. Same as my brother accepting his first wife's verbally abusive and physically abusive behavior. Always enabling and always choosing the abuser, not the healthy people, to be part of our lives. That is totally an alcoholic sick dysfunction. It's a merry-go-round, and we keep going in circles.

Yes, my father was a full-blown alcoholic, and sadly, that was how his life ended—from health issues related to long-time alcohol abuse. He died alone in a disease-ravaged body, his life unresolved. He died six years ago, while I was living in Arizona, in a nursing home in Belvidere, Illinois, from Alzheimer-related health issues due to his alcoholism. I never went back to Illinois for the funeral. I remember my brother had called and told me of his death. I felt numb. I felt nothing. My brother made the arrangements or at least helped his widow, Mary, who was mentally not capable of doing so. Mary was a lady my father married shortly after my mom and dad were divorced basically because my dad could not stand on his own two feet. Mary was the sister of one of his drinking buddies and very mentally unstable. She had several nervous breakdowns and actually, if I remember correctly, was about to be institutionalized; and my father married her to prevent that from happening, saving her. They were a great pair, alcoholic and mentally unstable, odd and oddball. I felt bad that my brother, after all those years of being mistreated, felt such a strong obligation to do this last thing for my dad, but I think it was his way of forgiving my dad for all the pain he inflicted on him, me, and my mom. Making my father's funeral arrangements gave my brother some sense of closure, a feeling of being needed from all those years of mistreatment and neglect from my father not showing him the kind of love a father gives a son. I vaguely remember telling my brother, "Thank you for telling me," then asking him, "Is it bad that I don't really feel anything?" I felt almost guilty at admitting that to him. He reassured me no, that there was nothing I could do, and that if I made peace with forgiving Dad, then that was all I needed to do. I am not sure my brother understood where I was coming from although he did not voice his opinion and probably at the time, he may have thought I was being very coldhearted. After all, he was my father. In my head, I felt a tinge of the good Catholic girl turn the other cheek and just forgive, forget, and do the obligatory daughter thing of putting on a front and run home and go to his funeral and pay my last respects to the man who gave birth to me. Showing his family—what was left of his family, the ones who had not yet died from an alcohol-related illness—that his children were there on his behalf to say goodbye. That thought left as quickly as it popped into my head, like a rocket. Hell no. That man put us through hell and back. No, I just couldn't go back. I could not pretend. Maybe my brother could, but not me. I could not put on a false front because the only thing I felt was a sense of utter sadness that this man who was my father died alone in a nursing home. His brain at the end was like a pile of mush from all the booze, and he died estranged from his only daughter and his grandchildren. He only had my brother, who was still hanging in there. I tried that, too, when my daughter was two and my son just a newborn, but I realized very quickly how one-sided that relationship was. I was always making the effort and trying to keep in contact with him. There was no reciprocation on my father's part. Therefore, when my two-year-old daughter asked me why that grandpa did not love her as much as the other grandpa, I severed the chord. Enough was enough. How do you explain to a two-year-old the behavior of a sick man? You don't. At that time frame, two years earlier when my daughter was first born, my mother had established a new relationship with a man ten years younger than her, the relationship I mentioned earlier that started out as positive but now is nothing but negative and toxic. That being said, it is very sad that person could turn into such a hateful being and cause so much discord in our small family unit. That toxic relationship also showed my children that pattern of behavior is normal, and thus, the merry-go-round goes around and around again. My dear sweet brother tried to have a relationship with my father. He just wanted my dad's love so badly, and because I bowed out totally from having or wanting any relationship with him, he thought maybe it was his opportunity to finally establish one in adulthood. That was one situation I always felt guilty about: why my dad treated me like a princess as a little girl and my brother like a dog. I never understood it. It made me feel terrible all those early years growing up, that my brother was always one step behind in the shadow of my daughterly limelight since I was forever daddy's little girl, always the princess, the kid who could never do any wrong. My brother, who was just the sweetest little boy, was the kid who, no matter how hard he tried, was always being picked on by my father. So in the end, who was by his side? Not the prodigal daughter who could do no wrong but the son who was treated like a dog all his life. That always struck me as odd.

Yes, you are probably wondering: did that mean my dad died alone? Yes, he sadly did. I remember telling my brother I felt sorry that my father left his physical body in such a lonely state, that he never learned to live, love, or get help for himself and his illness. That he never made peace with his life. I told my brother I would pray for his soul. After I hung up from my brother, I did not cry. I remember looking out my kitchen window at the desert dust, and I did what I told my brother I would do. I put my hands together and prayed a prayer that he could finally heal and that my father could be at peace from the ravages of the disease that took over his life all those years. This horrific disease that robbed him of having precious relationships with his children and grandchildren. The disease that consumed him and hurt so many people he encountered throughout his life. The same disease that literally consumed me and would have destroyed my life if I had not chosen sobriety. I also said in my prayer that I forgave him for all that he had put us through. I prayed that he was finally illness-free and at peace with himself. Forgiving him was one of the hardest things I came to grips with. I had such anger and resentment toward him, but once I allowed forgiveness in my heart, it gave me peace and closure. I prayed that one of us could fall off this merry-go-round of dysfunctional relationships. We were all a mess inside and outside. The dysfunctional carousel had taken its toll on everyone in my family. I was still messed up emotionally. Those scars still were not healed. You can put ointment on the boo-boo and keep scraping it in the same spot, but don't expect it to heal. That boo-boo, with time, becomes infected, and that infection grows without proper treatment. Then that was it. The door was closed. I felt no more. Nothing. I didn't feel guilty for not going back to Illinois for his funeral. I did not feel remorse for the way I handled his death because that part of me that loved my father had left my spirit many years earlier. He, as far as I was concerned, was a very sad, pathetic person who let his life be controlled by alcohol and who was a shell of a human being, a person with no personality, no empathy, and zero ability to love. It was over. He was gone, and I really did not feel bad, I did not miss him. Yet I still did not fall off the merry-go-round. I was still on the ride and had no idea how to fall off.

Let's go back to those good times and happier moments that I can say that I did have. Those I can thank my mother for making them happen. Despite the fact that she is probably one of the most dysfunctional people I know, she did her best. Those happier moments in time were probably the only way us three survived those years. Although our family was made up of four, we were a family unit of three: my mom, me, and my brother. The family of four never was a family. It was always the three of us, unified and connected and stuck like glue to one another for moral support, love, and survival. In my silly youth, I would consider us the three musketeers. It was my way of fantasizing, to make believe all was well even though our life was far from being well.

Hmmm, if you were to ask me to describe my mother, this would be my description: a strong, vivacious, beautiful woman who never and still does not realize how amazing she is as a person. Kind beyond belief, a giver, not a taker, she's a human being and person who deserves love and respect. Someone who deserves to feel needed, to be, for once in her life, put above everyone else, and to be cared for, not to be the caregiver. Caregivers are fixers. Remember? You cannot fix anyone except yourself. Yes, I have to keep reminding me and you of that. My mom, a woman so worthy of love, was, all her life, feeling worthless; or should I put it "not worthy of love." She deserves and deserved an equal partner in life—a friendship and love that would let her keep her individuality and allow her intelligence to shine, but a love that would admire and respect that intelligent mind, that spirit, and that kindness. She deserved and deserves that and more. Actually, all of us human beings deserve that, not just my mom. All women including me, and not just women; men as well, men such as my brother—they deserve to feel loved. To feel worthy of the kind of love that Spirit or God—whatever you want to call that Higher Power that created the universe—wants for all human kind. All of us are worthy of being loved truly deeply and accepted unconditionally for who we are as a people from our past to the present. To be heard, to be listened to, and to have someone understand our story. To not judge us or condemn us for how we feel. We all need to be needed but to be separate and to feel loved and wanted. Each of us deserves that kind of love no matter what our personal stories tell because we all have them to tell. Some are good; some are bad; and some are amazing, exceptional, and life changing. Our stories are unique and individual and when shared, shows the world who we really are. Sadly, though, most of us keep them to ourselves; therefore, they become untold stories. Then again, some are brought to the surface by exploring the depths of our inner spirit when we soul-search or when we reach a place where we want answers or if we hit rock bottom and need to release the pain or share the joy. If all of us learned the simple fact of not being afraid of what people would think of us and if we shared these stories, barriers and walls would be broken down, and we all would be more apt to open up and start to sharing the painful and the happy stories that make up who we are as human beings. And by doing so, we not only can help others but we would also be helping ourselves. By unlocking the past, opening the closed door, and telling the truth, then maybe—just maybe—we can learn, stop negative patterns, and grow.

All right, let's get back on track. My mom was the only female role model I was exposed to growing up, so I was taught everything she knew. And of course, I followed in her footsteps. Most daughters do, and most sons follow in their daddy's footsteps. Thankfully, my brother did not. I so admired my mom and still do. As all little girls do, I wanted to be just like her. "Oh no," you say. Where is this going? Is this another mom-bashing story? No, far from it. I am saying that because not all steps should be followed or behaviors inherited. This is not because my mom was not a good person. She is one of the most decent, kindest human beings I have ever met. She is also one of the most unhealthy people I know in mind, body, and spirit. It was never her fault, of course. She grew up in unhealthy circumstances, and therefore, it led her to marry my father. So the pattern of disease and unhealthy behavior and choices continued. Then, of course, she had no clue she was marrying an alcoholic, let alone a family of alcoholics, a disease that is not curable. So of course, it then becomes the factor of doing whatever you can to survive the madness, thus passing those behaviors down by generation to generation. That being said, you can only imagine the realm of unhealthy relationships I had, my brother had, and of course, my children have had in their life. It's called the life of the enabler, the fixer, the over-giver, the codependent learning early on in different ways to escape from facing pain. Mom had no clue that is what she was teaching me and my brother. How could she? She was trying to survive herself and at the same time, raise two young children on her own. She had two babies to feed and protect. She had a persona to keep up with in front of her family, the neighbors, and her friends. She had to portray the perfect all-American suburban family. Mom is strong and kind, but weak. She is a woman who has compensated and made excuses and still makes excuses for the men in her life. Men who she enabled, men who used her good nature and her strength, men who saw potential in her fix-it abilities, and men who ridiculed her intelligence but used it to their advantage. Men such as her own father, my father, and even with the man she is with currently. Men who said they wanted a strong woman but really just wanted a maid, a door-mat, and someone who would take care of their needs in all ways. Like I said, men who sucked the spiritual well dry. Men who always made poor choices for themselves, men who are disrespectful to all women in general, and men who are abusive, hurtful, and dysfunc-tional. It is amazing seeing it from my perspective and looking back at those men included not only my father but also her father and the current relationship she is in at this very time frame. All those choices happened because she grew up with no self-worth. From the time she was a toddler, she grew up feeling no love and grew up feeling abandonment. I looked at a picture of my mom when she was three from Germany before she came here. There is no smile on that little blond German girl's three-year-old face as she sat for the picture. Her face was blank. That in itself tells the story of a little lost soul and then the little I know of my grandfather who lived till he was forty-two. I heard he was pretty much a tyrant. So it was not a surprise that my mom escaped at eighteen, jumping into marriage as a way out. She chose what she thought was the doorway out. It ended up being the doorway to *hell*. When my dad latched on to her, she was enamored. She also was so unhappy at home she wanted an escape route, and she is super stubborn. She did not like that her parents did not like my father from the start.

My father was extremely good-looking, except the minute he smiled, you could see the rotten yellow teeth in his mouth from lack of healthy hygiene. My mom was a stubborn cookie. She did not like that her parents did not like my dad, so she decided it was her job to mold and fix his outer appearance to convince them he was worthy of her, defying her parents' discipline and rules. So my mom spent a good amount of her courting time with my dad fixing his outer appearance and showing everyone that he could be a good mate for her. I really don't even know if she loved him. She just was feeling pretty euphoric, accomplished, and maybe even rewarded that she did it. She was eighteen, and she was going to marry this creation despite her parents' dislike. My dad, of course, was on cloud nine, being that he never did anything for himself. Here he nabbed a good one, someone who would take over and be his personal director.

Unfortunately, my dad did not show his true colors to my mom. They only dated a year or so before they got hitched. So he kept his drinking rampages in check. One thing I do know is that when you attempt to change someone who doesn't want to change, it is like a fruitless tree. Most of the time, the person they are trying to help and change ends up resenting them, hating them, and treating them even worse than trash; and you, as the fixer, just don't understand why when you are trying so hard to help. What the heck happened? And why you are being treated so badly for trying to do something good for someone else? Those signs don't appear until you are way caught up into the turmoil. It's hard to fathom that person is ill. That person has a disease, is an abuser, has a disease, illness, resentment, and hate; and all go hand in hand and are all tied together. So basically, what I am saying is that my mom never had a chance. She was doomed from the moment she was born. Because of that, my mom's abusive childhood led her to basically choose wrongly and choose someone she could enable, whose enablement led to continue the disease. The abusive childhood she survived led her to think and believe she could never be a singular person of value, a pattern that she has not broken yet. I am not sure what you call it when you want someone to treat you badly. There has to be a name for it. It is a lifestyle and pattern that you are used to, so you think it is normal. It's the only kind of relationship that you know, so you keep going back for more. My mom is seventy-nine, and she would rather be with a companion who treats her like a dog and pats her on the head in a condescending manner, who beats her up verbally on a daily basis and condones it by ignoring it. My mom never changed the pattern. She just went from one abusive situation to another. I think that it is worse than my father, the alcoholic she lived with all those years, because this person is not a raging alcoholic but a raging abuser, a narcissist. He has the symptoms of the disease. The verbal abusive behavior was as horrendous as the physical abuse My mom had said that he possibly had a drinking problem. I don't know. All I know is that she would rather settle for no respect than to be alone. It is all part of the code-pendent, enabling illness.

She has lost so many friends who truly love her as the beautiful person she is. They have said no, they will not allow this toxic entity into their life. They did in the past out of respect for her, but his behavior has gotten worse as the years roll forward and the people that love my mom are no longer tolerant. When human beings see someone who truly is not a good person, who shows their true colors as being racist, a bigot, crude, rude, and completely nasty, and who treats the person you love like a dog without any qualms in front of all human beings; they know that really is sick behavior. Healthy people who have healthy balance and healthy boundaries choose to say "No, I am not going to let you into my circle. I will give you a few chances, but once you break the cardinal rules, I will set up boundaries." Unfortunately, that has happened to my mother, and unfortunately, many good people who love her have told her this. Yet she chooses to be with the person who treats her like a dog over being with the people who love her. Fear of being alone overrules her healthy judgement, and because she is used to a life full of unhealthiness emotionally speaking, it is an easy choice for her. That doesn't stop her from feeling the sense of loss and loneliness that choosing that unhealthy relationship has brought to her life because she feels all that and more but doesn't understand why those friends and loved ones cannot make an exception for her. The sad fact is, it's a pattern that has been repeating itself since she was married to my father and has been happening for over fifty years. That is a habit too difficult to break and to change at seventy-nine years old.

I only hope and pray that I can break the pattern, that I still have a chance, and that there is still hope for me because I understand totally where she is coming from. I can totally relate. I have such a fear of being alone. Because of that fear, I have made poor relationship choices. I have settled for less than I deserve. I have made excuses and justified poor behavior in the men I have known. I have accepted abusive verbal and physical behavior versus being healthy and singular. It's all in the illness we grew up with, the learned behavior patterns. See, it was always easier growing up to ignore bad behavior, make excuses for it, and compensate for it and way easier to accept than confront. You ask me for examples. If my mother's significant other was saying the word *nigger* or calling her stupid or correcting and being condescending in front of others, she would not say a word. She would take it and then tell us she had a talking with him. For me, an example would be like my ex-husband. One day, he was at Home Depot looking for a screw or a nut and thinking nothing of it and sticking it in his pocket and walking out. I was looking at him incredulously, saying, "That's stealing." He was saying, "It is only one nut. They won't miss it." No, not okay. Or my ex calling me a bitch; or like the time he would go behind my back; or when I would discipline the kids, such as not allowing my son to have a paintball gun at thirteen, and he would tell me in front of the kids I was crazy and "What's the big deal?" making me look like the bad guy. That behavior is wrong. I should have stopped it, but then again, so should have my mom. We are on this ride and keep repeating the same exact patterns. It makes me angry.

I am getting off this ride. If I cannot jump off, I am going to fall off. I am recognizing repetitive patterns in my relationships, and I am setting up the *no* boundary line. I am a person who chooses not to accept that is okay. My mother unfortunately is resigned to staying on the ride. I cannot help her, as well as I cannot help my daughter or son off of it either. All I can do is set a healthy example. Mom may not be able to change at this stage in her life, but I can say, "No." This has to stop. I can recognize what's going on and move on. Falling off is easy, but not hopping back on the merry-go-round—now that is the key to becoming healthy. I don't believe my mom will ever get off the merry-go-round. She is afraid, like we all are, of being alone, and of ending something that isn't right because that would mean you would have to learn to love yourself. To love being with yourself, to enjoy peace, to enjoy you, and to look in the mirror and have a conversation with the beautiful person that gazes back at you. To feel comfortable to stand on your own and to realize that you don't need a man. You don't need to self-destruct and hit the bottle or the pills to escape, or for that matter, you don't need anyone but yourself. You have to learn to be happy with yourself and know you can have fun with you. That is a mouthful to swallow because I, for one, have the most difficult time with doing just that for me.

Life can change. It can be better. Our family had one year of normal from all that hell. I think I mentioned it before, but it was crushed in a heartbeat after my father chose to pick up that first drink after a year of sobriety. I think that is how I have been able to stay sober all these years. Sober through all the heartache, hardships, abuse, pain, and loss because I remember all it took was one drink and that beautiful year was wiped out. Although it was brief, I can remember it clearly. We all were getting healthy. We were not on this crazy, unstable, dizzy ride we keep riding. Then the ride started up again. We never knew what to expect day to day, week to week. Is he going to come home smashed? Is he going to crash the car or kill himself or someone else? Is he going to hurt us? Is the hospital or morgue going to call us? Mom would always make excuses: "You know your dad is sorry. Let's eat dinner as a family." Then we would have to sit at the table, eating gross Hamburger Helper because that was all my mom could afford after my dad drank his check away the week before. All the love of a daughter loving her daddy dissolved when he became creepy. No matter how hard my mom tried to get him to fit in with the groups and the clubs, the binging lifestyle made it so difficult. It just was enough to keep him on track for short periods. Because my dad lacked depth as a person, my mom made up for his lack of it with her compassion and human kindness. So most people didn't pay attention to him because she was such a fun, vivacious, good person. I am sure this was not my dad's fault. It was his heritage, his bloodline. He was never taught those important human traits from his parents or grandparents. He grew up in the small town of Wild Rose, Wisconsin, right outside of Plainfield, which incidentally was the same town where the crazy Mad Butcher Ed Gein lived. Yes, you know the story. Ed Gein the Mad Butcher was the dude who exhumed corpses from local graveyards and fashioned trophies for keepsakes from the bones and skin. He also confessed to killing several women. Actually, my mother shook hands with the notorious Mr. Gein. She was with my father, pregnant with me, and was visiting his great aunt in Wild Rose, Wisconsin, the neighboring town. He was the local handyman around the area, and he was doing work in my great, great aunt's home. So yes, my mom shook hands with the crazy Mad Butcher. Now you can get the mental picture. Yep, that was the town my dad was born in and where he grew up as a young boy. Go figure why he turned out the way he did. I remember my mom telling me the story that my dad was actually a stillborn and that my great, great aunt took his little lifeless blue body and rubbed it vigorously and wrapped it in a blanket and turned the stove on and put him in it and, lo and behold, cooked my father back to life.

Amazing that we have all this modern medicine and that was how my great, great aunt revived a stillborn baby. Not sure if she did him a service or not, but if she didn't, then you wouldn't be reading this as I would not have existed.

I can give you a bit of background since I really don't know the complete history on the side of my father except for bits and pieces my mother would sometimes divulge. My mom kept us a good distance from that side of the family, and actually, my father did as well. See, his nature of closeness or emotional attachment to his family was evident in his relationship with them. That being said, he really did not have the ability nor was he able to show love or real affection, let alone have a meaningful conversation or real emotion and empathy toward any human being, animal, and even his own family. Maybe that's why his entire family grew up leaning on alcohol, or maybe it was because they lived in a hick town in Wisconsin and there was nothing better to do except drink your brains out and go screw cows and sheep. Yes, I am not kidding you. That's how they would get off, and it was disgusting. My mom told me my father and his Wisconsin buddies did that for fun, all during his teen years. When she told me, it physically made me sick. All I kept thinking was those poor animals. How cruel. The history of my father's family is quite scary. Beginning with his birth mother, she died of liver disease. His father remarried, and he, too, died of alcoholism. His second wife died from an alcohol-related illness. Along with his two sisters and brother, all were considered heavy drinkers or alcoholics. My mom, for the most part, kept us as far away as possible from getting too close to my father's side of the family once she knew they all were big-time drinkers. I vaguely remember meeting them just a few times. I remember a drive up to Rockford to his brother's house a couple of times. His brother was Uncle Johnny, and his wife, Aunt Lenore, and my cousins. I also vaguely remember meeting his sister, Candy. She scared me because she had eyes that bulged out of her head. She had some sort of eye disease. I remember when I got older, all of this made me wonder why my mom even considered marrying my dad if she knew all that about his family, but see, since my dad was not close to his family nor did he see them, she didn't know really the history until way after she was married to him. I remember my grandfather and his second wife, Verne, came and visited us. I was young, but I remember they both reeked of alcohol. My mom said they started drinking and chain smoking the minute they woke up. They added booze to their coffee instead of creamer and by noon they were trashed. We had steep basement stairs and Verne stumbled down them and fell. She was all bruised up and later passed out and didn't remember a thing. No wonder my mom wanted to disassociate from that side of the family.

There were also many factors why my mom married my father. I only know what I remember my mom telling me, so it may be a bit confusing. I guess learned behavior starts as young as three because that was how old my mom was when my grandparents, who were German immigrants, came over on the boat landing in Ellis Island. From there, they traveled and went directly to Chicago. My mother was just three years old. The Chicago area was where they came to settle as my grandfather had a living blood sister already living there. They were very strict, and my grandfather, who was an extremely talented tailor, was becoming very successful, making business suits that were impeccable. Although his work and his ability to create a suit to perfection was impeccable, his tongue, however, was not. He was hardheaded, stubborn, and quick-tempered; and he took out that temper on my mom very quickly and easily. Sadly, my grandmother did not intervene much. My mom was the oldest of three siblings. At the age of fourteen, her sister was seven, and her brother was just an infant and an unexpected surprise birth. Because my grandmother also worked as a house cleaner for the wealthy Wilmette Doctor Community, she would make my mom babysit her siblings.

My mom's childhood was not a very pleasant one. She told me she had very dark thoughts and remembered very horrible things. Basically for the first several years of her life, they ignored and abandoned her. My grandparents secretly married at sixteen because my grandmother had become pregnant, which was not a good situation living in Munich, Germany, back in the 1930s. So basically, they married secretly, and my grandmother kept the pregnancy quiet and hush-hush. When they had my mother, they were just not equipped to take care of a baby. So for the first three years of my mother's life, they dumped her off and left her in a children's orphanage. They would visit her now and again, but they never took her home. My mom never even had a birth certificate. Shortly after my mom turned three, my grandfather got called and drafted into Adolf Hitler's army regimen, which he was against and was adamant about not being involved. He hated Hitler and what he stood for but could not voice that for fear of being arrested or killed. Therefore, my grandfather devised a plan to leave Munich quickly with my grandmother, and they were going to finally retrieve my mother from the orphanage. So in those early formative years for my mother, the only ones she could remember were feelings of abandonment. The time in Munich was getting very intense, and they had to make the arrangements quickly. They basically packed a few things and the clothes on their backs, retrieved my mother, and grabbed the next boat out to Ellis Island. My grandmother said one last goodbye to her mother. It was to be the last time she ever saw her because they knew once they took this leap, they would never be able to come back, not if Adolf Hitler was still the leader of Germany. World War II was about to break. Hitler was rounding up all military men. Fear was abundant throughout Germany, especially for Jews. What he was doing to the Jews was horrific. My grandparents were terrified. They would be caught, but they were willing to take that chance. They barely were able to get on the last boat over from Germany, barely escaping.

If they had been found, my grandfather would have been arrested for deflecting and put to death. You can just imagine the fear and confusion of a little three-year-old girl who didn't really know her parents, who saw how terrified her parents were and now was thrown on a boat with two strangers she hardly knew. She could not speak anything but German, so when they got to Chicago, it was very difficult for my grandparents to secure work, not being able to speak English proficiently. They virtually had no money since that was used to pay their passage. All they had was the few clothes and a few personal items, and that was it—thus forcing them to move in with my grandfather's sister, Tessa, and her husband, Jonas. They were older than my grandparents and had no children. Tessa was

barren. Every day they lived with them, they would go out searching for work. It was very difficult with their broken English. Again
dumping my mother into the hands of my grandfather's sister and
then trying hard to forget Germany and to fit in, they thought the
only way to Americanize my mother was to refuse to communicate
with her except in English. So they stopped talking to her in her
native tongue, German.

My grandfather's sister, Aunt Tessa, was a wicked woman. Since
she could not have children of her own, she became a bitter, cruel,
angry woman. Behind my grandfather's back, she had been secretly
trying to convince my grandmother Annaliese into giving my mom
up to her and her husband, Jonas, my grandfather's brother. At first,
my grandmother considered it, but my grandfather Anton would
not allow it. I can only imagine the isolation she must have felt when
her parents refused to talk to her in German and when she did not
understand English. How cruel. They assumed that would be the
fastest way she would pick up the English language. It was actually a
form of child abuse, not speaking to her at all and expecting her to
only respond in English, or they would not pay attention or respond
to her. That was their teaching methods. Not only was it cruel—here
was my mom taken from an orphanage and then thrown with two
people who were virtually strangers to her and who would not speak
to her. Her whole environment was changed in a heartbeat. They
even refused to give her dinner if she did not speak English words. I
can only imagine what her little three-year-old brain and heart were
feeling: loss, fear, abandonment, and confusion. The real unfortu-
nate thing was that my grandparents actually thought they were
helping my mother by doing what they were doing. But really, they
only made her feel lost and alone, and they denied her the chance to
be bilingual. During those first few months when my grandparents
secured jobs and finally began working, they had no idea how abusive my great aunt Tessa was to my mother. Not Great Uncle Jonas—
he was as meek as a mouse. She would only be mean when he was not
looking. When Uncle Jonas was gone during the day, if my mother
did not do chores or respond in English, Aunt Tessa would refuse
her lunch and shut her in a dark closet. This happened quite often.

My aunt Tessa thrived on that power of authority. She would always make sure my mother was out in time to look well, put together, dressed, and washed before Uncle Jonas and her mom and dad came home. They never knew. This ritual and cruelty would continue for many months as it took quite some time before my grandparents were able to manage to get enough money saved for their own small one-room apartment. Still, because they worked such long hours, they had Aunt Tessa watch her, and most nights, it was late by the time they came home. My mother was already in bed, so they never really talked to her. They would grab her little body up and bring her back to the one-room flat where they all slept in the same bed. They never knew what was happening to my mother during the day. Aunt Tessa was a wicked woman. It must have been God's will that she be barren and not able to have children of her own because what she did to my mom those early years would haunt my mother and leave deep scars. Aunt Tessa would make awful dinners on purpose so that she could torture my mom and force her to eat it, knowing it was horrible, because when she couldn't, she would lock her up for hours in the dark cold closet with nothing in there except the hardwood floor. Things like liver and onions or liver sausage or blood sausage. That pitch-black silence scarred my mother. That is why she always needs the television on when she falls asleep. Noise and light, the only things that would calm her and lull her to sleep. She still, till this day, needs the television on. Then there were the other times where because my great uncle Jonas was wealthy, they had many nice things—Oriental rugs, antique furniture, and crystal—which, of course, my mom was not allowed to touch or set foot on. Playing was nonexistent in that home. My great aunt Tessa would force my mother to do chores and make her take naps when she did not want to, and then when she had to nap, it would be on the cold hardwood floor. My great aunt did not want her touching the Oriental rug for fear she would soil it. She just was a wicked woman. Once again, my mother felt no love—only fear, loneliness, and abandonment.

It was close to a year by the time my grandparents were able to move out of my great aunt and uncle's home. My mom was four years old. Because they wanted her to be Americanized, they rarely ever spoke to her in her native German language as they wanted her to be able to speak English as quickly as possible when she entered school. When they would converse with each other, it would be in German, but when my mom would try to join in, they would completely ignore her and not respond. By the time she was four, she was able to speak some broken English. During the move into the one-bedroom flat, my grandparents had to enlist the help of babysitting my mother to my great aunt and uncle. My mom tried to tell my grandma and grandpa in broken English how mean my great aunt was, but they would not hear it. They thought she was being disrespectful. They reprimanded her and admonished her and told her she was being ungrateful. How could she be so ungrateful and disrespectful to Aunt Tessa and Uncle Jonas, who had been so good to her and to them? Again she was shut down and ignored. My mother closed up further into herself. My mother never spoke of it again.

The one-bedroom flat that they moved into had a tailor shop in the lower level that my grandfather secured work at. When they finally moved, my mother had become so introverted and quiet. The damage to my mom's psyche had been done during all those formative years and could not be reversed. My grandparents just assumed it was because of the change of environment, new home, and new school. They did not put much precedence or question why she hardly spoke or smiled. I think this is when the innate need to win the love of my grandparents—the need to be recognized, to be heard, to be loved, and to have her parents show affection and have pride in her—became so important it was an obsession. She desperately wanted their approval. She wanted her parents to compliment her, to tell her she was a good girl, and to hug her or hold her. Any crumb of love they could throw her way would have been gobbled up with joy. She was like a puppy dog in a kennel all day waiting for table scraps to be thrown down to the floor after dinner. Whatever little crumb of positive compliment, something as dumb as "I am glad you were able to finish the laundry after your studies," she would relish in it. Those were the kind of scraps that were thrown to her. It is no wonder my mom had no idea what love was or could be. She never felt it once from her own parents or saw it displayed in her parents' relationship. I don't even think my mother saw my grandfather kiss my grandmother once. Only on the cheek, and it was quick. A display of affection was considered inappropriate and in my grandfather's eyes, a sign of male weakness. My grandparents just were not those kind of people. Plus they had absolutely no parenting skills whatsoever. All they ever knew to do was to get up, go to work, pay the bills, eat, and go to bed. They had absolutely no time for love, relationships, fun, and recreation. I am not even sure they knew what a relationship or what family meant. The only form of recreation my mom experienced was once in a great while, my grandfather would take some time off to go fishing. and since he did not have a boy, he would take my mother with him. Believe it or not, my mom was on cloud nine when he did because he was showing her attention. It may not have been positive because she knew he longed for a son to do this with. Nonetheless, she did not care. She treasured every moment of those times. It was the only time she could remember doing something together with her father. Henceforth, I now can see where and how the people-pleasing syndrome that was ingrained in my mother and passed down to me came into play in her personality and would continue with my mom and still continue throughout the years of her life and to this day. She didn't feel love. She didn't feel appreciated. She never felt needed. So she is trying so hard to get that recognition from others—pleasing teachers, girlfriends, boyfriends, and eventually, the men in her life—just to get that brief pat on the back, the recognition of a compliment, and to be liked, to feel needed, and to feel cared about.

That people-pleasing syndrome never leaves you, and of course, it then gets passed down from generation to generation. The trickle effect. It also did not help that she grew up for the first seven years of her life as the only child of my grandparents and that she was abandoned by them in the first three years of her life. When Mom turned seven years old, my aunt Lenore came along, and then when she was fourteen came my uncle Marvin. Mom was fourteen, and thus, she became the caregiver, the babysitter, their mommy figure. That is what my grandparents expected of her. That was her job: go to school and watch and take care of her siblings. Nothing else. When she tried to defy them, she got the brunt of disciplining from my grandfather's hand and tongue-lashing when he lost his temper. By the time my mom turned fourteen, she became a bit tougher and more defiant. She had much of her father in her with the quick German hot temper. She was stubborn. So the two of them butted heads quite often, and when my mother voiced her opinion, my grandfather considered that a complete denial of respect. The consequences that came from it would have been considered child abuse. If there was a thing called Child Protective Services back then, my mother would have been taken away from Grandfather and Grandmother and put into foster care, they would have been deemed abusive and unfit parents when investigated, and my aunt and uncle would have probably been thrown in jail as well. How in the world can you make a seven-year-old be the sole caregiver and babysitter of an infant? When she herself was just a child, my grandparents did, and my mother was smart enough to know that she had to do what she was told or she would get the back of my grandfather's hand to her behind or get smacked across the face. So she became the dutiful daughter, hoping deep down if she did what was expected, she would win their love and approval. No, never happened. Imagine a lonely seven-year-old child in a new country for only four years and wanted so badly to be loved and was so isolated and alone.

They were German immigrants. They were not brought up to be loving, affectionate beings, and really, you cannot fault them. It was the way they were raised. That culture where you pretty much grew up as a robot—work, eat, sleep, procreate, and attend Church and nothing in between. The word *love* and *fun* were unheard of. There were no such things in their culture that would be considered a sign of weakness or a sign of irresponsibility. Being rigid and frugal and following rules, that was how you got somewhere in life. The same thing was expected of my mother as well. When my aunt and uncle came along, things got a little more lenient, but not much. Every time my mom would try a little harder in school or in sports, no one noticed. It was expected. Even if you got a commendation, you still were not patted on the back. I can only imagine how hard that must have been for her all those years, which really explains why her need to please and her need to escape to find that kind of recognition and positive reinforcement and love became so prevalent.

By the time my mom was fourteen, she was getting pretty teenage mouthy and a bit defiant. She had to keep herself in check, or she would really get a lashing from my grandfather. I remember this one story my mom told me that made me laugh at her boldness to take chances. She so badly wanted to see the horror movie playing for a nickel at the movie theater, but she was stuck watching my aunt. My uncle, who was an infant, was brought with my grandmother to her cleaning jobs as he slept most of the time. Don't misunderstand. My mother loved her sister and her brother, but she also resented the fact that she could not be a normal teenager. She had to be a permanent babysitter. If she complained or was defiant, she got a crack in the face by my grandfather. That, in today's standards, would be considered child abuse. Forbidden to go to the movies, she stubbornly devised a plan. My mother defied my grandparents and snuck my aunt out of the house and to that movie, and every time a scary scene would pop on the movie screen, she covered my aunt's head with a bag. Then she told my aunt she would take away her favorite toy if she told. LOL. That was pretty darn bold of my mom. Kudos to Mom. She at least snuck out and had some fun.

By the time my mother turned sixteen, she turned into a curvy knockout, and at sixteen looked like she was eighteen to twenty years old. She was well-endowed, curvy, sexy, and a male magnet. She so desperately wanted to be loved and find love. She didn't receive it at home from my grandparents, who were so cold and not affectionate. My grandparents were even uncomfortable when you even hugged them. By the time she was seventeen, she had lots of boys asking her out. Although it was difficult to go out and date because of her responsibility to my aunt and uncle, she managed getting out there once in a while. She so wanted to find someone to escape her home life. I often wonder what would have happened because she showed me some of the boys she used to date. One in particular that she really liked and who cared about her very much wanted to marry her when she graduated. They were getting pretty serious, and he was a nice boy from a good family. My mom's best friend, her name was Mary Sue, had an older boyfriend. One weekend, Mary Sue decided to have a party, and she, of course, enlisted my mom's help. My grandparents did not know there was a party. They thought she was just spending the night at her house. That was the night she met my father. He happened to be the buddy of her best friend's boyfriend. She was still dating the other guy at the time, and they had been talking about getting engaged. I know my mom immediately thought my dad was good-looking. By today's standards, he was handsome. He was totally smitten by her. He was drawn to her like how a spider wants to suck the blood of a moth.

There is a funny story about this party. My mom, who had been helping to decorate for the party, bent over in her Bermuda shorts, and they split open. She did not have time to go home and change, and her parents would have questioned her why. So when the party started and my dad who immediately was smitten by my mom came over to talk to her, she never left the wall. She stood there for several hours with her back against the wall so no one would know her pants were split, including my father. LOL. That was hilarious. I don't know who was more attracted to who. I think my mom was so embarrassed by the shorts situation. Plus she was very flattered that this older boy—actually, I should say *man*—was interested in her. My mom looked way older than she was, and she was very reserved, shy basically because of her inexperience. Even though she was dating someone, this did not deter my dad. He did not care. He talked with her all night until she finally agreed to go out with him one time. I actually think the fact that my dad was so much older than my mom and seemed sophisticated and worldly intrigued her.

My dad was this tall, dark, and handsome guy with black wavy hair and big brown eyes. He acted suave and confident and sophisticated and acted as though he was successful, boasting to be wealthy. He was ten years older than my mom. She was only seventeen; he was twenty-seven years old. To have a good-looking twenty-seven-year-old guy pay interest to her was exciting. It built her ego up. He was so much older and seemed more sophisticated than the young boys she was dating in high school. Mom was a knockout, but she looked way older than seventeen. It didn't deter my dad that she was underage and ten years younger than him. At the time she met my father, she was not available. She had been dating a senior boy for a year, and they had been going steady. His name was Paul. This did not stop my dad from pursuing her. Before the party ended, he convinced her to go out on one date with him. She did go out once with him, sneaking out to meet him down at the soda shop on the corner. They had root beer floats even though my dad was old enough to have a beer float. He was on his best behavior with her, trying to impress her. They took a walk, but my mom said she was going steady with someone. Thus, she became a challenge to him. They played the cat-and-mouse game, flirting with each other at various gatherings of mutual friends when they saw each other. Then my dad made his move when he had heard that she broke up with her boyfriend, Paul, because he was leaving for college and Mom wasn't able to go to college. She had received a scholarship, but my grandparents forced her to turn it down. Her dream was to become an architect and designer and decorate homes. That was unheard of, and my grandparents stated that they would not allow it nor pay for it. Even though she received a scholarship, she was to refuse it. That was not a woman's career. She needed to go to work after graduation and be an assistant accountant. So that is what my mom did. I often wonder what her life would have been like if she hadn't, if she accepted the scholarship and went on to be an architect and married Paul. Her life would have been so different, the dysfunction may have ended right there, and I would not be here as well, telling the story. My dad took advantage of the situation and jumped in to ask her out. My grandparents were horrified and totally against them dating. Even though my father was extremely handsome on all outer appearances, he had one really bad, nasty flaw: his teeth. All of his lower teeth were rotting in his mouth from lack of dental care and the result of heavy drinking and cigarettes. He was only twenty-seven; my mom was just seventeen. My mom wanted an escape, so when my grandparents were so against my father, that made him all the more appealing to my mother. So behind their backs, they dated. During that time, my mom insisted that my dad fix his teeth, or she would not go out with him. He did. How my mom even kissed him after seeing that his teeth were rotting is beyond my comprehension. I may have puked if he was smiling. Mom showed me the picture of her former boyfriend prior to my dad, the one whom she almost married. He was handsome too and had an engaging smile; but he was not as debonair, tall, dark, and handsome like my father. Of course, except for the smile.

Since my mom had grown up in a very strict German immigrant family, my father had to abide by their rules. Home by nine, and most of the time, they had to take my aunt with them. Although it was babysitting, the German way considered it a chaperone, a report-back scenario. My grandparents were so against my mom and my father's relationship for all the right reasons a parent should be: he was too old and not secure in his career goals. He was a laborer. The more my grandparents were against my father, the more appealing he became to my mother. My father became her project. She was going to do everything in her power to fix him and convince her parents he was suitable marriage material. Not only did she set up to do so but she also looked at my dad as her escape hatch. She wanted desperately to get away from her dad's wicked temper, get away from being the babysitter, and just get away from all the strict rules and the cold atmosphere she was surrounded by. The fact that they could forbid her because she was only seventeen irked my mother, and her German stubbornness came out. She had a lot of her father in her, and that is all they needed to say because she defiantly said, "You can't stop me. When I am eighteen in January, I plan to marry him." She did abide by their rules and not date him, but secretly behind my grandparents' back, she continued to see my dad in group situations on the sly until she turned eighteen. Because of her parents' dislike of my father, this only fueled her fire to prove them wrong. So for the next several months, she made it her goal to fix him, starting with his teeth, then his clothes. She was refinement at work. Her goal was to impress her parents and make him respectable and prove that their first impression of my father was wrong. During this grooming period, my dad made it a point to behave on the drinking. He had to because my mom was only seventeen. She was underage. He behaved himself when he was around her and was able, at that point, to conceal the fact he was already a heavy-duty drinker on his way to being an alcoholic. Easy to hide when you are dating a seventeen-year-old who cannot drink and who is a good Catholic girl and whose parents already made it known they were not too happy about their association.

When my mom turned eighteen in January, they went public with their relationship, and shortly thereafter, they got engaged. My grandparents had no choice but to bite the bullet and accept that she was going to marry him with or without their approval. They were married on June 18 that year. Mom's stubbornness won. Although I don't think she ever proved to them they were wrong, she convinced herself she had. Mom was so caught up in everything—the excitement of escaping the hell of her home life, the newness of what the future might hold, and the whirlwind courtship and adoration of an older man. I really think that she convinced herself that she loved him, that he was not a bum, and that she was going to make a beautiful life despite what her parents thought. She was so wrong, but too naive and stubborn to see it or admit it. I found out in later years that my mom was my dad's second wife. One week before my mother's wedding, when they went to apply for the marriage license, my mom had found out my dad lied to her. He had been married before. *Ding, ding, ding!* Hello, Mom, a red flag was right there. Mom was mortified and embarrassed and in no way in shape or form was she going to admit that to anyone, especially her parents. My father, of course, played it down, stating he didn't consider it a marriage. They were young and out of high school, and they had it annulled. That he forgot all about it. Ha! How can you forget you were married before? I cannot believe my mom accepted that answer, but see she was in too deep already. They married as planned in June and moved to Lake Villa, Illinois, out in the middle of nowhere. My grandparents were still living in the two flat off Roscoe Street in Chicago with my mom's siblings—her sister who was then fifteen, and her brother who was eight. My mom still commuted to her accounting job in Chicago by train. Things were okay in the beginning of the marriage as my dad kept his drinking to a minimum. He was trying to be on his best behavior. He did slip up now and then, but my mom thought that was what men did. She had seen her own father tie a few ones on and get mean and nasty to her grandmother, knocking her around, so she thought that was normal. So when my father did that to her a few times, she chalked it up to stress and overwork.

For two years, things were going okay. Then shortly after my mom turned twenty years old, she received a devastating phone call. Mom was called to come to the two flat immediately. Her mother was distraught and inconsolable, and there she found her forty-two-year-old father dead from a stroke and lying on the ground inside the tailor shop where she had to identify him. My mom had never made peace with her father, so she was completely devastated. This left my grandmother a widow with two young children to raise on her own. It was an awful time for my mom. She felt guilty. She felt lost. She never had the chance to have the relationship she always wanted with her father, and he would never be alive to meet his grandchildren. The fact she lived so far away made her even more sorrowful. She was not close enough to help with her brother and sister. She also realized that things were not right in her house, and she so badly wanted to tell her parents the truth. And it was too late to do that with her father. My dad had started drinking heavily, going on major binges, and my mom was desperately trying to pretend and hold it together and that everything was fine. But it wasn't fine. He was going out with the boys after work, stumbling home drunk and drinking away his paycheck. My mom could not admit that to my grandmother, her mother, especially while she was grieving and angry that she was left to raise two children on her own. With my grandmother having no formal education except grade school, she did the only thing she could do: be a housekeeper on the North Shore and clean for all the wealthy doctors' homes in Wilmette. She worked on her hands and knees, scrubbing floors. In return, the doctors gave free health care to her children when needed. So how could my mom burden my grandmother?

By the time my mom was twenty years old, before my grandfather died, she had two miscarriages. My father's drinking started escalating and got worse. The verbal abusiveness started and then the pushing and shoving. Pretty soon, the group of neighbors and friends they had made started avoiding them as my father would pick fights with whoever got in his way or looked sideways at him when he was drinking. My mom was so alone. She had no one to confide in, and she was embarrassed and ashamed. How could she now go to her own mother and admit the truth that she had made a mistake? The timing was awful when she herself was going through her own grief-stricken state. My mom kept up the front, begging and pleading with my father to stop drinking. Each time, he would promise not to, and then the cycle would happen all over again. Payday arrived, then he would promise he would only go out for one drink or maybe two with the boys after work. She needed to stop nagging him. It would be hours later when he would stumble in drunk and try to sleep with her. If she didn't comply, he would beat the crap out of her and pass out, and the paycheck would be gone. The next day, he would beg her for forgiveness, hold his head down in remorse, and barely look her in the eye because he could not face to see the black-and-blue marks he inflicted. It was like a never-ending merry-go-round. They started to go through friends like water as no one, once they figured out my dad was a drunk, wanted to be around him. They loved my mom. She was a bright, vibrant light, but that light dimmed being around him. His drinking had caused too many verbal and physical fistfights. Then the inevitable happened: she got pregnant then miscarried. She got pregnant again then miscarried. I am not sure if this was God's way of warning her, trying to give her a wake-up call. One will never know because then she got pregnant with me, the year 1961. It was a difficult pregnancy. She developed toxemia, and I was taken by C-section and was four weeks premature, weighing only four pounds, five ounces on June 21, the first day of summer. She was told not to get pregnant and to avoid sexual relations until she was healed, but in one of my father's drunken states, he did not abide by the doctor's order. Thus, my Irish twin, my brother, was born eleven months later on June 13, giving my mom horrific stretch marks and scars because her body had not had time to heal before the next life growing within her expanded body.

When I was a year and half and my brother six months old, my mother finally tried to take her life back. My father beat my mother so badly, causing her to miss a day of work as she could not hide the damage he had done. It was her breaking point. She could not take it anymore. The very next day when she could collect herself, she packed a few items, got on the train, and told my father she was leaving him. My father, remorseful as always, begged and pleaded with her not to leave. She did leave that time, left and went to my grandmother's to finally tell her the truth, to ask for help, and to get the love she so desperately needed. What she had not expected was the unwelcome greeting she received. My grandmother took one look at my mother and said, "What did you do to make him mad?" My grandmother was cold and unwelcoming, and when she saw my mother, she told her, "You need to go back home to your husband. You made your bed. Now you lie in it. Take your children and go back home." She did not want to hear nor did she want to listen to my mother's heart-wrenching story of abuse and alcoholism. She blamed my mother for my father's drinking and abuse and that my mother was somehow causing him to go to the bottle. My mom left my grandmother's flat devastated, more broken and lost than before.

In the illness of alcoholism, the nondrinkers are just as sick as the alcoholic. We enable, we pretend, we cajole, we blame ourselves, we are ashamed, and we are filled with guilt. My mom took on all that and more. She had the full-blown illness, just not the alcohol-induced one. She wanted desperately to fix it, but in the end, all she did was enable. So then it became her mission to hide and pretend we had a perfectly normal family. Give off the persona that we were the all-American family. That it was normal to worry every other Friday when it came to be five o'clock and there was no sign of my father. That it was normal to walk on pins and needles, never knowing what to expect. Talk about living life filled with anxiety and stress. Leading a double life is never easy. One thing that I used to think was quite comical and actually fun for us kids because it became sort of an adventure. I felt like we were like pirates looking for the treasure chest, only we were looking for my father before he blew the paycheck. So if it was past five o'clock, she would load me, my brother, and her best friend and her three kids in the Ford station wagon and go from bar to bar in Glenview to try and find him before he drank the entire paycheck away. She would try to make it seem like a fun road trip—like I said, somewhat of a comical adventure—even though she had that look of panic and dread every time we had to do this little road trip. She was like "Okay, kids. I am pulling in here. Look for Mint Green Matador. First one that finds it gets fifty cents." If we found him, she would go in and take whatever was left of the check and leave my father there in the hands of his crony work buddies all sitting on the bar stools. She didn't care what happened to him. All she cared about was being able to put food on the table and to pay the bills. This kind of roller coaster went on for years. Sometimes if we found him right away, for a special treat for dragging us all over to every pub and bar in Glenview, my mom would take us to Lum's, a restaurant in Wheeling that us kids loved. They had the best had fried clams and fries ever. My brother and I and her best friend's kids would get so excited when the find was quick. It didn't matter that my dad was drunk in a bar, and that's why my mom was rewarding our good behavior for being dragged everywhere looking for him. We thought it was fun. Isn't this what a normal Friday night family ritual consists of? Doesn't every all-American family do this on a Friday night? As we got older, we didn't do the road adventure as much. My mom was a bit more stable with her job, and she was getting more savvy, saving money when she could to make up for the benders when there would be none. In those times, we lived on Hamburger Helper meals. Needless to say, they make me sick now. LOL.

Starting, I think, when we were in about fifth and sixth grade, when he wasn't home by five p.m., my mother would tell us to stay in our bedrooms and keep our doors locked and let him pass out on the couch and not to antagonize him for fear of being knocked around. See, as we got older, we were more boisterous, louder, sassier, and more bothersome to my father. We weren't the pliable toddlers to hold and cuddle and slobber on. We were more defiant, and that just irked my dad even more. My mom saw this change, and to protect us, she always took his wrath. She never wanted us to be beat or verbally abused like she was, so she allowed herself to be the constant punching bag.

It became very clear to me at an early age that I was Daddy's favorite. It was obvious and apparent 'cause he did not easily hide his feelings, and this was when he was not drinking and on his dry binges. He treated me like a princess and my brother like a dog. We could be doing the same exact thing, the same exact situation, and my father would praise me and ridicule my brother. My mom saw it, and my mom compensated and showered my brother with positive reinforcement to make up for the way my father treated him. That made me sort of mad, jealous even, and sad at the same time. I, too, wanted the same attention from my mother. I felt bad when my father treated my brother so badly and me so good. I felt guilty that I could do no wrong. I would even try and stick up for my brother to my dad, but he would just ignore me. Even though I felt guilty, being a child, I saw it as an opportunity to manipulate the situation to my advantage. I taught myself tricks of manipulation, the ones that worked where I could wrap my father around my pinky finger and get him to do whatever I wanted, except for getting him to stop drinking. So I was the princess, and my brother was the scapegoat. When my mother realized the ability and influence I had over my father, she used it, and she used it constantly. I hated it. I resented her for many years for making me do it, but as an adult, I see now she was only using me to survive because my mom wanted so badly for us to be normal or have some normalcy as a family and portray that family image.

This is what would happen if dad had a bender on a Friday night and was passed out most of the day on Saturday. The ritual would be my mom coming to me and saying, "Okay, we are going to do a family thing on Saturday now that your dad is home and not drinking. We are going to go to Shakey's Pizza and have fun. Katie, you're the only one that your dad will listen to, so you need to go talk to your dad and ask him to come with us and be a family."

I would have to start working on this in the early afternoon to get the plan to work by evening. I started with hugging and begging then pleading and cajoling. This could last sometimes close to an hour to two hours before he would even respond. I would say, "Daddy, please, can you get up? Please? We want to go to Shakey's, Daddy, as a

175

family. We love you, Daddy. Daddy, it will be okay." I would rub his back as his remorseful face was always faced toward the couch back and the wall. I would try to pull on his arm to turn him over. "Come on, Daddy. I love you. I know you can do this. Do it for me, Daddy. I want you to go with us. It will be fun. Aren't you hungry, Daddy?" After two hours of this ritual of begging and pleading with him to finally move his ass off the couch, take a shower, and act like nothing happened the night before; it was victory! He finally stirred and moved, with me kneeling down next to the couch, rubbing his back to try and stir him out of his sleep-induced hangover. "Please, Daddy. Please, Daddy. Please get up?" It worked. I felt a sense of accomplishment; at the same time, I felt sick. When he would finally turn to me with his beard already forming into a stubble and his bloodshot eyes sunk in his head and his breath sour, I would say, "Daddy, it is okay. I know you didn't mean it. Mommy isn't mad. We love you. Come on, Daddy." I would pull him up to sitting position. I would act excited and animated, hugging him, smiling, and dancing around. I could tell he always loved that, and I would say, "Yeah, Daddy. I knew you could do it. Yippee! I knew you would get up for me."

I'd be hanging on him till he would crookedly smile and gruffly say, "Okay, sweetheart. For you," and he would slowly stumble to his feet and get up off the couch, hangover and all, reeking of alcohol and cigarettes and his feet smelling like a boys' locker room. It was vile and gross.

When he was safely in the shower, I could relax. I did it. I always felt yucky and dirty after doing it, but I also felt power and control. So many odd feelings for a young child to feel. Once he showered, none of us would mention the night before. It would be like it never happened. We would go off and do some kind of fun family thing that my mom would plan—whether it be going to Shakey's Pizza or our other favorite, Pit-n-Pub or Barnaby's, or to the stock car races, movies, picnic, camping, etc. Whatever my mom organized, it was such a farce and a joke. Part of me would feel all proud of myself when I saw my mom sigh and look relieved. The other part was filled with resentment toward her for making me do that vile act. I am really not sure what my brother felt. He kind of always stayed far away from that scene when it played out. Once out in the public eye, we would all be happy honky dory, pretending the night before never happened. My dad would always be very quiet and easy going mostly because he probably still felt hungover… On the outside surface, to the public, we looked like this all-American family that was out for Saturday night family fun; and yeah, for us, by Sunday night, the hangover had subsided. This kind of ritual went on for years. I began to physically get sick knowing I would be asked to do it, but I could not say no to my mom. I just wanted us to be normal. So I became the surrogate wife, so to speak, because I could get my dad to do most anything when he was not under the influence.

So through the years of tears, we, as a three-family unit, did everything in our power to pretend we were a normal happy family; and because my dad was a binge drinker, it was an easy task to hide his alcoholism. Sometimes, throughout the years when my brother and I would have friends over, they would ask, "Where is your dad?" if he had a binge during the week or on a Friday night when he was out all night. We would lie and say, "Oh, he is working late." Once in a while, we occasionally had a friend over when he was passed out on the couch, and we would just say he had to work late and that's why he was so tired. Always hiding and covering up it became second nature to our family to bear the shame and embarrassment. We wanted everyone to see us as one happy family in a pretty little package—a beautiful house, three-fourth of an acre yard, great vacations, hosts of great parties and neighborhood gatherings, and involved in church functions. The perfect little family. Because in a nutshell, on all those occasions, my dad did behave himself, and he was able to control the demon. It was easily done because he was a binge drinker, but in between the binging, he was a dry drunk. Meaning that to control the demon, he would pace, drink tons of coffee, smoke like crazy, and eat an abundance of sweets. But that did little to control his agitation and irritability in between binges. We couldn't keep a dozen donuts, coffee cake, cake, ice cream, and Little Debbies in the house for more than a day. During those dry drunks, he was irritable and cagey, but if we kept him busy with activities, he seemed to fare better only because he was out in the public eye and had to put on the perfect-dad-and-husband suit. There are so many times I can remember being so scared for my mom, afraid to do anything because I would always remember back to when I was five and remember the purple-and-red bruises and the blood dripping from her lip. Memories that have been etched from five years old that cannot be erased.

I remember my mom telling me the story of my aunt Lenora's wedding, her sister. I was four, the flower girl, and my brother was three, the ring bearer. She said my dad almost destroyed the whole event. He had started drinking at who knows what time, but all day long, and during the reception, he started to be loud, boisterous, and belligerent and pick a fight with one of the band members. He had to be physically carried out of the reception before he caused any more havoc, embarrassment, and damage. All because he didn't like the music they were playing and started mouthing off, being loud, rude, and obnoxious so much so that the band member was going to take him outside and knock the living daylights out of him. I can only imagine how mortified my mother was that he did this at her sister's wedding. It took the whole wedding party to drag my drunken father's ass outside and hold him down until he passed out before shoving him in a car. It didn't stop the horrible embarrassment and the shame my mom felt. My poor mother. And of course, my mom never heard the end of that event for years to come at family functions. My grandmother would always make sure she would bring it up, blaming my mother for not being able to control my father. Shortly after that event, my father's and mother's best friends, Kate and Howard, who were my godparents, told her that they no longer could be around my dad. His drinking had become unmanageable. He was no longer the happy drunk. He was a vicious beast—crude, mean, and incorrigible—and they did not want to be out in a public place with them for fear he would do something vile or hurt someone. My mom was devastated and again left alone with two little ones.

Thus the merry-go-round continued for years. One week good, two weekends horrific, another week tolerable, and the next one horrific. Always living on the edge of insanity and anxiety and walking on eggshells to try avoiding a crack. I do have to say, even the most dysfunctional families can still have some good memories to hold on to, and those memories and moments my brother and I had were the camping vacations my mother planned. Some of our family vacations, when my mom could plan them, were camping, which were away from the booze and away from his boozing work buddies. Those times were quite almost idyllic and sometimes very comical. See, my dad was not a man who had much common sense, not sure if that was because of all the heavy drinking and brain-cell killing. My mom, on the other hand, was smart, intelligent, and organized. She was the glue, always putting back the pieces. Camping was a good thing for our family. It got us away from scrutiny, away from temptation for my dad. Although always the first few days of the trip were a little hairy and tense as he would be coming down from a dry drunk, my mother would always make sure the cabinets were filled with Ho Hos, Little Debbies, and Twinkies galore. We started out tenting, moved up to a pop-up trailer, to a trailer, to a Dodge Camper with the bunk bed over the top of the cab, and to a Minnie Winnebago. Each time was an adventure with my dad because he never seemed to remember all the steps for setup. I really don't know how we survived those trips if it hadn't been for my smart mother.

I remember one time he forgot to block the wheels of the trailer, and we were in the Smoky Mountains. It started rolling back, and my mother, brother, and I were trying to hold the back of the trailer before it rolled down the mountain and into a ravine, plus crushing us three to death. Thank god the neighboring campers saw what was happening and came running over and saved us from being crushed to death and threw the blocks under the wheels.

Another time, I remember my mom telling my dad to make sure he turned the water off outside as there were signs posted everywhere, warning you to make sure you turn off the water at the spigot after you fill your holding tank because of the water pressure. My dad would say, "Yeah, yeah, I got it. Quit bitching at me." Well, in the middle of the night at that campground, my mom woke up hearing gushing water. My brother and I were on the top of the bunk beds, and there we saw my mom open the kitchen cabinet and an explosion like a giant tidal wave came flooding out of the cabinet and flooded the entire floor of the camper floor with a foot of water. My dad had forgotten to shut the water off and blew the lines in the camper. It took several days for the camper to dry out, and my dad had to sit there with his thumb holding back the water until my mom ran and got the campground host to shut the valve off outside. Such ignorant stupidity.

There was another time we were in Juniper Springs, Florida, with my cousins and aunt and uncle. Dad was taking a sharp turn in the Winnebago in the campground, and my mom said to him, "Kevin, that is too low and too sharp. You are too close to the out-house." "Oh no, you are crazy," my dad would say to my mom, and there went the outhouse. We took a piece of it with us—dragged the roof and side of it several feet. Even though these may seem like crappy situations, they were ones we could sit back and laugh about because my dad did these things when he wasn't drinking. Hahaha! You may not think that is humorous, but to a dysfunctional family grasping on to alcohol-free moments to laugh about, it was fantastic.

Dad also had no sense of direction, and that maybe because his brain was fried from all the boozing. Who really knows? I remember my mom would always have to stay awake and navigate with the map where we were going step by step. One time, she was so tired she said, "Kevin, all you need to do is take this exit when it comes up and stay on that highway till you reach the campground." We were heading to Yellowstone. She fell asleep at eight and woke up at eleven, and we were at the same exact spot where she had dozed off. My dad had been driving in circles for three hours. My Mom was like "What the hell? We were just here." She looked at her watch. Three hours had passed. She was like "Kevin, why didn't you think to wake me up?" "Uh, uh, I dunno," he would mumble. Those were the times we could sit back and actually laugh at the stupidity and absurdity.

Mom—well, she was a great organizer and party thrower and would have these amazing parties at our house—I think mostly to help validate my mom's ability to be amazing and to prove to everyone that we were this awesome family unit. All our friends and neighbors would get so excited because those parties truly were fantastic. I have the many photo albums to prove it. Of course during those times, my dad would hold it together and not drink, and if he did, he just snuck a few in on the sly. I always wonder how he was able to control his drinking in front of everyone, but he did put on this perfect persona of the great husband and father. It was quite weird how he could be around all that booze and not slip, and then when he was not around people he knew, he was a raging boozer. I remember friends and neighbors coming up to me saying, "Your dad is such a nice guy. Your family is so lucky." He would be helpful, personable, and polite. He had that kind of quiet-puppy-dog manner that people who met him found endearing and attractive. If they only knew the truth—the truth being that he could turn into a dog with rabies in a heartbeat after drinking a six-pack. Sometimes when people would say that to me, I wanted to yell back, "Well, he is this week! You missed him last week. He was in rare form then. Can't you see the remnants of that big bruise on my mom's shoulder? And oh by the way, did you see the smashed bumper on the Ford station wagon? Compliments of my dad's night out!" But I never did speak those words. I just kept silent. All three of us did. My mom, brother, and I went to great lengths to keep his drinking and binging hidden from everyone. Sleepovers with friends rarely occurred on weekends because that would mean having to explain why your dad was fully clothed and snoring like a pig on the couch and reeking of alcohol.

Throughout the years, my mom was really the sole breadwinner. She took on accounting jobs and did taxes as side jobs along with working full-time for the accounting firm in Chicago. She made an arrangement with her boss to take care of all their suburban clients. This allowed my mom to be home and work out of the house, thus protecting us as much as possible. She dragged me and my brother to all her clients to drop off or pick up work as to not leave us at home in the hands of our dad as he could not be trusted. Here is a truly funny story. I remember one time we were in Des Plaines, Illinois, at the Arlington Meat Packing Company. My mom was dropping off a file, and she said, "Kids, stay in the car and don't touch anything. I will be right out." We were probably about six and seven years old. She had parked right next to the brick building off a side street from the main busy highway. It was a business then residential street that the driveway sat off of. Well, me and my brother decided to pretend we were driving the car. Oops. We had no idea if you put the car in neutral, it would move. It rolled out into the street. My brother and I were so scared we hopped in the back seat and pretended that's where we were the whole time, and then the car horns started blowing because now the car was in the middle of the street, blocking traffic. My mom came out of the building, and I thought I could see steam coming out of her ears. Needless to say, we never did that again. See, my mom worked so hard to make ends meet because half the time, my father would drink his paycheck away. My brother and I rarely did things that would upset my mother because we just could not do that to her. We became like the three musketeers. At least that's what it felt like. We were a threesome, a united front. All we had was one another to lean on.

My brother's escape route. My brother, during high school, worked two jobs to save money, and when he wasn't working, he was with his girlfriend, who was a girl who lived right down the street. He would spend most nights there after work and school just to stay away from the crazy house, which made him even more attractive to the females in my high school. He also was way different than most of the teenage guys. He was mature beyond his years because he had to be the man of the house at a very early age. He was and still is such a truly genuine, kind person. A nice guy, more sensitive, and a gentleman. He was taught by my mom to treat women with respect, not the way my dad treated her. He became a heartbreaker in high school without even realizing it, and it was because of the close bond he shared with me and my mom. His escape from the crazy looney-tune house was to work, work, and work his brains out, save money, go fishing, and of course, date—until Annie nabbed him; and then it was date and sleep with Annie. That was his out. Instead of facing it and getting help, he pretended that everything was fine, and he chose to run. How many eighteen-year-olds do you know can put ten thousand dollars down on a house, get married, go to college, and work a full-time job after graduation? That was my brother. As soon as he was eighteen, he did all that, except the only thing he didn't do was take me with him. He left me behind.

Going back to that marriage and family class I took in high school, I remember writing, rewriting, and turning in that assignment so I would not get an F was the best thing that ever happened to me. R. L. said to me, "I really think that this was a good assignment for you as I can tell it brought out all of your fears to the top. I want you to know that what you and your family are living through is not normal, and I would like to talk to you and meet with you once a week on your free period to talk more about this illness."

Looking at him perplexed, I said, "Illness? Who is sick?"

His response was "You and your entire family. Your mom, your brother, and you, Katie. It's life-threatening for your father and incurable. For your family, it won't go away. It's something that we can try to work on. Give you some coping skills. It's time to talk about it, not hide it or pretend it's not there."

Immediately, I felt a weight being lifted from my shoulders. I almost felt like a feather. What I felt was hope. "Wow! So I am not crazy."

He laughed and said, "You are far from being crazy. You are a smart, you are intelligent, you are kind, and you are a beautiful young lady that has been living with a sickness."

He saw my perplexed look. "Now one thing I want to make clear, it is not my illness. It was my father's. But because we are living so close to the illness, it was contagious. You all have the illness." I remember furrowing my brow.

He then said, "When you live with an alcoholic, it is like being exposed to someone with a contagious virus." He said that my father was the virus and had infected our whole family. Hmmm, I never thought of it that way. "It's also an incurable disease." Wow, our family had a disease. Who would have known? Mr. Hansen then said, "I would like to meet with you on your free period two times a week so that you have someone to talk to and discuss your feelings openly without fear of being judged. It is strictly confidential. I would, however, like to speak to your mother and let her know and get her permission as you are a minor."

I hesitated. *Hmmm, I don't know,* I thought. Would Mom be mad that I wrote about our family and exposed our little secret? I felt sick to my stomach. I so did not want my mom to be upset, but I just could not take it anymore. I could not hold my feelings in—my anger and my anxiety. I was ready to explode. I needed to tell someone. Here was my lifeline. I decided to take the plunge and go for it. "Yes," I said.

Mr. Hansen said, "Okay, let's plan on meeting next week. This will give me time to have your mom come in for an appointment and talk to her about the plan." I had that look of dread on my face. "Your mom loves you. She has the virus too. Let's just hope that when I talk to her, let her read what you wrote because I am sure you did not show it to her. Am I correct?" he asked. I nodded. "I thought so. By writing your story, it is the first step to treat the illness because you are speaking the truth. Truth and honesty free you."

I wasn't sure he was right, but I was so alone and so broken I was willing to try. I met with R. J. Hansen for little under two years. I believe my mother was quite shocked when she read my essay. I don't think she ever realized how deep the scars were. I was seventeen and a junior in high school, my brother a freshman. R. J. Hansen also was a great support to my brother, who was not like me at all.

When R. J. started to get to know our family dynamics, he pretty much took my brother and me under his wing. He saw how I was willing to open up the door and set the demon free or at least unleash so it was not stuck in the dark depths of our souls, eating away at us. I was reaching out desperately, even if it was baby steps, for help. I was still reaching. On the other hand, my brother was a clam. He saw no problems except to be the protector of me and my mom. He never wanted help. He did not want to talk about the situation. He pretty much just wanted to get the hell out of dodge. My brother, such a charismatic, sensitive, giving, and caring person. He had to be. He was the man of the house since he grew taller than me. Girls saw how different, how sensitive, and what a kind, caring, giving guy he was; and the girls migrated to my brother because he was so good-looking. He lacked such self confidence in himself that he truly had no idea how attractive he was, and that made him all the more attractive. When we were young adults, my friends my cowork-ers who were girls just sucked up to me to get to him. It was because of how he was raised by my mom and me. Because he was not stuck up and did not realize it, that was what the girls went crazy about.

R. J., which I am so happy about, took my brother under his wing and helped him even if my brother was not willing to open up and speak about the dysfunction we were living in. He helped bring out all the good and potential for success in my brother. For that, I am forever grateful to R. J. Hansen, who is unfortunately no longer in flesh on this earth but an angel in another dimension. He helped my brother and became a male cheerleader to boost his confidence. R. J. helped my brother find his potential and achieve the Michael Caruso Scholarship. He saw a young man broken but a young man of such strength and character. It did not stop my brother though from escaping the madness at eighteen with a girl that fell madly in love with him to the point of obsession and latched onto him with her cat claws deeply. My brother just got roped along because he finally felt like someone loved him. He was so lacking in that emotion since my father never gave it to him. So to the first person that obsessively showed him this, he allowed himself to be swept off, seeing his escape route laid out before him. Unfortunately, that left me behind to deal with the hell on my own.

By that time I graduated early from high school at eighteen, I started cosmetology school, working nights at Roy Thomas doing data entry, the company where my mom was employed at as the head accountant. Because I was with a group of older, over-the-age-of-twenty-one students, that was when I first got my fake ID and started to go out and party heavily with the gang after school. One of the friends I met was a super tall girl who was five feet, eleven. She belonged to a Tall Singles Club that worked out great for me, being on five feet, two. She had a tall girlfriend, Barb, who was six feet, two; and her boyfriend, who eventually became her fiancé, was six feet, eleven. I would fit in, sandwiched in between them, when we would go out bar hopping, and not one bouncer would even notice me slide in. Never even saw me because they were too busy looking at the giants. That would be my first heavy-duty introduction to the world of heavy partying and getting totally trashed, wild, and crazy. Needless to say, I could not handle it. Many of those times, being so wasted, I would get so physically ill, sleeping by the toilet. Not a good feeling waking up totally hungover and trying to function by going to school and working at nights.

So ask yourself this question: How does one survive a dysfunctional family? How does one break the cycle and fall off this merry-go-round? By telling this story. I am and always will be a work in progress myself. I believe the only way my family could live through those dark times was because the fact we leaned heavily on one another. We used our inner strength, but because we grabbed so tightly to one another, we added another tier codependency—thus causing the lot of us to not set healthy boundaries and to have this innate need within our soul to always try fixing the broken. Healthy people will not understand why nor will they fathom this happened and happens. Some of those healthy people will be some I have known all my life—family, friends, coworkers, my doctors, teachers, and priests. They will be shocked we kept such a good secret. They will be shocked that I had a drinking problem and became a closet alcoholic for five years. Although there will be those that can empathize and sympathize and who have been right in my shoes and where we were at then, there will be those who may see their own lives intertwined in this story and possibly see a bit of themselves and will be able to relate more than they would like to admit. Intimate stories of illness and family discord and dysfunction don't normally get told. They stay hidden, buried deep inside, and rarely come to the surface because they are too painful to face and too painful to relive. Many times, family members end up going to their grave with it, and the torch of dysfunction gets passed to the other surviving members of the family to either keep it stored secretly or to release it.

I pray every day that we can all finally jump of this merry-go-round. Telling these stories can be the catalyst of what will break the cycle so it doesn't repeat itself again. The long effect of alcoholism and the dysfunction it causes within the family is truly a brutal, sad fact. If we do not face our pain and face our fear, we will succumb to the numbing and escape through alcohol or drugs. It is only a temporary fix and is not the answer. In those five years, I drank myself to oblivion to try and numb myself, only to become sicker both physically and mentally by leaning on alcohol. It was awful, but it brought me to the realization that this is an illness and you cannot survive it alone without help, without support, and without allowing yourself to heal. If I can jump off the merry-go-round, you can too. I thank God and my Higher Power every day for the support of AA; for the therapist who helped me; and for my mother, my brother, my children, and my friends who now know my struggle and who love me even more. I am sharing my pain, my mother's pain, my brother's pain, and my son and daughter's pain so that it will end our dysfunction and end someone else's pain. For you to know you are never alone, then this is my ultimate gift to others who have lived and shared a similar burden. Even if it only helps one person, it will be worth it.

The End

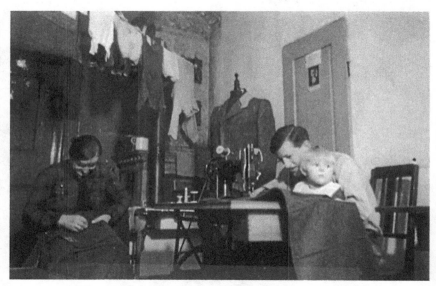

Mom with her parents in the one-bedroom apartment

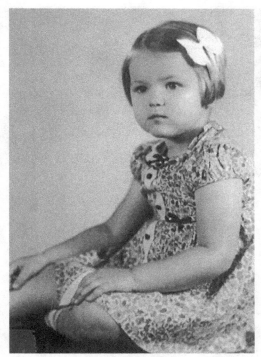

Sad, lost, lonely little girl—Mom at age 4

My mom, sexy at 17 1/2 years old, a beauty, and looks way older than her age

The early courtship dates

My father all fixed up and wedding ready! Mom did a wonderful job!
Picture-perfect wedding bliss before the reality hits

The disease taking a toll—eye issues and teeth issues
My father is aging quickly while my mother still smiles through it all.

My father and mother pretending a wedded bliss of 25 years

1954, my father and his father and his grandmother

My father and his mother
Wicked Aunt Tessa

My mother and her brother and sister and parents

My very strict German grandparents

Picture-perfect family
Early Years

My brother and I were inseparable when we were young.

The years of idolizing your father before the storm

The Three Musketeers

My rock, my mom

ALAN J. DIXON

SECRETARY OF STATE

SPRINGFIELD, ILLINOIS 62756

STATE OF ILLINOIS **OFFICE OF THE SECRETARY OF STATE** SPRINGFIELD

NOTICE OF SUSPENSION

KENNETH C STEWART
210 E CLARENDON ST
PROSPECT HEIGHTS, ILLINOIS 060
5363-5032-8119   000000015240

	Mo.	Day	Yr.
Effective Date of Suspension	07	26	77
Termination Date of Suspension	10	26	77
License Number	5363-5032-8119
Authority: Section	11-501.1
Illinois Vehicle Code

Pursuant to the provisions of Section 6-209 of The Illinois Vehicle Code, YOU ARE HEREBY NOTIFIED that an Order suspending your Illinois drivers license or permit, your privilege to operate a motor vehicle, and your privilege of obtaining a license within the State of Illinois, has been entered for the period of time indicated above.

This action has been taken as a result of this office being notified of your refusal to submit to the breath analysis which was requested following your lawful arrest for driving while intoxicated on

05 / 05 / 77
Mo.   Day   Yr.

William F. Logan, Executive Assistant
Driver Services Department

ILLINOIS OFFICE OF THE SECRETARY OF STATE SPRINGFIELD

NOTICE OF SUSPENSION

Kenneth C. Stewart
210 East Clarendon St.
Prospect Heights 60070
S363-5032-8119

EFFECTIVE DATE
OF SUSPENSION   04-25-

DRIVERS LICENSE

LICENSE PLATES   01-23-79

MO. DAY YR.
03   09   79
S363-5032-8119

Current Plates

Pursuant to Section 7-304, Illinois Vehicle Code, you are hereby notified of the suspension of any and all registration certificates and license plates issued for any motor vehicle registered in your name. Such licenses and registrations shall remain suspended and shall not at any time thereafter be renewed nor shall any license be thereafter issued to you until permitted under the Vehicle Codes of this State and not then unless you shall give and thereafter maintain for a period of three years Proof of Financial Responsibility as provided in Section 7-315 of the Illinois Vehicle Code.

This suspension is based on a notice of the revocation, by the Driver Services Department, of your drivers license or permit, or your privilege to obtain a license.

Financial Responsibility Section

William F. Logan, Director
Driver Services Department

IMPORTANT—SEE REVERSE

ILLINOIS STATE POLICE
Bureau Of Identification
260 North Chicago Street
Joliet, IL 60432-4075

L03807810

Criminal History of:	STEWART,KENNETH C	**State Identification Number:** IL03807810
(Last Known Name)		

Conviction Status:	MISDEMEANOR CONVICTION(S)
Custodial Status:	RECEIVED

Custodial Status Date: 02/17/1996

Juvenile Data:

Informal Adjustment: 0	**Formal Adjustment:** 0	**Probation Adjustment:** 0

Alias Name(s)
STEWART, KENNETH C
STEWART, KENNETH CLADEL

Date of Birth
04/26/1925

SUBJECT IDENTIFICATION DATA

Sex:	MALE
Race:	WHITE
Height:	511
Weight:	220
Eyes:	BROWN
Hair:	GRAY OR PARTIALLY GRAY
Skin:	FAIR

Date Reported:
Date Reported:
Chicago IR#:

Scars/Marks/Tattoos	**Place of Birth**	**Drivers License Number**	**DL State**
BLND L EYE	UNITED STATES OF AMERICA WISCONSIN	S36350328119	IL

Social Security Number	**Miscellaneous Number**	**Palm Prints Available**

Photo Available	**IDOC#**	**FBI#**
MC HENRY COUNTY SHERIFF'S OFFICE	612834	

Occupation	**Date Reported**
Employer	**Date Reported**

CRIMINAL HISTORY DATA

Custodial

DCN:	22977536X	**Date Received:** 02/17/1996
Name:	STEWART, KENNETH CLADEL	**Date of Birth:** 04/26/1925
Residence:		

Subject Institution Number:	612834	**Photo Available:** Yes
Confining Agency:	MC HENRY COUNTY SHERIFF'S OFFICE	**NCIC:** IL056000
Agency Received From:	MC HENRY COUNTY SHERIFF'S OFFICE	**NCIC:** IL056000

Custodial Status	**Status Date**	**Agency Name**

page 2 of 3

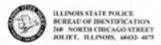

ILLINOIS STATE POLICE
BUREAU OF IDENTIFICATION
260 NORTH CHICAGO STREET
JOLIET, ILLINOIS, 60432-4075

KATHI STEWART ANN
DAUGHTER
106 CARSWELL CIRCLE
SUN CITY CENTER, FL 33573

THIS CRIMINAL HISTORY RECORD IS BEING ISSUED BY THE ILLINOIS STATE POLICE, BUREAU OF IDENTIFICATION PURSUANT TO THE UCIA NAME BASED INQUIRY SUBMITTED BY YOUR AGENCY. THIS RESPONSE DOES NOT PRECLUDE THE EXISTENCE OF CONVICTION INFORMATION UNDER OTHER PERSONAL IDENTIFIERS. TO ENSURE THAT INFORMATION FURNISHED BY THE ILLINOIS STATE POLICE POSITIVELY PERTAINS TO THE SUBJECT IN QUESTION, A UCIA FINGERPRINT INQUIRY SHOULD BE SUBMITTED.

ONE COPY OF THIS RESPONSE HAS BEEN PROVIDED. REQUESTS MADE FOR LICENSING OR EMPLOYMENT PURPOSES REQUIRE THE REQUESTER TO PROVIDE THE APPLICANT WITH A COPY OF THIS RESPONSE. THE APPLICANT THEN HAS 7 DAYS TO NOTIFY THE ILLINOIS STATE POLICE OF ANY INACCURACIES. THE APPLICANT MAY INITIATE PROCEEDINGS TO CHALLENGE OR CORRECT SUCH ERRORS BY CONTACTING THE BUREAU OF IDENTIFICATION.

ANY PERSON WHO INTENTIONALLY AND KNOWINGLY REQUESTS, OBTAINS, OR SEEKS TO OBTAIN CONVICTION INFORMATION UNDER FALSE PRETENSES, DISSEMINATES INACCURATE OR INCOMPLETE CONVICTION INFORMATION OR VIOLATES ANY OTHER PROVISIONS OF ILLINOIS COMPILED STATUTES, CHAPTER 20, ACT 2635 ET SEQ. MAY BE GUILTY OF A CRIME PUNISHABLE BY UP TO ONE YEAR OF IMPRISONMENT AND/OR MAY INCUR CIVIL LIABILITIES.

THE SEARCH ROUTINE USED TO PROCESS YOUR SUBMISSION DID NOT INCLUDE AN INQUIRY INTO THE ILLINOIS STATE POLICE SEX OFFENDER REGISTRATION FILE. TO DETERMINE IF THE SUBJECT OF YOUR INQUIRY IS A REGISTERED SEX OFFENDER, PLEASE CHECK THE ILLINOIS STATE POLICE REGISTERED SEX OFFENDER INFORMATION WEB SITE AT "WWW.ISP.STATE.IL.US"

IF YOU HAVE ANY QUESTIONS, PLEASE FEEL FREE TO CONTACT THE BUREAU OF IDENTIFICATION CUSTOMER SUPPORT UNIT BY EMAIL AT BOI_CUSTOMER_SUPPORT@ISP.STATE.IL.US OR BY PHONE AT 815/740-5160.

IDENTIFIERS

AGENCY:	DAUGHTER					
REQUEST DATE:		**INQUIRY TYPE:** UCIA	**RESULT:** HIT			
TCN:	FRM11300.79813997	**DCN:** L79813997			**SID:**	3807810
Name:	STEWART, KENNETH C					
Sex:	MALE	**Race:** WHITE			**DOB:**	04/26/1928

STATE USE ONLY
WARNING: RELEASE OF THIS INFORMATION TO UNAUTHORIZED INDIVIDUALS OR AGENCIES OR MISUSE IS PROHIBITED BY FEDERAL LAW TITLE 42 USC 3789G PERTAINING TO CRIMINAL HISTORY INFORMATION

Summer of 1980
Dear Mr. Cash,

Thank you for showing me that life will go on to the good things it has to offer and not the bad. If only one chooses to do so, by putting matters in God's hands.

My family and I visited Nashville, home of the Grand Ole Pry last week, my mother, brother and father. We took a tour and saw your beautiful home, and then went on to the House of Cash, where we met your lovely mother, and saw all your precious treasures, but the one thing I thought was your most valuable treasure was your book, "Man in Black." I did not realize then, that reading your book would give me a whole new outlook and understanding. My mother originally bought the book for my father, to try and give him an inspiration, to give him the will and the strength to turn to God for help.

My father is an alcoholic, very sick, sick man. In my 19 years I have watched the changes in him. These past 2 years have been the very worst. It's been hard for our family to survive in living with the sickness. I know it must have been just as hard for your family as well.

I guess it's been the hardest for me to cope. I thought I was strong, keeping the problem to myself, never opening up to friends and family, always covering up for my dad.

I reached my breaking point last year. I thought or wanted to believe everyone had deserted me, even God, because I blamed Him for making us suffer so. I thought God was punishing me—my mom and brother every time. My brother came home drunk, violent and abusing.

I honestly was so mentally disturbed, I couldn't cope with life, when I thought life was treating me so miserable. All my pent-up emotions for all those years exploded, the love, hate, anger, resentment, caring and always hoping, was all too much for me to handle that I actually wanted to die. I was in a severe depression, I had no more faith in God, because I believed God betrayed me for not creating a miracle to end my dad's drinking.

My father did quit drinking for one year, my freshmen year in high school. It was miraculous the change he went thru, he was a different man, a happy one. I have never seen my mom so happy and at peace in all my life. My dear brother finally had the father he never had before. My dad was back, until the bubble burst. We had a heaven for a little while and we hoped too much. It was a devastating thing to happen once he took his first step backward.

My mother is a strong lady, she has suffered so much in the past 25 years, and yet she still goes on one day at a time. I have seen a change in her this last year that I really couldn't understand, or didn't want to. She does what you and your family have learned to do. She puts the problem in God's hands. She prays to God to help my father in his sickness, and leaves it entirely in his hands. I think she has received this inner strength from ala now and God, I admire her. My brother Kenny, is a lot like her in many ways. I wish I could be too. You and your brother, Jack were very close and special to one another.

My brother, Kenny and my mom are my best friends. I think that's why we have survived and made it this far, because we are very close and we have each other to lean on for strength.

I have been having a hard time this past year to cope with my father without taking the problem in my hands. My mom is constantly trying to help me, by telling me to leave it to God, that's it's my father's sickness not mine. I guess it affects me more than I realize.

I think I have grown a lot this year, I've opened up more. I don't hide the problem, although it still embarrasses me and I feel ashamed sometimes. But I have to start realizing that people will accept me as I am with or without my father's sickness. I'm going to join a local ala-teen or ala-non group, and become involved in the alcoholics anonymous program for better understanding.

I want to thank you again for letting me realize that other people have gone thru as much as I have and survived with the strength of God and loved ones. Your book really touched me down deep in my heart.

Now, maybe I know I can say this prayer to the Lord and truly means it, because I never really did before.

God, grant me the serenity to accept the things I cannot change.

The courage to change the things I can, and the wisdom to know the difference. Amen.

I will try my best to put things in God's hands, thanks to the deal, "Man in Black."

And whether it inspires my father or not, I know it has helped and bought me to a new understanding. Because thru your life story, you were able to show me that God will always be there, and he wont let me down, if I learn to leave things in his hands.

I feel very close to you and your family, even without ever truly meeting them. Maybe because we have all shared and experienced some feelings together. You all are very special people, and you have a special place within my heart.

May God Bless you and your family always!

Love and Happiness,
Kathi S

The Beginning—My Early
Sobriety Journal Entries

Sobriety Birthday, February 16, 1999

2/19

    Today I had a very excellent therapy session with Dr. H. Told him I was very honest with myself and considered myself an alcoholic. That I finally admitted this to my Internist, which both shocked and mystified him, and which brought light to my never-ending illnesses. I also told him that to the Thursday morning Women's meetings, I since have admitted to being an alcoholic. I had a very bad binge which made me remorseful, ashamed and did so humbly admit this relapse at the meeting. Starting a new date for my sobriety, 2/16/1999. My emotional well-being has a long way to go. Although I cannot and do not blame my husband for this addiction. I have much anger towards him. I asked Dr. H. how he thought I was doing and he said I have made some giant progress to both my physical and emotional well-being. I felt very good when I left. Before I went I was still beating myself up over my big binge the Tuesday before. After much thought I stopped at Borders Book store and bought a journal, a recovery meditation book and a book on woman and drinking. I thought it is time to continue to educate myself so I don't feel like a flawed worthless person, but only a person with an illness who chooses to get help and recovery.

2/20/99

    I now have been dry for 4 days. I finally last night slept almost entirely thru the night without the shakes. Hopefully the circles under my eyes will disappear. I found the hidden vodka bottle from my binging spree Monday/Tuesday. I plan on throwing the deadly thing in the recycle on Monday. The recycle men will be surprised to only see one bottle not 30. It still sickens me and frightens me to know I still have to replace the Case and Half of beer along with the half bottle of Wine, of my Mother's that was hidden under her desk in her basement apartment. I'll have to do that one last time before she returns from Hawaii. My husband seems to think that hiding the demon helps but knowing how controlling it is and how easy society is on selling the demon juices. I could pick up a bottle at 8:00 a.m. at the local Grocery store. I still wonder what the thoughts of those sales ladies were when I was buying booze at 8:00 a.m. every other day? Even though I slept last night my dreams were plagued. I dreamt that everyone where I worked, even people I worked with years ago found out I was an alcoholic. My biggest fear. Hearing them stating it out loud, "I didn't know you were a problem drinker, an alcoholic" seeing their faces and the looks of pity, disgust and surprise. I woke up, my body drenched from sweat—scared and frightened. I do not and still do not want anyone I work with, my friends, their husbands, the extended family, the people I deal with at the kids' school to know that I had a hidden side; a frightening hidden secret life. Although some might suspect or have speculated since the disease was and had been taking over more frequently at gatherings, I would get drunk or almost drunk more often, than not.

Yet most of the time I still was able to maintain my functional personality, and once they left or I left, I went to the land of oblivion. Did I really fool them? Or was I just fooling myself? I just pray now I can start a new beginning and make up for all the foolish things I said or did during those times.

2/21/99

I'm thankful to God for helping me make sobriety one more day. I did have another sleepless, restless night although my dreams were not plagued by nightmares of my addiction. I read that the alcoholic when he/she chooses help or treatment that it may not be immediate, it may take weeks, months, years for the obsession to drink the poison to lift. That scares me. Because I consistently obsess about it. Even during my periods when I wasn't getting this additional support and trying to quit on my own. The longest I quit on my own was 17 days last January 1998. I consistently thought about alcohol. I constantly wanted to numb and escape. Not so much me drinking. Just thinking about alcohol wanting it; wanting not to want it; wanting to say no at a social function; Wanting to be able to stop after two drinks; wanting so bad to feel that euphoria, to numb, to escape. And not wanting to go home and crave more.

2/22/99

I actually made it through an entire weekend without alcohol. I still am sleeping on the couch, my excuse is that my back hurts, but the real reason is that I fear to be close to Jack. That he will want to touch me, or want sex. I don't want him to sap my strength or energy, because I am not ready, and I don't want to just do it to satisfy his urges, that will just make me feel cheap, angry with myself. I really cannot remember a time where I truly wanted to make love with my husband without alcohol. We had always for the first 5 years drank together, our first date was at a bar. I don't know if I am ready to experience sex sober. Alcohol made me amorous, sexy and uninhibited, and helped make it okay to dress up the way Jack wanted me to look while making love. I can tell Jack doesn't understand why I am being so distant, and so jumpy when he touches me. I hope I can get past this. Because right now, if he comes up to me, touches me, and says, "Can I get lucky tonight?" I cringe. Why am I feeling this way?

2/23/99

My higher power is God. I still recall 2 years ago when I was at work, I had the shakes so bad, anxiety, chest pains, and nausea. How I prayed to God to just get me through the day. I would sit in the handicap stall at work on the floor crying tears of despair and fear. Gagging and dry heaving after making sure the bathroom was empty or having diarrhea from the after-effects of too much alcohol the night before. When I drank too much my bowels had no control. My bodily functions and insides could not handle it. I sometimes could not make it to the toilet at times. Luckily, these times always were at home. How humiliating would it have been if it had not been? I would stagger removing the soiled underwear & toss it in the garbage so that my husband would not see it. I have to keep reminding myself the many awful things I experienced while drinking. Each time I remember, it is making me stronger to stay sober.

2/24/99

I made it through another day. I feel stronger. I am still very frightened because almost every minute when I am not doing something my mind drifts off to some aspect of alcohol and drinking, or at least some scenario or situation that involve alcohol. This scares the Hell out of me. Yesterday I got very angry with Jack, he made a comment to me over the phone. He said, "Isn't it great how we are getting along so good this week? See—when you're in a good mood, I'm in a good mood. Whatever mood you are in that day, that's the mood you put me in. See how nice it is to get along?" WTF, really? My response, I said, "Don't blame me for what mood you are in. I don't control you." He said, rather dejectedly, "I know." I had a tinge of guilt when I said good-by to him on the phone. What is wrong with me?

2/25/99

I keep replaying the scene in the Meg Ryan movie *When a Man Loves a Woman* where she falls through the shower door in front of her daughter. Then I replay the scene on February 15th when I lay so drunk on the couch and began gagging on my own vomit in front of the kids, scaring the hell out of them. God forgive me for putting them through that, being the Daughter of an Alcoholic I know how badly that can affect a child, yet I did it anyway. Alcohol, cunning and unmerciful Or the time I left her only being 8 in the car with the doors locked so I could run into the grocery store for a small bottle of Vodka. Thank You God that nothing happened to my baby. Then when I got back in the car, I used to take everything out of my purse and put it in my coat pockets and then hide the bottle in my purse so I could sneak it in the house.

2/26/99

Yes I made it another day sober. I made a big breakthrough at my Women's AA meeting. I was the last person to read the Big Book, that meant I had the lead. The pain of hiding this horrible disease for so long poured out of me. That I knew long ago how I began the downward spiral. It started with sneaking booze from my parents' bar at 17. How if I had a date and was nervous I would down several drinks to relax and be able to deal with it. How when I was nineteen and drunk driving from a night out at a bar with my fake I.D. taking the side streets to avoid being stopped or pulled over and on that side street that was snow covered I slid into a street sign and knocked it over. How I panicked that the cops would give me a DUI, if they found me. Praying someone did not see it and call them. How I pushed my car out, and drunkenly drove away. The ladies told me that they were so proud of me for opening up.

2/27/99

Thank you for another day sober. I have come to the realization that I know Jack loves me in his own way, but I feel if he knew the enormity of this demon that has taken such hold over my life, and controlled my body and mind, that he would be scared shitless. His emotional maturity level could not handle it. Therefore, I have retreated, from communicating with him these thoughts and fears. Dr. H. said I need to be honest with him on why I cannot be intimate with him. That right now it could be more than I can handle. I have to have the emotional capacity to give my body to him sexually. After a night out with friends, we came home and he approached me yet again, and I backed away. I told him, "It's not you, it's me," yet I am not sure about that either.

2/28/99

Yay!! I am sober another day. Jack and I came home from a night bowling with my neighbors, and he said, "How about making love?" He was tipsy, I was not. I said, "No." He then tried to beg and pout like a child. He said, "I am so horny for you. I bet I can make you horny." I said, "No, Jack, I am not ready." He whined, "Please can we just lay naked together on the bed?" Then his tone changed, and he said sarcastically, "Or are you sleeping on the couch again?" "Jack." I told him that I just can't right now. I have too many things I am trying to sort out in my head, and one big one is not to think of Alcohol or drink. He walked away grumbling, I knew he was mad, and I felt guilty, but I just could not bring myself to go there. When are these feelings going to pass? I also resented the fact that he could still drink, and I couldn't. Was that it?

3/4/99

Thank you, Lord for yet another new day. It has been 14 days. My thoughts are still obsessed with alcohol but I think being an alcoholic that will never change. I am just thankful I have not picked up a drink.

3/6/99

17 days of sobriety. This is the longest I have made it sober since I tried it last December 1998 to quit by myself and failed. I could only last 12 days that time. I still obsess about drinking, but not as much as in the beginning. I am starting to see a side of Jack that I tried to ignore, his verbal barrage of cruelty to me and the kids. I realized my job now is to be protector and mediator. Why did I never see that before? These angry, violent outbursts for the most ridiculous things. Oh Dear God I have the urge to drink after this last episode with Jack, but I didn't. Dr. H. was proud of me, he did say that I need to come to terms that since I am becoming sober and growing. I have changed the rules and dynamics of our relationship, and I may decide that it won't work, because I am getting healthy and Jack is staying in the same place, emotionally and physically. Hmmm, that is food for thought.

3/10/99

Thank you God for day 21 of Sobriety. This morning I almost broke my routine of doing other things instead of sitting down with no sound, no TV no music, and reading my meditation book, my Daily Word prayer. My 24-hour thought for the day to Thank God for putting myself in his hands. I have to do this, and make it a routine, otherwise I will stray, I am not strong enough yet.

3/17/99

It has been 4 weeks of hard work. Staying sober, changing patterns, trying to get healthy, all the while being a Mother, Wife, and friend. What frustrates me the most today, is that I actually woke up feeling like crap. And today I even feel worse. I'm angry, actually very angry and pissed. Here I have been trying so hard to get healthy physically, mentally and I have another damn cold. But on a positive note, I am still sober.

3/19/99

I made it 30 days Sober. We did a first-step meeting at my Ladies AA meeting. It was for a newcomer, a petite, pretty 33-yr-old girl who was addicted to pain killers. She was desperate, and struggling to detox and she was scared, she reminded me of me, those first few days when I walked into that AA meeting. Late that afternoon I got a surprise phone call from Dr. H. He called to congratulate me on my 30 days. He said, "Has the family noticed your mood changes? That you aren't angry and irritable and uptight all the time? That your anxiety is not as bad?" I said yes. What a great feeling. He ended the call by saying how great it was that I made 30 days and that he knew how hard it was for me.

3/20/99

Today I had to miss my appointment with Dr. H. I didn't feel well enough to go. This damn cold. I reassured him it was not because of a hangover, lol, like in the past. Which he had quickly figured out that routine. This time it was the sober truth.

4/17/99

I made it!! 60 days sober! Thank you! Thank you! Thank you! I was very agitated all day. It was a good day with the kids, no disasters, so I cannot put my finger on it why or what I was feeling, but I didn't want to do anything to celebrate. Jack kept pressuring me to go out and celebrate, but I said no. I don't know why I didn't want to, because this was a big milestone. 22 years of drinking, and over-indulging but now I have managed for 60 days to not have a drop of alcohol. Why am I not wanting to celebrate, that is my soul-searching question today, that I have yet to answer.

4/24/99

Thank you, God, for another day. I'd like to say it's been easy trying to stay sober, but it hasn't been. I still crave it. I still wish for a chilled glass of wine in an elegant wine glass. Pretending to sip it slowly instead of gulping it down. Reward myself, saying this will help me relax. Pretending and trying not to fool myself that I'm just like everyone else.

4/26/99

I am reading a good, a very good book which is reinforcing that fact that I sometimes have a hard time believing or accepting that I am an alcoholic. Saturday, Jack said a weird remark which really aggravated me. He said, "No one knows what goes on behind closed doors." He said, "No one knows you are an alcoholic." It was the way he said it. Like it was a great thing. That made me angry and defensive. How dare he use that word, only I am allowed to call myself an alcoholic, me and my friends in my Thursday group. Alright that's not the right answer, so why and what is the real reason I am so defensive and angry? All he was doing was stating the truth.

4/27/299

Thank you for 69 Days of sobriety. It has been tough. I try to fool myself that its easy, but it's not. I am plagued with constant nightmares and thoughts of alcohol. Then I try and think to myself, maybe I am better. I can control my drinking at social gatherings. I can just have one and enjoy it; relax; be like everyone else without wanting more, or craving more and wondering if it would be okay to not only have one cocktail, but two? They call that Stinking Thinking in AA. The summer is near and the calendar is booked with parties and events and I am utterly terrified. Will I be able to be happy and have a good time without alcohol? Will friends who don't know, which would be all of them, pressure me to drink? Question me why I am not drinking? Give me a hard time? How will I respond? Will I be strong enough to say no, without feeling sorry for myself? I pray that I can. I know deep down inside as I read books on Alcoholism, that I am on the slow road to recovery of getting my identity back, that was lost completely for 22 years of my life but most definitely how badly I lost these last 4 years.

4/28/99

Today I ask, will I ever be able to forgive myself, for putting my daughter through some miserable times under the influence? Can I forgive myself for drinking while taking care of friend's children, while half in the bag? I am pretty sure I hid it well enough to be functional but once the kids were all asleep or picked up I would drink myself to oblivion, the fantasy world of escape and sleep. Relieved I got thru the incident without being caught, relieved my duties as a good Mom/friend were over so I could drink more. I felt such remorse even while I downing the vodka and OJ's. We are working the 12 steps in our meeting and it has been very humbling, to have to make amends to the people I love, and myself.

4/30/99

I have been going thru a binging period, no, not alcohol, but of stressing myself to the max. I am overloaded and exhausted. It's like I need to be constantly busy or doing something or a project for fear of sitting down and drinking. That's the one thing that has taken over and possessed me—this innate need to constantly be on the go. I cannot sit still. The only time I do is at 10 p.m. when I am about to fall asleep from exhaustion. Help!!! What is wrong with me?

5/1/99

I constantly want Jack to understand, this new me. I let him listen to Betty's message. I want Jack to know that even though I have admitted to this illness of Alcoholism that there are so many women who have this disease. Strong, beautiful, successful, kind, good women. It really irked me that he was surprised that there were 1,900 women at the AA luncheon. He was in a state of shock. Really? WTF

I actually was in awe myself at the luncheon, seeing so many beautiful women, all races, all ages. It was incredible to hear their stories.

5/4/99

I began reading a book called the Joy of Recovery. There was a checklist of questions to ask yourself to see if you were an alcoholic. I answered "yes" to almost every one of them. Which reinforced the fact that I am an "Alcoholic." Any question in my mind was dashed away. I guess in my recovery I am going to have to keep going back to that checklist, and also remember several months ago when I was actively drinking how awful it was. Being 69 days sober, you try and push out the agony of the worst days of your hangovers. You pretend that they weren't as bad as you remember, yet in reality they were way worse.

5/15/99

I realize I am an enabler. I have made my husband's life so easy. I clean the house, take the kids to their activities, help with home-work, have a cleaning lady once a month, a lawn service, I pretty much took over where his Mom left off. We are not a team, and that is half my fault. I get so frustrated when I ask for help, for his help on just regular household maintenance and he grumbles and complains like a baby, and just wants to play Nintendo, or with the kids. It is no wonder I don't want to have sex with him. I did the other night just to gratify his sexual need so he would not be grumpy, then I got mad at myself because I feel like a cheap slut just spreading my legs. It pisses me off, and God would I love to drink. But he is just waiting for me to slip up, I can feel it, so I will not give him the satisfaction of failing. I never saw this behavior in him before we had kids because we both were party animals. It was all about the drinking and fun. The two of us were drinking and inebriated the whole start of our dating and marriage. Now I am sober and he drinks, the dynamics have changed. I am not sure we have much in common anymore except for two beautiful kids. Jack's personality has started to change, he has become nasty, verbally abusive, and has angry outbursts. It is scary. I did not see it as much because I was always numbing myself.

5/19/99

90 Days sober! I made it. I never thought I would make it. The cravings are getting less and less and for this I am so thankful. I am feeling stronger being around others who drink. It's still not an easy road, but I am doing it. I am so proud of myself. The Thursday Ladies from AA are super proud of me, Dr. H. is proud of me, My Mom is proud of me and yeah, well Jack is too in his own selfish way. I am going to keep on going One day at a Time, Keep reading the Serenity prayer and my Daily Word. I have made somewhat peace with Jack to an amicable state, and have now eased myself into having sex with him, I say sex because it is just that, not making love, not a give-and-take and sharing type of intimacy. Jack gets what he wants, and because I don't know yet how to be assertive and communicate my needs, I am left behind, and just resigned to that's the way it is. In all reality I am sort of relieved because he does not turn me on the way he did when I was drinking. I saw him in a totally different inebriated state of mind, which if I am honest helped me fantasize how great it was, and how sexy he was, but now not so much. Sad but at least I am sober, and just not sure where this will go in the future.

Present-day journal entry, 6/19/20

Today, I am so grateful, for where I am at in my life. I have 21 years of sobriety under my belt. My life has not been easy during that Merry-go-round ride. I have had many emotional hurdles, and events that are frightening, horrible, and scary happen during those 21 years. Two brutal divorces, death of loved ones, loss of a home, having to move 6 times in 8 years. I have made mistakes, and decisions that were not the best, and suffered the consequences, yet never once did I falter and pick up that one drink. Believe me, I have been offered, I have been taunted, I have been cajoled and told, "What's the big deal if you just have one?" or "Just a taste or a sip." That "if you fall off the wagon, I will be there to catch you." Yes, I miss the taste of an ice-cold Beer and the soft warm pretzel, so thank you, Heineken "0"!!! Now I can indulge myself without the hangover, or guilt. All I can say, it would just be that one drink, that one time, that would lead to 100 more and then a living Hell. Every day living sober is a challenge, life is hard. I still have a lot of work to do on myself. I still need to heal from the past, and keep growing but guess what? I am doing it Sober, and I am not on that Merry-Go-Round anymore. I pray every day that I am never on that ride again.

Reviews

The following individuals have read this manuscript:

Vance Nesbitt, Cover Illustrator—"Umm…I'm emotional, fatigued, and extremely teary eyed. I'm happy and torn together. I'm left totally bewildered and angry. I have a void that can't be filled. I feel horror and shock and the overwhelming desire to hold back a wall from demons coming in. I have grown in a short period. I'm educated in wisdom with the sacrifice of a part of my soul. I bear witness to an experience that 'monsters' do exist. I felt pain and relief of pain in just moments apart. I have been influenced by your gift once I get past the tears to see my way forth. Kathi, what I just finished reading was so profound that I am having troubles finding the word that can color my emotions right now. I just want to hold you and assure you that you are an amazing woman that is touching the core of humanity with a gift of freedom and life. I can't begin to thank you enough for sharing this experience with me on a firsthand basis. You just made me desire to become an even better man."

Erin M.—"After reading the manuscript, I found it emotionally painful, but very well written. Because of knowing the author on a personal level, I found I could only read it in short segments due to the graphic painful nature of the material. It's a truthful and honest account of what dysfunctional families living with addiction go through. At the end, I told the author in a humorous manner that she should provide a therapy coupon at the end of the book to be used later."

Pam T.—"I found the book fascinating and could not put it down as soon as I began reading it. It brought up so many emotions: anger, frustration, strength, courage, and the ability to see how the power of the mind works in trying to overcome and survive the obstacles of abuse. At first, I was angry at the author's mother, but that quickly changed as I continued to read the story. I found it to be well written and an honest account of hidden secrets within the family."

Joy B.—"The book is a testament of survival of how one woman pulled herself out of a dysfunctional merry-go-round, one who had watched her family go in circles for years and how she chose to change the course so that it would stop with her and that her goal is and was to help her children and to help other families and individuals going through the same situation to let them know they can survive dysfunction, survive addiction, and come out healthy."

Susan W.—"I have known the author for over fifty years, and yet I never knew the pain and anguish that was so secretly hidden behind the walls of her home and in her childhood. This was so well written and such a testament to showing me that by releasing these fears and demons and destroying the power they have over us, we can do anything. By doing this, it allows us to forge healthy friendships and create healthy personal relationships. It was extremely painful for me to read but so enlightening and had lighthearted sections that the author could rise above and make a bad situation humorous. That truly is a gift."

Tracey S.—"Kathi, I am sorry it has taken me so long to be able to return your manuscript and write a review. I did give this my full attention and am amazed at your courage to give this accounting of your life. It hurt to read the details of so much trauma and from such an early age. My heart aches thinking of you. Such a dear one—handling so much emotional stress first as a child, then as a parent. What a task you gave yourself with this writing. I hope it was therapeutic (though these events must have been painful to return to even now, well into your recovery). I had no idea how such a personal story could be adapted for publication, but I imagine others, who have suffered similarly and still hide their histories, could benefit from reading your honest accounting of things. Please keep me up-to-date on your progress. I am honored you shared your writing with me and that you are doing things that make your heart happy."

About the Author

Kathi Ann Stewart was born on June 21, 1961, raised Catholic in the northwest suburbs of Chicago with instilled Midwestern values, where getting married and raising a family were prevalent. She was married at twenty-four, raised two children, in a seemingly perfect suburbia lifestyle. Where in her forties she relocated to Phoenix where a series of traumatic events ultimately led to divorce and then a rebound marriage. Through all this loss  and suffering, you begin to see a picture emerge of Kathi's character. You will witness her strength, her courage, her sense of humor, her humility, but most of all, her vulnerability. Through prayer, spiritual growth, you see Kathi rise above addiction and abuse. The author now resides in the Tampa area with her schnoodle, Jacey, enjoying the peace and tranquility of being surrounded by the white sandy beaches and gulf ocean breezes.